ARL-SR-93 September 2000

50 Years of Army Computing
From ENIAC to MSRC

Thomas J. Bergin, editor

A Record of a Symposium and Celebration
November 13 and 14, 1996
Aberdeen Proving Ground

Sponsored by the Army Research Laboratory and
the U.S. Army Ordnance Center & School

Approved for public release; distribution unlimited.

This volume is dedicated to Michael John Muuss (1958 - 2000), whose video record of these precedings made this publication possible. His loss is felt personally by many of the participantshe recorded, but more poignantly his loss is felt universally, for his talent, his spirit, and his wisdom cannot be replaced. He was truly a national treasure.

Welcome

U.S. Army researchers played a fundamental role in the inauguration of the modern computer age. The urgent need for high-performance computing during World War II led the U.S. Army Ordnance Corps to fund the design and implementation of the world's first high-speed electronic automatic computer, the ENIAC. The price tag for this groundbreaking invention was $486,804.22, but its lasting impact on Defense science and technology, and indeed on the world today, is incalculable.

What began with our early technology pioneers, both military and civilian, continues today with numerous contributions in hardware, software, networking, and computational methods. The Army Research Laboratory, the Army's premier research organization, celebrates its heritage with the publication of this volume. I hope it is a welcome addition to your library.

> Robert W. Whalin, PhD, PE
> Director,
> U.S. Army Research Laboratory

In November 1996, a symposium was held to commemorate the 50th anniversary of the dedication of the ENIAC. The commemoration also marked another important milestone in the history of Army computing, the ribbon-cutting ceremony for the Army Research Laboratory Major Shared Resource Center (MSRC). This large high-performance computing facility features heterogeneous supercomputing systems, massive near-line storage, robust high-speed networking, and scientific visualization with video production capabilities.

The symposium provided a wonderful opportunity to recognize the contributions and dedication of the Army computing pioneers and to trace the growth of an industry and its impact on the Army over 50 years. The accomplishments of the early computing pioneers, many of whom participated in the proceedings, are an indelible part of the legacy of the Army research.

As the successor to the organizations described in this book, the ARL Computational and Information Sciences Directorate proudly carries forward the tradition of its distinguished predecessors. On behalf of our Directorate and the ARL MSRC, I am pleased to present this volume as a historical perspective on the Army's role in the birth of the computer age.

> Dr. N. Radhakrishnan
> Chief, Computational and Information Sciences
>   Directorate
> U.S. Army Research Laboratory

Foreword

A symposium and celebration was held at Aberdeen Proving Ground (APG), Maryland, in November 1996, to recognize and commemorate seminal Army contributions to the birth and development of modern computing. Primarily inspired by the 50th anniversary of the invention of the world's first general-purpose electronic computer (the ENIAC), this two-day event also celebrated the dedication at APG of significant new computational resources provided by the Office of Secretary of Defense. On this occasion, scores of "computing pioneers" gathered at APG to reminisce about the accomplishments that stemmed from the Army's computation needs during World War II—in particular, the need for the firing and bombing tables that were essential for accurate targeting of ground- and air-delivered ordnance.

How did this grand celebration happen? Pretty much by accident! In August of 1995, a letter arrived at my home from Dr. Judith Rodin, President of the University of Pennsylvania. This was a generic letter to "parents of University of Pennsylvania students" which, much to my interest, announced an upcoming celebration of computing to be held in Philadelphia. The focus was to be the 50th anniversary of the invention of the ENIAC, and the festivities were to be sponsored jointly by the University and by the Association for Computing Machinery (ACM). As part of the event, Vice President Al Gore would ceremonially activate a small piece of the original ENIAC.

At the time of the Rodin letter, many of us at the Ballistic Research Laboratory (BRL) had just been sensitized to our own Army ENIAC history. In September 1992, the old BRL, along with a number of sister laboratories, was reorganized into the newly established Army Research Laboratory (ARL). During a contemporaneous retrospective[1] the history of Army computing at APG was reviewed, including the concept, design, and construction of the ENIAC, activities sponsored and managed by the Army. To ensure that the Army would not be overlooked at the Philadelphia celebrations, I contacted Dr. Rodin's office. Fortunately, both the University and the ACM were happy to refine the planned program to give the Army the credit it deserved. Over the next few months, ARL worked with contacts at the University of Pennsylvania (Mr. Steve Brown and Dr. Greg Farrington) and with the ACM (Dr. Bert Herzog, Dr. Dianne Martin, and Dr. Tim Bergin); finally, we met with Dr. Herman Goldstine himself, who had been the Army technical representative overseeing the ENIAC project 50 years earlier.

[1] For insights into early ballistic studies at BRL, see Klopcic and Reed (1999).

One result of these activities, due particularly to Dr. Bergin, was that an Army history panel was added to the ACM History Track. And thanks to Dr. Farrington, Dr. Goldstine assisted Vice President Gore in the ceremonial restarting of the ENIAC. In addition to the assistance of Dr. Bergin, enthusiastic support was received from Dr. William Moye (ARL Historian), Mr. Harry Reed (former BRL Division Chief), and Mr. Mike Muuss (Senior Computer Scientist at ARL). After the Philadelphia celebration, those of us who had witnessed the event were so impressed with the importance of the Army story (and the significant contributions of our computing pioneers) that we dedicated ourselves to sponsoring an APG-based symposium. For this event, we wanted to focus particularly on the people and activities that had typically been ignored by the extant articles and monographs on the history of computing. We additionally wanted to celebrate a new beginning with the dedication of the DoD-sponsored ARL Major Shared Resource Center. With the encouragement of Dr. John Lyons, then Director of ARL, an *ad hoc* committee was formed to bring about the celebration documented in these pages. The activities of the committee were supported by Major General Robert Shadley, Commanding General, U.S. Army Ordnance Center and Schools, and his staff, who sponsored the military review and award presentation on the second day of the celebration.

Although more than three years have passed since this event, time has not dimmed the importance of the role played by the Army. We are pleased that these pages can finally be shared with the Army family and all those who may be interested in the roots of 20th century technology. In no small measure, credit for these pages goes to Dr. Bergin, Dr. Moye, and Dr. Barbara Collier (ARL Technical Publishing Branch). Finally, thanks go to Dr. Robert Whalin, Director of ARL, and to Dr. N. Radhakrishnan, Director of the ARL Corporate Information and Computing Directorate, for ensuring that this story was finally told.

Paul H. Deitz, Ph.D.
Technical Director
US Army Materiel Systems Analysis Activity
ATTN: AMXSY-TD
392 Hopkins Road
Aberdeen Proving Ground, MD 21005-5071
phd@arl.mil or *phd@amsaa.army.mil*

Preface

My part in this story began in the summer of 1995, when a colleague asked if I would serve as the "liaison to some people working on the ACM's Computer Science Conference." When she put it that way, how could I refuse? Over time, I found out that the ACM[1] was about to celebrate its 50th anniversary and wanted to have a commemorative program on the history of computing. After much e-mail, I decided to have a "history track" for the Conference, as well as a half-day commemorative program on the day before the Conference.

My first task was to invite a number of prominent computer historians to a two-day planning meeting in Arlington, Virginia. At this meeting, we outlined the commemorative program, assigned historians to topics, and outlined four panels for the history track: (1) "Hardware History," (2) "Software History," (3) "The ENIAC," and (4) "Antecedents of Personal Computing."

In November, I received e-mail from David Rutland, who had worked at the National Bureau of Standards and wanted to propose a panel on NBS's early computer efforts. So the first history track in the history of the ACM now had five panels, including "Early Electronic Computing at the NBS," which had Harry Huskey[2] as a speaker.

By now, dear reader, you may be asking, "Why is he telling me all this?" Well, in December, I received a phone call, at home, on a Sunday evening, from Paul Deitz, who identified himself as the Chief of the Army's "Vulnerability and Lethality Division." That title sounded ominous, so I decided to try to help this fellow. He said that he had a story he wanted to tell about Army computing, and he had learned that the Association for Computing Machinery was having a history track at the 1996 Computer Science Conference to be held in Philadelphia. Paul asked if there would be room for a panel that explored the early days of Army computing at the Aberdeen Proving Ground. I told Paul that it sounded like a wonderful idea, but that I would have to get approval from the Chair of the Program Committee for an additional room. In two days, we had an agreement for a sixth panel, entitled, "The Army, the National Need, and the ENIAC."[3]

After the ACM Conference ended, all those involved agreed that it had been a wonderful conference, and that the History Track and the History Commemorative Program had added much to its success. Indeed, after the final panel, "The Army, the National Need, and the ENIAC," Paul Deitz, Harry Reed,[4] Bill Moye,[5] and I talked about the need to do more. The Army did indeed have a story to tell, having been a pioneering organization in the earliest days of computing. Most importantly, we agreed that the *people who worked at Aberdeen* needed to be recognized and given an opportunity to tell their story.

Well, through the efforts of Paul Deitz, Harry Reed, and Bill Moye, a Program Committee was assembled to plan *Fifty Years of Army Computing, from ENIAC to MSRC*, the Commemoration documented in this volume. The results of their

[1] Association for Computing Machinery.

[2] ENIAC team member. See Presenter Biographies, this volume, p 138.

[3] A transcript of this panel is included in this volume (pp 142–158).

[4] ENIAC team member. See Presenter Biographies, p 139.
[5] ARL Historian. See Presenter Biographies, p 139.

hard work were presented on November 13 and 14, 1996, at the Top of the Bay (Officers' Club) at Aberdeen Proving Ground. The Commemoration honored the memory and accomplishments of the earliest computer pioneers at Aberdeen, as well as celebrating the future of Army computing with the dedication of the Major Shared Resource Center.[6]

The Commemoration also included two exhibits, a photographic display and a collection of artifacts. The photographic display was created for the ACM Conference by Sharon McCullough and her colleagues at Special Events, Inc. Sharon invited me to create an exhibit of artifacts to accompany the photographs (possibly inspired by a visit to my rather cluttered office).[7] The two exhibits appeared at both the ACM Conference and the Commemoration.

On behalf of everyone who attended the Commemoration, I would like to thank the members of the Program Committee: Ray Astor, Bill Barkuloo, Hal Breaux, Paul Deitz, Tad Edwards, Bob Eichelberger, Carol Ellis, John Gregory, Sharon McCullough, Bill Moye, Mike Muuss, Charlie Nietubicz, Harry Reed, and Jill Smith.

I would also like to acknowledge the tremendous effort it took to plan and manage the Commemoration itself. Without the efforts of the Administrative Committee, we would not have had such a wonderful two days: Virginia Bailey, Elizabeth Barber, Judith Celmer, Patricia Cizmadia, LouAnn Conway, Connie Gillette, Rodger Godin, Dave Jennings, Judy Johnston, Thomas Kile, Angie Levrone, Charles McDevitt, Ronald Mihalcin, Bob Reschly, Jr., Brenda Rice, Kathryn Sorensen, and Edward Starnes. We owe all of them a big "thank you" for a job well done.

And last, but not least, I want to thank Bill Moye, the ARL Historian. Bill has worked with me through all the rough spots in this project and I appreciate his assistance, support, and friendship.

I wish to apologize for the delay in the production of this volume. A week after the conference, my wife, Diane, was diagnosed with ovarian cancer. I completed the first draft in late fall 1998, and received it back for final editing in February. Diane died on March 5, 1999, and I have had a difficult time finding the time and focus needed to finish the job.

I would be remiss if I did not thank the people at Business Plus, Inc., especially Jon Morell, for their support, patience, and understanding during the preparation of this volume. I have been fortunate to have worked through this fine company.

In addition, I would ask that all attendees look in their attics, basements, and garages, to see if they have materials or artifacts to donate. The Computing History Museum at American University is a direct outgrowth of this Conference and the ACM Conference which preceded it. Indeed, Armand Adams, one of

---

[6] A Major Shared Resource Center is a Department of Defense high-performance computing asset available to the DoD R&D community. See also Bergin and Moye (1997).

[7] With the addition of some first-rate artifacts donated by members of the Program Committee, as well as by attendees at the Army Commemoration, this exhibit became the backbone of the Computing History Museum at American University. See "ENIAC 50th anniversary continued," in "Happenings," *IEEE Annals of the History of Computing* **18**, No. 3 (Fall 1996), p 75.

the participants, has already donated artifacts from his personal collection. The Museum is an opportunity for you to continue to contribute, by sharing your memorabilia with present elementary, secondary, and college students. Please contact me if you have something to donate.

Finally, I want to reiterate what I learned many years ago: Wonderful things happen when a group of dedicated people works together to achieve a goal. This was true for the pioneers who were honored during these two days, as well as for the people who worked so hard to make this Commemoration possible. It was an honor to work with all of you.

>	Thomas J. (Tim) Bergin, Ph.D.
>	Director, Computing History Museum
>	Professor, Computer Science and Information Systems Department
>	American University
>	4400 Massachusetts Avenue, NW
>	Washington, D.C. 20016-8116
>	*tbergin@american.edu*

Contents

Welcome iii

Foreword v

Preface vii

Introduction 1

1. Opening Session: History of Early Computing 8
   Welcoming Remarks 8
   Announcements 10
   Keynote Address: A Short History of Computing or
      How Did We Get to Aberdeen? 12

2. ENIAC: Development and Early Days 24

3. Women Pioneers 38

4. Digital Computing at BRL: 1938–1969 50
   1939–1954: ENIAC and the First Computer Survey 51
   EDVAC, ORDVAC 55
   BRLESC I and II 58
   HEP 60
   Software 61
   ENIAC Put to Work 66
   Applications 68

5. The Early Computer Industry 74

6. Recent History: Supercomputers and Networking 86

7. Military Ceremony 102

8. Civilian Recognition and MSRC Ribbon-Cutting Ceremonies 104

Presenter Biographies 136

**Appendix. ACM History Track Panel: The Army, the National
   Need, and the ENIAC** 142

Epilog. High-Performance Computing at ARL 160

Literature Citations 163

Sidebar articles

Mauchly and Eckert 26
Adele Katz Goldstine and stored-program machines 27
"Intermediate programming"—converter code 30
Babbage 32
His engines 32
Bletchley Park 33
Turing 33
The "first draft report" 34
FORAST 38
How a core memory element works 56
Machine language 62
FORTRAN and FORAST 62
JK switches 63
Interpreting punched cards 63

Figures

ENIAC at BRL: Homé McAllister, Winifred (Wink) Smith, George Reitwiesner, and Ruth Lichterman 1
Mauchly, Barnes, and Eckert peruse ENIAC manual in February 1946 2
Console of BRLESC I computer 3
ARL Major Shared Resource Center 4
Photo exhibit at 50 Years of Computing celebration 9
Computer technology stamp 11
Martin Weik's "computer tree" 53
Truman visits ENIAC, 1951 66
Muuss and Weaver with PDP-11 displaying wire frame diagram of XM1 tank 92
Uncrating the Cray Research XMP 95
The Ordnance Corps honors two of its own 102, 103
Barnes and Brainerd in front of ENIAC Function Table "A" 109
Ribbon-cutting for ARL MSRC 113
Speed of networks versus time 118
Speed of supercomputers versus time 119
Computational grid 122
Flow field visualization 122
Computational grid for transonic computations 123
Pressure contours on a wrap-around finned projectile 124
Image of steel rod penetrating steel plate, obtained by flash radiography 125
Modeling long-rod penetration with combined yaw and obliquity 126
Tank simulation: medium resolution 128
Applying our expertise to new areas 129
Terrain model showing quantization error ("steps") 130
Model of terrain at Fort Hunter-Liggett 131
Corps Main Command Post: detail of truck 131
Energy versus frequency for one pixel in a sensor 132
Scene generation elements 133
Model of tank in smoke 133
Software simulation back plane 134
Energy transport: basic sensor scenario 134
Simulation showing effect of distance on color 135
Barkley Fritz, Herman Goldstine, and Harry Reed at ACM Meeting 144
A simple set of trajectories 155
Firing table for 105-mm howitzer 156
Quadrant elevation table 157

50 Years of Army Computing
From ENIAC to MSRC

Introduction

This volume is a record of a conference held at Aberdeen Proving Ground, Maryland, on November 13 and 14, 1996. The conference sessions included talks and panel discussions on topics ranging from the earliest days of computing at the Ballistic Research Laboratory (BRL) (now part of the Army Research Laboratory, ARL) to projections for the future use of ARL's Major Shared Resource Center, which was dedicated during the event. As part of the dedication ceremony, awards were presented to honor three of the most important pioneers, Herman Goldstine, Paul Gillon, and John von Neumann.[1]

[1] Biographical sketches are provided on pp 5–6 (this volume).

Much of the following material was included in the conference program, along with some of the accompanying photographs. Because of its historical nature, we decided to include this program material here for readers who did not attend the event.

Historical Background

The Ballistic Research Laboratory of the Ordnance Department, established in 1938 from the Research Division of Aberdeen Proving Ground (APG), was charged to produce firing tables for the Army. For artillery, for example, these tables showed the soldier what angle of elevation was required for a specific projectile to impact a target at a specified range with a given propellant charge. The tables also indicated corrections to apply for variations in atmospheric temperature, air density, wind, angle of sight, weight of projectile, muzzle velocity, and compensation for drift. Especially in wartime, firing tables had to be prepared and sent to the field as rapidly as possible, because without the information, artillery became less effective.

ENIAC at BRL: (*left to right*) **Homé McAllister, Winifred (Wink) Smith, George Reitwiesner, and Ruth Lichterman.**

To speed the calculation of firing and bombing tables, BRL's predecessor organization acquired its copy of the Bush differential analyzer in 1935. Early in World War II, the lab also contracted with the Moore School of Electrical Engineering, University of Pennsylvania, to take over operation of the school's somewhat faster differential analyzer. Hoping to improve on the Bush analog device as a means to generate firing tables, John W. Mauchly and J. Presper Eckert, Jr., proposed building an electronic numerical analyzer.

Two Ordnance Department officers, Colonel Paul N. Gillon and Captain Herman H. Goldstine, recognized the potential of the proposal to build an electronic computing machine, nurtured it, found money to support the project, defended it against critics, and helped publicize its achievements.

A contract was signed in June 1943, and construction began in June 1944, with final assembly in the fall of 1945 and the formal dedication in February 1946. Later that year, ENIAC was dismantled, and it was delivered to APG in January 1947. It was operational again in August 1947, representing "the largest collection of interconnected electronic circuitry then in existence."[2] With refinements suggested by John von Neumann and others, ENIAC provided years of successful service until it was retired in October 1955.

[2] Weik (1961), p 6.

By this time, BRL had acquired two more computers. Beginning in the fall of 1944, the ENIAC team, working with von Neumann, designed EDVAC (Electronic Discrete Variable Computer). The new device, a collaborative effort by BRL, the Moore School, the Institute for Advanced Studies (IAS), and the National Bureau of Standards (NBS), was the first computer to be designed with an internally stored program. EDVAC was installed at BRL in 1949, but design problems delayed acceptance and practical operation until 1952.

BRL was already at work on a new system. ORDVAC (Ordnance Variable Automatic Computer) belonged to the group of computers whose basic logic was developed by the IAS. It was built by the University of Illinois and brought to Aberdeen in 1952. Thus, for a brief time in 1952, with ENIAC, EDVAC, and ORDVAC, BRL was the world's largest computer center.

By 1955, available time on each computer had been pushed to 145 hours per week of error-free production to support ballistic research and compute firing tables and other ballistic data for artillery, rockets, and missiles. The computers also performed calculations in other fields, including weather prediction, atomic energy research, thermal ignition, cosmic ray studies, and wind tunnel design.

In 1956, engineers and scientists in the BRL computing laboratory began to develop a new computer, to be called BRLESC (BRL Electronic Scientific Computer). At the same time, the Ordnance Department transferred money to NBS to develop logic modules—the arithmetic, logical, and control units for the new system. BRLESC went on line in 1962, and tests indicated that it was two to eight times faster than commercial systems.

Planning for BRLESC II began in 1965. BRLESC II was a solid-state digital computer designed to be 200 times faster than the ORDVAC, which it replaced in November 1967. The integrated circuits for BRLESC were produced under an industrial contract, but BRL employees did all the logic design,

John W. Mauchly, Major General Gladeon M. Barnes (Chief, Research and Development Service, Office of the Chief of Ordnance), and J. Presper Eckert, Jr., peruse ENIAC manual in February 1946.

back-panel wiring, and assembly.

To facilitate use of these increasingly powerful machines, BRL personnel pioneered software. FORAST (Formula and Assembly Translator) was developed for ORDVAC in 1960 and implemented on BRLESC by 1961. During 1962–63, BRL wrote a FORTRAN (Formula Translation) compiler for BRLESC, one of the first uses of the FORTRAN language on other than IBM computers.

DoD directed BRL not to design and build any more computers in-house, primarily because of the extensive capabilities achieved by the commercial computer industry. Even so, lab personnel continued to experiment with computer hardware, software, and operations.

For example, during the 1970s, the lab worked with Denelcor, Inc., on its Heterogeneous Element Processor (HEP), the world's first massively parallel supercomputer. A 64-bit, floating-point digital machine with considerable multi-user and multi-task possibilities, the HEP was the first supercomputer to run the Unix operating system. In the late 1980s, BRL dedicated two of the Army's first supercomputers, a Cray X-MP/48 followed by a Cray-2.

Console of BRLESC I computer, side view. At the console: Lou Moeller. Note the ENIAC photograph hanging on the side of BRLESC.

From the early 1970s, BRL employees had a prototype BRLNET up and running, and by the later 1970s, they were pursuing the tools to permit local-area networking. In the early 1980s, the lab played a major role in working with the Defense Advanced Research Projects Agency (DARPA) to develop the ARPANET. By this time, BRL had adopted the Unix operating system, implementing many modifications along the way. For example, an engineer at the lab contributed substantially to the specifications for the ANSI version of the C programming language.

These tremendous tools greatly enhanced research capabilities in such areas as simulation, virtual reality, and scientific visualization. By the early 1980s, lab personnel were developing three-dimensional graphics display hardware to assist in the development of combinatorial-solid-geometry descriptions of military vehicles. In 1991, the lab began shipping BRL-CAD release 1.0, which included a network-distributed image-processing capability.

The scientific visualization program was started in 1984 to provide tools and expertise to help researchers graphically interpret the voluminous results of scientific supercomputer calculations. Visualization techniques provide three-dimensional, color representations of calculated variables that characterize ballistic phenomena such as density, pressure, temperature, and strain.

Now, under the Secretary of Defense's High-Performance Computing Modernization Program, ARL has been designated a Major Shared Resource Center (MSRC),[3] one of four being funded by the Modernization Program. ARL already operates an 8-node, 96-processor Silicon Graphics array system that became operational in April 1995, and a classified Cray-2 system that was made available to the DoD user community in June 1995. DoD awarded the contract for the ARL MSRC to Raytheon E-Systems—an eight-year integration effort with a total life-cycle value of more than $150M. These computational assets will greatly enhance Defense research and development capability, especially in the technology areas of structural mechanics, fluid dynamics, chemistry and materials, forces modeling, nanoelectronics, electromagnetics and acoustics, signal image processing, and simulation and modeling.

[3] For more on the Major Shared Resource Center, see the remarks by Kay Howell on pp 114–117 (this volume).

The ARL Major Shared Resource Center is dedicated to supporting the high-performance computing requirements of ARL and other DoD organizations.

Special Honors

On November 14, 1996, special awards were presented to honor computer pioneers Herman Goldstine, Paul Gillon, and John von Neumann. Herman Goldstine was presented with the U.S. Army Distinguished Service Medal in a military ceremony (see pp 102–103); later he was also awarded the Decoration for Distinguished Civilian Service at a Recognition and Dedication Ceremony, at which the computer pioneers were recognized and the new Major Shared Resource Center was dedicated (pp 104–113). Paul Gillon and John von Neumann, represented by their families, were also posthumously recognized at these ceremonies for their significant achievements.

Herman Heine Goldstine.
During World War II, as an Ordnance officer assigned to BRL, Goldstine played a major role in the development of ENIAC. Initially, Goldstine was put in charge of the BRL section at the Moore School of Electrical Engineering, University of Pennsylvania, which operated a Bush differential analyzer and produced firing tables for the Army. At the Moore School, he met John W. Mauchly and J. Presper Eckert, Jr., and helped them develop their plan for an electronic computer. After the Ordnance Department signed the contract with Moore School to build the ENIAC, Captain Goldstine served as the Army's on-site technical representative overseeing the project.

While at the Moore School, Goldstine helped develop the operating routines for the ENIAC, and he also helped develop the original plans for the Army's second computer, the EDVAC.

When released from the service in 1946, Goldstine joined von Neumann at the Institute for Advanced Study, working on the IAS computer project (partly funded by the Ordnance Department). During the late 1940s, Goldstine, von Neumann, and others wrote a series of reports on the logic and operation of a stored-program computer, very largely defining the structure of modern electronic computers.

The IAS group fathered a generation of machines, including the ORDVAC, installed at BRL in 1952. ORDVAC was one of several direct descendants of the IAS machine, but there were also several collateral descendants, perhaps the most important being the 700 and 7000 series of IBM machines and the UNIVAC 1100 series from Sperry Rand.

In 1985, President Reagan presented Goldstine the National Medal of Science, recognizing "his fundamental contributions to the development of the digital computer, computer programming, and numerical analysis."

Paul Nelson Gillon.
A 1933 graduate of West Point, Gillon earned his master of science degree from MIT in 1938. In 1939, he was assigned to BRL to work with R. H. Kent.[4] In 1940, he was named Executive Officer of BRL, and the next year, he was named Assistant Director, following Lieutenant Colonel Leslie E. Simon. In 1942, he was assigned to the Office of the Chief of Ordnance as Deputy Chief of the Service Branch, Technical Division. At BRL, Gillon pushed Simon and Colonel Herman H. Zornig to approach IBM to obtain a set of punch card machines to support the BRL Bush differential analyzer. In 1942, he contracted with Harold Pender (Dean of the Moore School) to

[4] Robert Harrington Kent served as Associate Director of BRL until 1948. His 40 years of service to the U.S. Army were commemorated with a symposium on December 7, 1955. A copy of the commemorative material was distributed at the conference.

take over operation of the Penn Bush differential analyzer. He put Goldstine in charge of the BRL operations at Penn, and he supervised the ENIAC project, visiting Thomas J. Watson (then CEO of IBM) and Oliver E. Buckley (then President of Bell Telephone Laboratories) to request help. In 1944, he was awarded the Legion of Merit for his R&D management accomplishments. Gillon was later the director of research at the Watertown Arsenal and the commander of the Ordnance Research Office (1954–56).

John von Neumann.
In August 1944, Goldstine told von Neumann about the ENIAC project and showed him the machine. That same month, von Neumann attended a meeting of the BRL Scientific Advisory Committee when it was decided to proceed with a second machine, the EDVAC. In the spring of 1945, Goldstine circulated copies of von Neumann's "First Draft of a Report on the EDVAC," a seminal document in the design of computers. Later that year, at von Neumann's instigation, Nicholas Metropolis and Stanley Frankel journeyed to Philadelphia to run calculations for the Manhattan Project on ENIAC.

Back at the Institute for Advanced Study, von Neumann launched his Electronic Computer Project. In the first conceptual paper on an internally programmed computer, "Preliminary discussion of the logical design of an electronic computing instrument" (June 1946), Arthur W. Burks, Goldstine, and von Neumann issued a classic report that profoundly influenced all subsequent computer developments. Among the family of machines built following the IAS concepts was ORDVAC, installed at BRL in 1952. Meanwhile, in 1948, after ENIAC had been reconstructed at BRL, von Neumann helped reprogram the

Day 1
November 13, 1996

1. Opening Session: History of Early Computing

Welcoming Remarks

Paul Deitz:

Good morning, ladies and gentlemen. I'd like to welcome all of you here on this very wonderful two-day celebration. My name is Paul Deitz; I'm with the Army Research Laboratory. For some of you who remember the old days, I used to be with the Ballistic Research Laboratories.

It's a very exciting time for us. We're actually here in part because our friends in Philadelphia had a wonderful celebration last February.[1] They reminded some of us younger folks about a bit of our heritage that we hadn't really truly forgotten but weren't as well informed of as we might have been. There are of course two major groups that sponsored the celebrations last February: the University of Pennsylvania and the Association for Computing Machinery. Dr. Greg Farrington of the University of Pennsylvania will be here tomorrow, and his fine staff welcomed us into their midst.

A number of folks at the Association for Computing Machinery were really instrumental in our being there. Among these were Dr. Bertram Herzog, of the University of Michigan, who I think is going to be here later; Dr. Frank Friedman, who is Chairman of the Computer Science Department at Temple University; and Dr. Tim Bergin, of the American University, who is up on stage with us and whom you'll meet in just a few minutes. Tim, who is a historian, had already put together a history track for the ACM meeting and very kindly extended the program so that we could have our own special session devoted to the work at Aberdeen Proving Ground (APG).

Through that experience, some of us younger folks got to meet some of the earlier workers and pretty much fixed in our minds that we needed to plan something like this commemoration, from our own somewhat parochial perspective here at APG. So here we are, and I welcome you as guests of the Army Research Laboratory and the Ordnance Center and School. General Shadley has provided wonderful support. Tomorrow we're going to see a wonderful event: there will be a parade in review tomorrow morning and we'll all be going over there by bus. After lunch we will have our civilian ceremony.

What are really the foci for this celebration? Some of us felt that it might be useful to help the public remember that it was the Army that initiated the computer revolution. I know that many of these ideas are arguable, but we'd like to think that the Army had a lot to do with this. It's fairly clear that very few inventions have had as large an impact on our civilization as the

[1] The Association for Computing Machinery held its Computer Week in Philadelphia in February 1996 to commemorate the 50th anniversary of computing. The History Track, chaired by Tim Bergin of American University, had a panel on "The Army, the National Need, and the ENIAC." The panel was chaired by Paul Deitz, with Herman Goldstine, Harry Reed, and Barkley Fritz as panelists. A transcript of this panel is provided on pp 142–158 (this volume).

computer. Modern computers are pretty much descended from the ENIAC, the EDVAC, the ORDVAC, and the BRLESC machines, which were all a part of the early history of the Army's Ballistic Research Laboratory here at APG. These machines weren't built for some abstract need, but were conceived and built to solve specific military problems. We're going to hear a lot more about what those problems were, later on today.

The second focus is to attempt to give credit to the highly skilled and dedicated military and civilian scientists and other workers who, along with their counterparts in the private sector, solved a great national defense problem. They had specific objectives and, ironically, the very first problem that the ENIAC was used to solve was not what the machine was built for. As many of you know, it was first used to perform hydrogen bomb calculations for Los Alamos.[2] Of course the machine was designed to compute firing tables and bombing tables for BRL. So the ENIAC met a tremendous defense need.

[2] Fritz (1994); also Randell (1982) and Metropolis (1980).

The third focus is to capture this information and document it. That's part of what this celebration is about, so we're filming and taping these sessions. We are going to endeavor, later on, to put together a compilation of the transcripts of what is said.

To my right are some wonderful exhibits.[3] In addition, we have provided lots of materials in your registration kit, so you can go home and at your leisure read up on the many fascinating details.

[3] A photographic exhibit, prepared for the 1996 ACM Conference by Expert Events, Inc., of Philadelphia, was displayed at the Commemoration. Tim Bergin of American University, who served as a consultant to Expert Events, created an exhibit of artifacts from this period to complement the photographic exhibit.

Our guiding principle was to look backwards. However, another very happy event was that the Army Research Laboratory was chosen as one of the four Department of Defense sites for a Major Shared Resource Center (MSRC). So tomorrow afternoon, there will be a panel on ARL efforts in supercomputing and the dedication of the MSRC. Some folks around here that you'll meet later on, including Charlie Nietubicz and Harold Breaux, have made

Photo exhibit at 50 Years of Computing celebration.

major contributions toward making this event happen and in helping to continue our proud ARL traditions.

Just a couple of related administrative issues. The principal focus today is not on the people with the red badges—those are committee members. If you have a problem, I suppose you would see one of us wearing the red badge. The people that are really important are those wearing the blue badges; these are our ARL computer pioneers. So if you're wearing a blue badge, get to know one of the younger people; if you're not wearing a blue badge, get to know somebody who is!

We're trying to be as inclusive as possible. Two days seems like a long time to do a program like this. However, when you start to look at the magnitude of the set of events that happened here at APG, two days isn't really very much time. So, we're inevitably going to miss important things and underestimate the importance of various contributions. We really do want to try to be inclusive, but that may only happen later on, as we put together our written compilation of the day's activities.

So I'd encourage all of you who have another view, or who have photographs or different ideas, to talk to somebody back there at the table and we'll do everything we can to ensure that this additional material is included in the final written record. Let's have a very good day.

I'd now like to introduce Dr. William Moye, who is the ARL historian. He has been one of the really active people in seeing that this event took place.

Announcements

William Moye:

I have just a few short administrative announcements. We're very glad to see all of you here this morning. I'm told that the heat is on and it should be warming up. [laughter] You're welcome to bring your coffee in here. As most of you know, there's coffee and doughnuts in the room immediately behind us here, so you're welcome to bring your coffee in.

Some of you took the buses from the motel this morning. There will be buses this afternoon going to the APG Ordnance Museum for the social. There will also be buses again in the morning. So if you didn't know about the buses, be advised that there is transportation from the Sheraton coming over here to the Top of the Bay [officer's club]. And if you didn't sign up for the social and you want to come, we can still do that.

You probably found the rest rooms. They're basically down this hall and down the outside hall. There's a pay phone in the coat room. There's also a pay phone upstairs. We will be eating lunch upstairs. I hope you picked up your bag at registration. Please remember that there's a coffee mug in there, so please try not to break that. It has the little logo on it.

I want to thank Ray Aster, who is sitting here in the front row. Ray is one of the APG retirees. He brought the large replicas of the computer technology stamp that are over here by the registration table. [see sidebar] There will be personnel from the Postal Service here at lunch time, both today and tomorrow, selling the stamps.

Sharon McCullough is walking around here somewhere. She's the one from Expert Events. They put together the big display on the ENIAC. This is the same display that many of you saw up in Philadelphia at the ACM Conference in February. Many nice pieces. I think a lot of you see yourselves in some of those pictures in Sharon's display. There's also a nice display against the back there on the Scientific Advisory Committee. Some of you will recognize a lot of the BRL staff, as well as the scientific staff of the Scientific Advisory Committee. There are also some video kiosks showing some of the later computer developments here at ARL.

Tim Bergin, who Dr. Deitz referred to a minute ago, provided a lot of the material and certainly provided all the little identification pieces in the display case over there. Some of the rest of you provided some of the booklets and items. Tim had a different array of items up at the ACM Computer Science Conference in Philadelphia. This is a very nice display of artifacts, pamphlets, and manuals on some of the early machines. Tim is a professor at American University, and he is our next speaker.

Commemorative Stamp

On October 8, 1996, the U.S. Postal Service issued a 32-cent "computer technology" stamp, which commemorates the 50th anniversary of the unveiling of ENIAC (Electronic Numerical Integrator and Computer) and the pervasive influence of computers and computer technology in modern life. The Postmaster General and the Commanding General, U.S. Army Aberdeen Proving Ground, sponsored the dedication ceremony at the Top of the Bay Club (formerly the Officers' Club). In his remarks, Dr. John W. Lyons, Director, U.S. Army Research Laboratory, noted that the Army stood in the forefront 50 years ago, that over the years, Army researchers and technicians supported development of faster and more powerful processors and networks, and that ARL would soon dedicate tremendous new capabilities as part of the Department of Defense High-Performance Computing Modernization Program. In a ceremony on November 14, 1996, ARL dedicated its Major Shared Resource Center, one of four such facilities in DoD. (See Moye, 1996; Weiss, 1997.)

Computer technology stamp.

Keynote Address: A Short History of Computing *or* How Did We Get to Aberdeen?

Tim Bergin:

Introduction

The history of technology in general, and of specific technology such as the automobile, the television, and the computer, tells us that a given technology springs not from a single idea, but emerges over time from the work of numerous individuals—some of whom are known to us, and some whose contributions are lost to history. Computing is a perfect example of this phenomenon.

Although we're here today to pause and reflect on the role of the U.S. Army Ordnance Department, and its successor organizations, in the development of the electronic digital computer, the Program Committee asked me to set a context for the day by identifying important milestones in the evolution of computing. I will also try to relate this to the Ballistic Research Laboratory's use of mechanical and electrical calculating equipment, punch card data processing equipment, analog computers, and early digital machines.

Before beginning, we might all stop and ask the question, *why*? Why was it that the Ordnance Department at Aberdeen Proving Ground got involved in computing? I'll first give you a short answer to the question. The longer answer is the actual lecture itself.

I first met Harry Reed in Philadelphia, last February, at the Association for Computing Machinery's annual conference. Harry was an early member of the team at the Ballistic Research Laboratories. And in the course of a discussion after the panel, Harry told me, "You don't fire a weapon unless you know where the shell is going to land." Although that might seem self-evident to most of you in this room, it seemed profound to me, as a college professor who did two years, eight months, and 21 days in the Army Medical Corps in the early sixties. So the important question is "how do we aim the weapon?"

Harry also shared some material with me, and after reading over some of it, I realized that "interior and exterior ballistics" are topics that are simply over my head. But I do know that the process of calculating firing tables is complex and time consuming. The number of individual calculations needed to prepare a firing table in the 1930s was staggering.[4] And in 1941, the United States entered a war.

The need for firing tables for existing weaponry, as well as newly developed weaponry, was overwhelming. The men and women of the U.S. Army and Navy were desperate for ways to improve the quality of firing tables and the timeliness of their delivery. There is some data that has been floating around from multiple sources, and it's actually on some of the display panels, that a person with a desk calculator could compute a 60-second trajectory in about 20 hours. The differential analyzer, which I'll mention, could compute a trajectory in about 15 minutes. The ENIAC could compute the trajectory in about 30 seconds, or about half the time that the shell would be in the air. Given these figures, it's easy to see that a firing table for a single weapon could take a number of skilled workers a number of weeks to complete using desk calculators. If you've never seen a firing table, there's one in the exhibit display case.

[4] According to *Ballisticians in War and Peace, A History of The United States Army Ballistic Research Laboratories* (Volume 1, 1914–1956, p 38), the Aberdeen differential analyzer computed 1560 production trajectories used in the preparation of 10 firing tables, between February 1 and June 30, 1945. Obviously the use of punched card machinery and hand-operated adding machines, as in the 1930s, was much more labor intensive, and took longer periods of time.

In a nutshell, that is why it was the Ordnance Department that led the way—because they had the need. Interestingly enough, the panel that Paul Deitz put together for the ACM's February meeting was entitled "The Army, the National Need, and ENIAC."

During the rest of this lecture I will try to identify some of the precursors of the modern computer and highlight the important role played by the Ballistic Research Laboratory, Aberdeen Proving Ground.[5]

Punched Card Technology

Although the punched card had been invented in the 1880s by Herman Hollerith for the U.S. Census Bureau, the first really scientific use was by L. J. Comrie in 1928, in the United Kingdom. Comrie used punched card technology to calculate the motions of the moon, but he was not alone in his endeavors. Wallace Eckert of Columbia University also experimented with punched cards. In 1929, Eckert convinced the IBM Corporation to fund the Columbia University Statistical Bureau, which would use IBM punched card machines for processing. Eckert not only performed essential scientific calculations using this equipment, but he proved the value of this technology to *science*.

Let me bring this discussion closer to home. In 1937, Colonel H. H. Zornig of APG (later head of BRL) became interested in the capabilities of punched card equipment and its potential application to the creation of firing tables and other ordnance processes. By 1941, BRL was using standard IBM tabulating equipment, as well as equipment specially modified to BRL's specifications. This equipment was used in the preparation of firing tables, as well as other problems such as the theory of breech rings, fuze-setting coefficients, shock wave study, and probability integrals.[6]

Analog Devices

Scientists and engineers have been using *analog devices* for many years. Indeed, for a lot of us in this room, our introduction to higher mathematics was accompanied by the acquisition of a *slide rule*. I still have the slide rule I got in 1958, when I went to college. When I show it to students today, they all say, "What's that?" There is a *military slide rule* in the display case that I found in Boston about five or six years ago. I've not yet found anyone that can tell me how to use it to calculate a trajectory. So if there's anyone in the audience who could help with that, I will be most appreciative.

Vannevar Bush, who later served as President Truman's science advisor, had a large analog machine known as the "differential analyzer" constructed at MIT in 1930.[7] This machine solved differential equations by mechanical integration. In 1934, the Moore School of the University of Pennsylvania constructed a similar, but more powerful machine based on the MIT design. In the same year, Bush suggested to BRL's predecessor organization that they use a differential analyzer for calculating ballistic trajectories. In 1935, a differential analyzer was built at Aberdeen Proving Ground and used in firing table preparation.

According to *Ballisticians in War and Peace*, "the differential analyzer was the most important tool acquired before BRL was formed."[8] The success of the Aberdeen analyzer marked the beginning of the development of specialized computing facilities for ballistic computations of various kinds. Since the Aberdeen analyzer could not keep up with the Army's needs, BRL arranged to have access to the larger and more powerful differential analyzer at the

[5] The best general text on the history of computing is Williams (1997). The best source for information on the developments at BRL is Goldstine (1993). Information on specific individuals may be found in Lee (1995a).

[6] See *Ballisticians* (vol. I), pp 38–41.

[7] See *Ballisticians* (vol. I), pp 17–18.

[8] *Ballisticians* (vol. I), p 38.

Moore School of Electrical Engineering of the University of Pennsylvania. Staff from BRL were sent to Philadelphia to operate this machine. During this period, a number of improvements were made to increase the speed, mainly by substitution of electrical for mechanical components.

Early Efforts

Starting about 1937, a number of projects began working on improving the speed of computation. In Germany, Konrad Zuse began experimenting with mechanical computing devices; in the United States, George Stibitz began experimenting with telephone relays, John Atanasoff started construction of an electronic calculator, and Howard Aiken designed an electrical analog of Babbage's analytical engine; and in Britain, Alan Turing and others began the construction of machines to decode messages.

Konrad Zuse

Although unknown until after the war, a young German engineer, Konrad Zuse, began experimenting in 1934 with a mechanical device to do calculations.[9] In a lecture that Zuse gave at the Computing Museum in the early 1980s, he explained that he was "lazy," and he didn't want to spend the time necessary to do the calculations by hand. By 1938, Zuse had completed his first machine in his parents' living room in Berlin. The Z1 had a mechanical memory capable of storing 16 binary numbers, each with 24 bits. Zuse's control mechanism used holes punched in discarded 35-mm movie film. By 1939, he had completed his second machine (the Z2), which used relay technology. By 1941, Zuse's Z3 was operational. This machine used relay technology and had a 64-word floating-point binary memory.[10] Zuse went on to design several other computers and after the war was the founder of a successful computer firm in Germany.

John V. Atanasoff

Across the ocean in Iowa, another young man was bothered by repetitive calculations, the waste of time that they entailed, and the problems of error. John Vincent Atanasoff was a professor of physics at Iowa State University.[11] In 1937, he started thinking about a machine that would use capacitors as a memory. From 1939 to 1942, he and his graduate assistant, Clifford Berry, built a special-purpose electronic digital calculator that later became known as the Atanasoff-Berry Computer, or ABC. This machine had a regenerative memory that could store 30 (50-bit) binary numbers and used digital logic for computation (addition and subtraction). Atanasoff left Iowa State in 1942 to work at the Naval Research Laboratories, and did not return to work on the calculator.[12]

John Mauchly met Atanasoff at a meeting of the American Association for the Advancement of Science in Philadelphia in December of 1940. After an exchange of correspondence during the spring, Mauchly visited Atanasoff in June of 1941. Mauchly, a professor of physics at Ursinus College, was experimenting with devices to assist in weather calculations. (I would be remiss if I did not mention here that faculty at Iowa State have started a project to build a model of the ABC.)

George Stibitz

George Stibitz was a mathematician working at the Bell Telephone Laboratories.[13] In 1937, he too was interested in calculation. He took some wire relays out of a scrap pile and took them home to experiment with. Stibitz had

[9] Lee (1995a), pp 758–774.

[10] This was the "first fully functional program-controlled electromechanical digital computer in the world" (Lee, 1995a, p 759).

[11] Lee (1995a), pp 27–46.

[12] Following a patent dispute between the Honeywell and Sperry-Rand Corporations, Atanasoff was designated the inventor of the digital computer (U.S. District Court, District of Minnesota, Fourth Division, October 19, 1973). For an excellent discussion of this dispute, see Rosen (1990).

[13] See Lee (1995a), pp 640–644.

noticed the similarity between binary numbers and the on/off states of the (telephone) relay. He created a small (binary) adder, which was later called the Model "K"—for the kitchen in which it was fabricated. There is a model of the Model-K in the display case, built by Raymon Richardson, a student at American University.

Stibitz showed this model to colleagues at Bell Laboratories, and a project was started in 1939 in which Stibitz and S. B. Williams built the "complex number calculator." Although not a computer, it was capable of complex arithmetic operations. On September 11, 1940, Stibitz demonstrated the machine to the attendees at a conference of the American Mathematical Society at Dartmouth College in Hanover, New Hampshire. Using a teletype connected over special telephone lines, attendees were able to type in mathematical problems. The answers were received in a matter of minutes. Mike Williams, in *A History of Computer Technology*, mentions that John Mauchly and Norbert Wiener both spent a great deal of time experimenting with the relay calculation system.[14]

[14] Williams (1997), p 224.

When the United States entered the War, the National Defense Research Council (NDRC) asked Stibitz to work on some projects. The first project was to build a gun director. Stibitz suggested, of course, a relay calculator, which was later called the "relay interpolator." The machine was operational in September of 1943. Stibitz's third relay computer was designed to test the accuracy of antiaircraft gun directors and became known as the "ballistic computer." A second ballistic computer, known as the Bell Laboratories Relay Calculator Model IV (or Error Detector Mark 22 by the Navy), was built for the Naval Research Laboratories in Washington, D.C.

Finally, in 1944, the U.S. government gave Bell Labs a contract to build two identical machines, known as the Bell Laboratories General Purpose Relay Calculators or Model V. The first of these was for the National Advisory Committee on Aeronautics at Langley Field, Virginia; the second was built for the U.S. Army's Aberdeen Proving Ground. These computers were so reliable that people would submit problems at the end of the day shift, the problems would run overnight, and they would get the output the next morning.[15]

[15] *Ballisticians* (vol. I), pp 39 and 40 (with photograph).

Howard Aiken

Howard Aiken of Harvard University's Computational Laboratory was also working on computing devices.[16] Unlike the others, Aiken borrowed from many technologies, including mechanical devices based on IBM punched card equipment and the relay technology used by Stibitz. Aiken was also saddled with complex problems, and decided he needed a machine that was at least an order of magnitude better than anything that existed at the time. Knowledgeable of the work done at the Watson Astronomical Computing Bureau at Columbia (by Wallace Eckert), and quite aware of Charles Babbage's efforts a century earlier, Aiken set out to design such a machine.[17]

[16] Lee (1995a), pp 9–20.

[17] Williams (1997), pp 154–186; Lee (1995a), pp 51–64.

Ultimately, Aiken convinced IBM to build a machine with financial assistance from the U.S. Navy. The Automatic Sequence Controlled Calculator was operational at IBM's Endicott facility in January of 1943, and was later relocated to Harvard. Commonly called the "Harvard Mark I," the machine was dedicated in May 1944. It contained 72 mechanical registers, each capable of storing 23 decimal digits and a sign, and it was controlled by punched paper tape. During the war, Aiken served as a Commander in the U.S. Naval Reserve, and the Mark I was used by the Navy's Bureau of Ships and later by the Navy's Bureau of Ordnance. One of Aiken's young assistants was Lieutenant Grace Murray Hopper, who was to play a major role in the development of standardized programming languages and rise to the rank of Rear Admiral.

[18] For Grosch's recollections on the "Aberdeen machines," see Grosch (1991), pp 88–91.

Another of Aiken's assistants was Herbert R. J. Grosch (an attendee at this meeting).[18]

British Code-Breaking Efforts

During World War II, the British government maintained its code-breaking establishment at Bletchley Park, outside London. Alan Turing was one of the people working there.[19] By April of 1943, Dr. C. E. Wynn-Williams had constructed a machine using mechanical relays and electronic components. The machine was called the "Heath Robinson," after a cartoonist at the time, who was known for designing strange and wonderful machines—like those designed by Rube Goldberg, the American cartoonist. Later this machine was surpassed by the Colossus, which used 1500 vacuum tubes (or valves as they were known in Britain at that time), which was more than any other device except for the ENIAC.[20] A museum has recently been built at Bletchley Park to commemorate these activities, many of which are still protected under the Official Secrets Act.

IBM and Mechanical Calculators

The last thing I want to mention is the mechanical calculators, which were used for scientific as well as commercial calculations. In truth, their use at Aberdeen preceded the other devices I just mentioned.

During this period, the International Business Machines Corporation (IBM) continued to design more powerful accounting machines, including a Card-Programmed Electronic Calculator (CPC). Of more importance to us, Herb Grosch, in his memoirs, mentions that the Ballistic Research Laboratories, under Major Leslie Simon, let a contract to IBM "to develop two high-speed relay calculators with plug board sequencing."[21] Constructed during 1944, these machines were called the IBM Pluggable Sequence Relay Calculators, but they were better known as the "Aberdeen machines" and were used for preparing firing tables.[22] Five additional copies of this machine were built, three for the Naval Proving Ground at Dahlgren, and two for the Watson Scientific Computing Laboratory. Ultimately IBM built its largest calculator, the IBM Selective Sequence Electronic Calculator (SSEC), which contained about 13,000 vacuum tubes and was dedicated in 1948.[23]

The topic of mechanical calculators leads us to the first use of the term *computer*, which was originally used to identify individuals who did calculations using mechanical and electrical calculators. These people were typically women with a strong educational background in mathematics. There's an excellent paper in your packet by Barkley Fritz from the *Annals of the History of Computing* on the women computers.[24] In the second panel this morning we will all have the opportunity to hear some of these women "computers" speak about their experiences here at Aberdeen.

ENIAC

The Moore School of the University of Pennsylvania was founded in 1923. By the 1930s, it had formed an arrangement with the U.S. Army's Ballistic Research Laboratory here at Aberdeen. As I mentioned earlier, a major result of this collaboration was the construction of two differential analyzers, one at the Moore School, and one here at Aberdeen.

By the 1940s, faculty at the Moore School were involved in radar and other electronics research. John Mauchly, whose interest in high-speed computation I mentioned earlier, was a professor of physics at Ursinus College outside Philadelphia.[25] Because of the war, he enrolled in a wartime electronics course

[19] Alan Mathison Turing was the creator of the concept of the "universal machine," later called a "Turing machine" in his honor. See Lee (1995a), pp 670–678, and sidebar, p 33.

[20] For an excellent discussion of British efforts, see Williams (1997), pp 284–293.

[21] Grosch (1991), p 89.

[22] "The two IBM Relay Calculators were used for a short time but were not successful." —Kempf (1961), p 17. (Copies of this monograph were distributed to attendees.)

[23] For more on the SSEC, see Williams (1997), pp 255–258.

[24] Fritz (1996).

[25] Lee (1995a), pp 453–460.

[26] Lee (1995a), pp 271–275.

at the Moore School; John Presper Eckert, Jr., was a graduate student overseeing the laboratory for that course.[26] Mauchly and Eckert spent many hours discussing electronics, especially Mauchly's fascination with weather prediction, an effort retarded by the lack of high-speed computational capacity. When the Moore School needed to replace faculty who were drafted into military service, Mauchly agreed to join the Moore School Faculty.

In August 1942, Mauchly distilled his ideas into a short paper, "The use of high-speed vacuum tube devices for calculating," in which he compared the advantages of electronic techniques to those of mechanical technology.[27] Mauchly estimated that calculations for ballistic trajectories would be in the 100-second range, compared to the 15 to 30 minutes required using mechanical technology. Mauchly's paper was not well received.

[27] First printed in Randell (1973), pp 355–358, from original typescript.

By 1941, the production of firing tables was far behind. The officers of BRL were searching for any opportunity to improve processing. Lieutenant Herman Goldstine, an assistant professor of mathematics at the University of Michigan before the war, was assigned to oversee the production of firing tables, including the supervision of the women computers at the Moore School. Hearing of Mauchly's ideas, he approached his former supervisor, Colonel Paul Gillon, about pursuing the construction of an advanced machine. Colonel Gillon, who now worked in the office of the Chief of Ordnance, recognized the potential for success and convinced the Army to fund the project.

Accordingly, on June 5, 1943, the Army Ordnance Corps and the University of Pennsylvania signed a contract for "research and development of an electronic numerical integrator and computer and delivery of a report thereon."[28] The initial contract was in the amount of $61,700.

[28] Kempf (1961), p 22.

It should be noted that Colonel Gillon was responsible for the addition of the words "and computer" to the name of the device in the contract. Gillon wanted to forestall future problems if the machine was used for more general problem-solving purposes later on.

The Electronic Numerical Integrator and Computer (ENIAC) was officially dedicated on February 14, 1946. It had 40 units with 18,000 vacuum tubes, 1,500 relays, 70,000 resistors, 10,000 capacitors, and miles of wire. It was eight feet high, three feet deep, and 100 feet long, weighed 30 tons and consumed 130 kW of power.[29] Although the Army had initially budgeted $150,000 for the project, the final accounting showed a total expense of $486,804.22.[30] So you can see that we got a real bargain for our tax dollars.

[29] Williams (1997), p 272.
[30] Williams (1997), p 272.

In March of 1946, after a dispute about patent rights, Eckert and Mauchly left the Moore School to found their own firm, the Electronic Control Company.[31]

[31] For their reflections, see Eckert (1980) and Mauchly (1980).

In the first panel this morning, we'll have an opportunity to hear from Herman Goldstine, BRL's liaison to the Moore School; Harry Huskey, one of the ENIAC engineers; and Harry Reed, an early member of the BRL team at Aberdeen. Your packet also contains some reprints from the *Annals of the History of Computing* devoted to the ENIAC and the ENIAC applications.[32]

[32] Volume 18, Number 1, of the *IEEE Annals of the History of Computing* was a special issue "Documenting ENIAC's 50th Anniversary." Two papers from this issue were reprinted for the attendees: Winegrad (1996) and Goldstine and Goldstine (1946). Reprints of Fritz's ENIAC history papers (Fritz, 1996, 1994) were also included.

After the planning and construction were well under way, the project members started discussing ways to improve the machine. Since it used cables to move pulses from place to place, setting up the machine was time consuming and subject to error. One idea was to create a memory that would store instructions and data. Indeed, Pres Eckert envisioned using a modification of the mercury delay line that he had developed for radar use.

It was during this period that John von Neumann, a member of the BRL Scientific Advisory Committee, met Herman Goldstine at the Aberdeen train station, learned of the project, and joined the ENIAC team as an advisor. In June 1945, von Neumann prepared a document called "First draft of a report on the EDVAC," which, as its title suggests, was preliminary and informal.[33] Goldstine distributed this report to members of the Moore School staff and interested outside scientists, and thus it was the first widely distributed report on electronic digital computers.[34]

EDVAC

EDVAC stood for Electronic Discrete Variable Automatic Computer. It was constructed by the Moore School for BRL and delivered in August of 1949. This *stored-program computer* was put into "practical use" at Aberdeen in April 1952.[35,36] The first panel this afternoon will provide insight into the EDVAC and its immediate successors, the Ordnance Variable Automatic Computer, or ORDVAC; the BRL Electronic Scientific Computer, known as BRLESC I; and its successor BRLESC II.

Moore School Lectures

Although the ENIAC served BRL well until it was turned off in October of 1955, perhaps the most important contribution of all these efforts was the Moore School lectures during the summer of 1946. Actually the first course on the "Theory and Techniques for Design of Electronic Digital Computers," the series included lectures by most of the members of the Moore School team, as well as prominent members from the small but growing computer community. These lectures spread the "good news" about computing to many of the scientific organizations across the country and the world.

Three Lines[37]

Evolving out of these projects, or inspired by the Moore School lectures, were many other projects to design and build electronic computers in the forties and early fifties. Three main lines of development can be traced:

(1) The **EDVAC** was the model for a National Bureau of Standards project that became known as the Standards Eastern Automatic Computer (SEAC),[38] as well as for the BINAC and the UNIVAC machines.

(2) The Institute for Advanced Study at Princeton established a computer project under the direction of John von Neumann. The team included Herman Goldstine and Arthur Burks, both associated with the ENIAC project. The **IAS** computer[39] inspired a second NBS effort, the National Bureau of Standards Western Automatic Computer (SWAC)[40] (which was headed up by Harry Huskey, who is one of our speakers this morning), as well as the ORDVAC,[41] MANIAC,[42] and ILLIAC projects.

(3) And finally, Maurice Wilkes, who was one of a number of people inspired by the Moore School lectures, returned to Cambridge to design and build the **EDSAC**, the Electronic Delay Storage Automatic Calculator.[43] Other projects were started by Manchester University and the National Physical Laboratory in Britain.[44] Harry Huskey, one of our speakers, spent 1947 in the UK, working at the National Physical Laboratory, and visited the other British computing sites.

---

[33] Copies of this report are contained in Stern (1981) and Randell (1973).

[34] Herman Goldstine points out that this distribution of the report "placed its contents in the public domain, and hence anything disclosed therein became unpatentable." See Goldstine's Jayne Lecture (Goldstine, 1992) (provided as a handout to attendees).

[35] *Ballisticians* (vol. I), p 73.

[36] For interesting first-person discussions of EDVAC and its capabilities, see Mauchly (1973b) and Burks (1980).

[37] Weik (1955) includes a three-branched "computer tree" of domestic computing history/evolution (included in the attendees' packets); see pp 52–53, this volume.

[38] Slutz (1980).

[39] Bigelow (1980).

[40] Huskey (1980).

[41] Robertson (1980).

[42] Metropolis (1980).

[43] See Williams (1997), pp 329–336, and Wilkes (1980).

[44] See sidebar, p 33.

Concluding Reflections

From these humble beginnings, an industry developed that has altered modern society more than any other. Each semester I teach an undergraduate course, "Introduction to Computing." Each semester I have to discuss new capabilities. A few years ago, it was personal computers, then it was the Internet, and now it's the World Wide Web. Such courses are only a barometer of the computer's impact on society at large.

The Army too has had to keep up with technology, and the first panel tomorrow morning will tell us about how the Army Research Laboratory has attempted to stay ahead of the computing field with leading edge research and applications such as supercomputing and networking. And finally, after the awards ceremonies tomorrow, a panel will explore the future of computing from ARL's perspective. Certainly all of us will get insights into the future of computing from that panel.

One of the metrics I use for measuring technological change is the extent to which new technology is discussed in the popular media, such as newspapers and news magazines. Fifteen years ago, computers were rarely mentioned in such media, and certainly they were never advertised in them. Now there's rarely an issue of the *Washington Post, Time,* or *Newsweek* without major stories on computing topics and multiple advertisements for personal computers. Where most people had not heard of the Internet just three years ago, a growing number of people are using electronic mail on a daily basis, and public and private organizations are planning for and exploring electronic commerce.

Finally, in the last year the world has jumped on the World Wide Web, so that you rarely see an advertisement that does not have a Uniform Resource Locator (URL) at the bottom. Indeed, the history of computing community, of which I am a member, has a number of Web sites, including one by Mike Muuss here at ARL. If you have some time, you can kill a couple of hours out on Mike's web site[45] examining all the materials he has collected.

How It All Began

So, tomorrow morning when you pick up your newspaper and see an article on the Internet or an advertisement for a personal computer, remember how it all began: a small research project funded by the Ordnance Department, to meet the needs of the Ballistic Research Laboratory, at the Moore School of the University of Pennsylvania, and a dedicated cadre of engineers and (female) "computers."

This morning, we have the incredible privilege of listening to some of the men and women who were there "at the beginning." Thank you.

Paul Deitz:

Thank you very much, Tim. We're going to take a short break. I wanted to mention to you that a few minutes ago, one of the returning pioneers mentioned that a decade or two ago, somebody said that "It would be a cold day at Aberdeen before they recognized Army computing." [laughter] Well, as usual, our pioneers were prescient in their judgments.[46] I do want to tell you

[45] http://ftp.arl.mil/~mike/comphist/eniac-story.html

[46] November 13, 1996, was a very cold day, and when the attendees returned to APG on November 14, 1996, there was an inch of snow on the ground.

Timeline of Selected Early Computing Activities

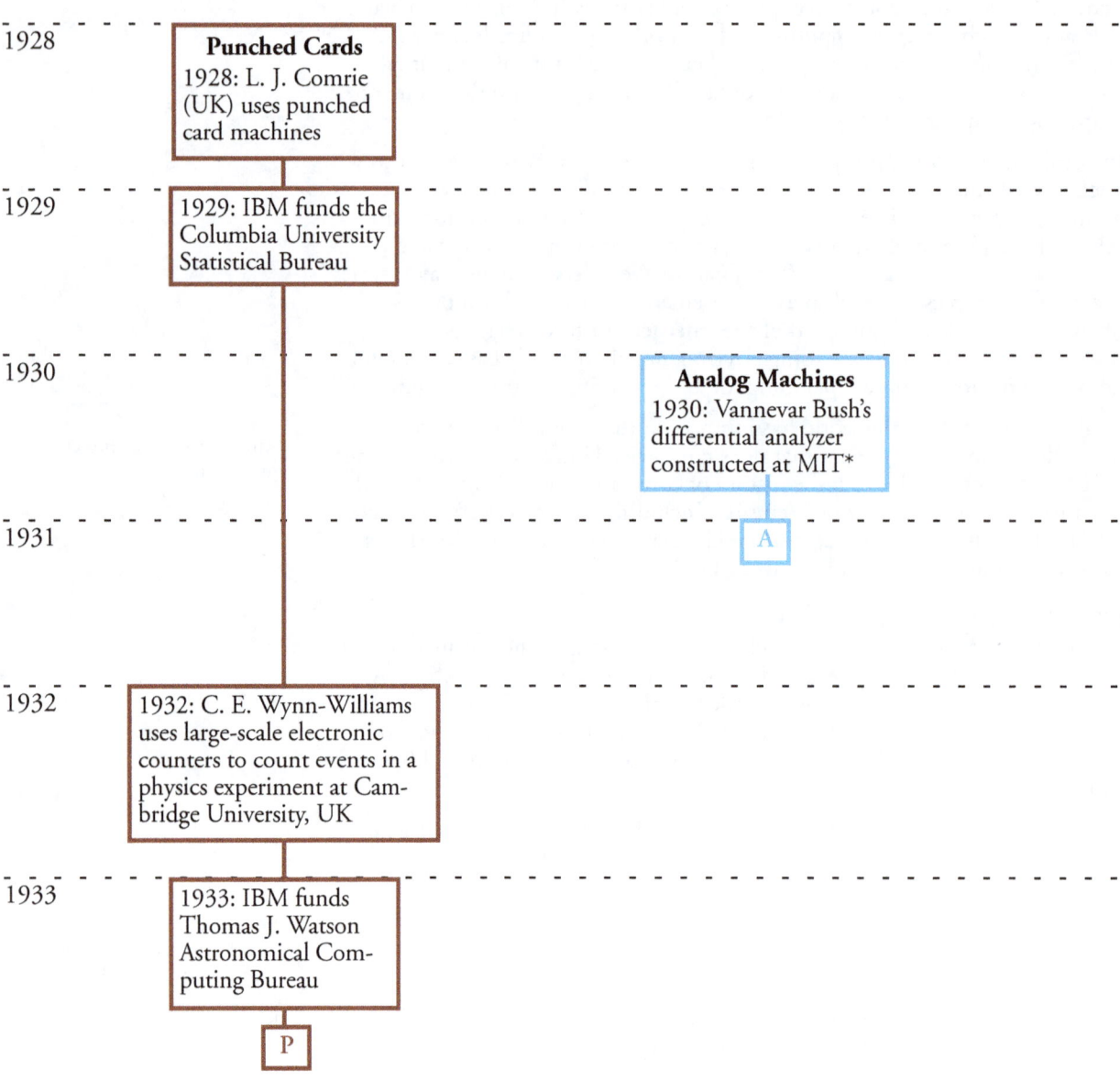

* "… the differential analyzer 'was the most important tool acquired before BRL was formed' [and] the success of the differential analyzer 'marked the beginning of the development of specialized computers for ballistic computations of various kinds.'" (*Ballisticians*, vol. I, p 38.)

Timeline

The information in this timeline, prepared by Tim Bergin, was handed out at the event; the timeline was based on Williams (1997), with additions from other sources.

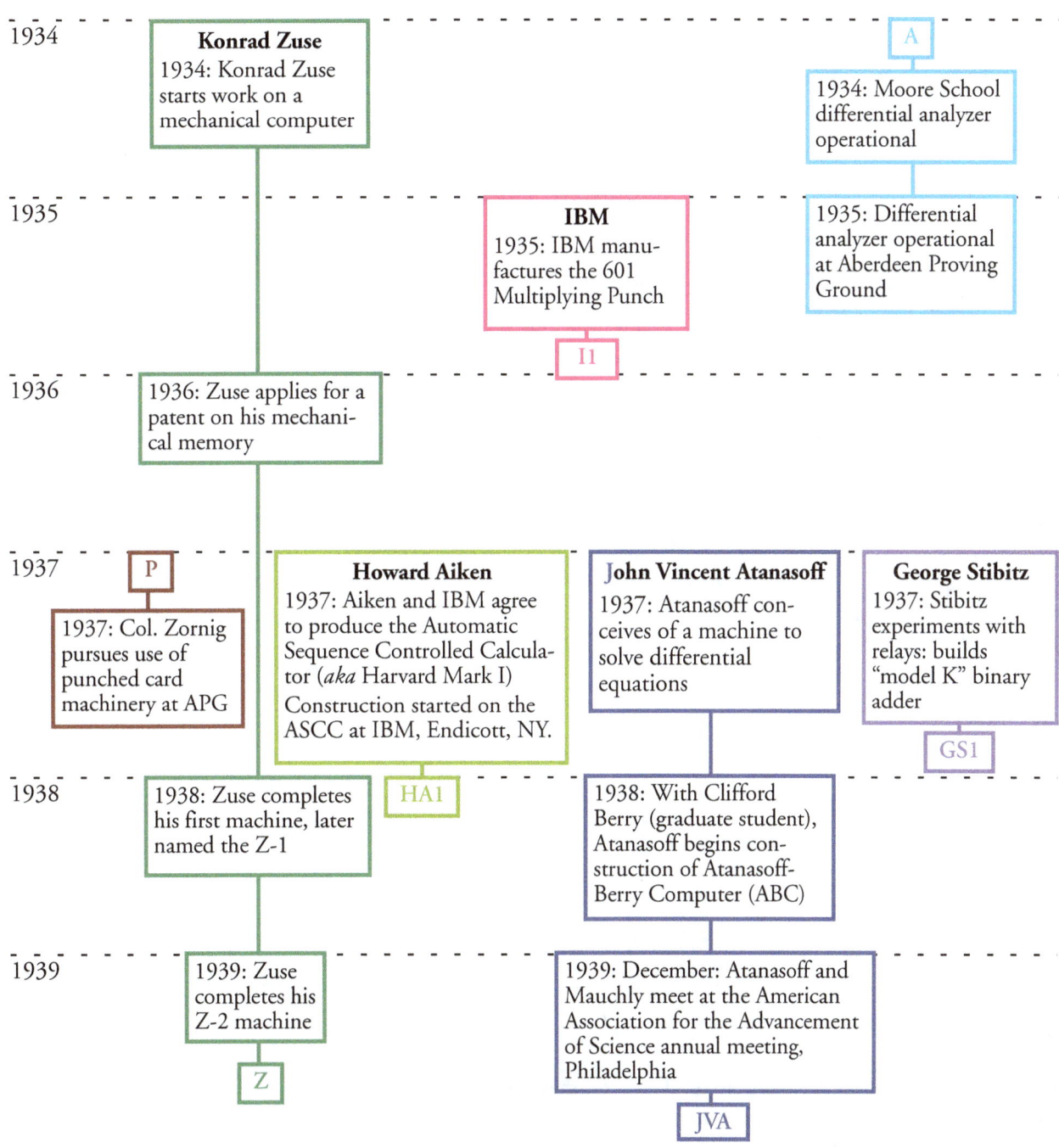

22 *Fifty Years of Army Computing*

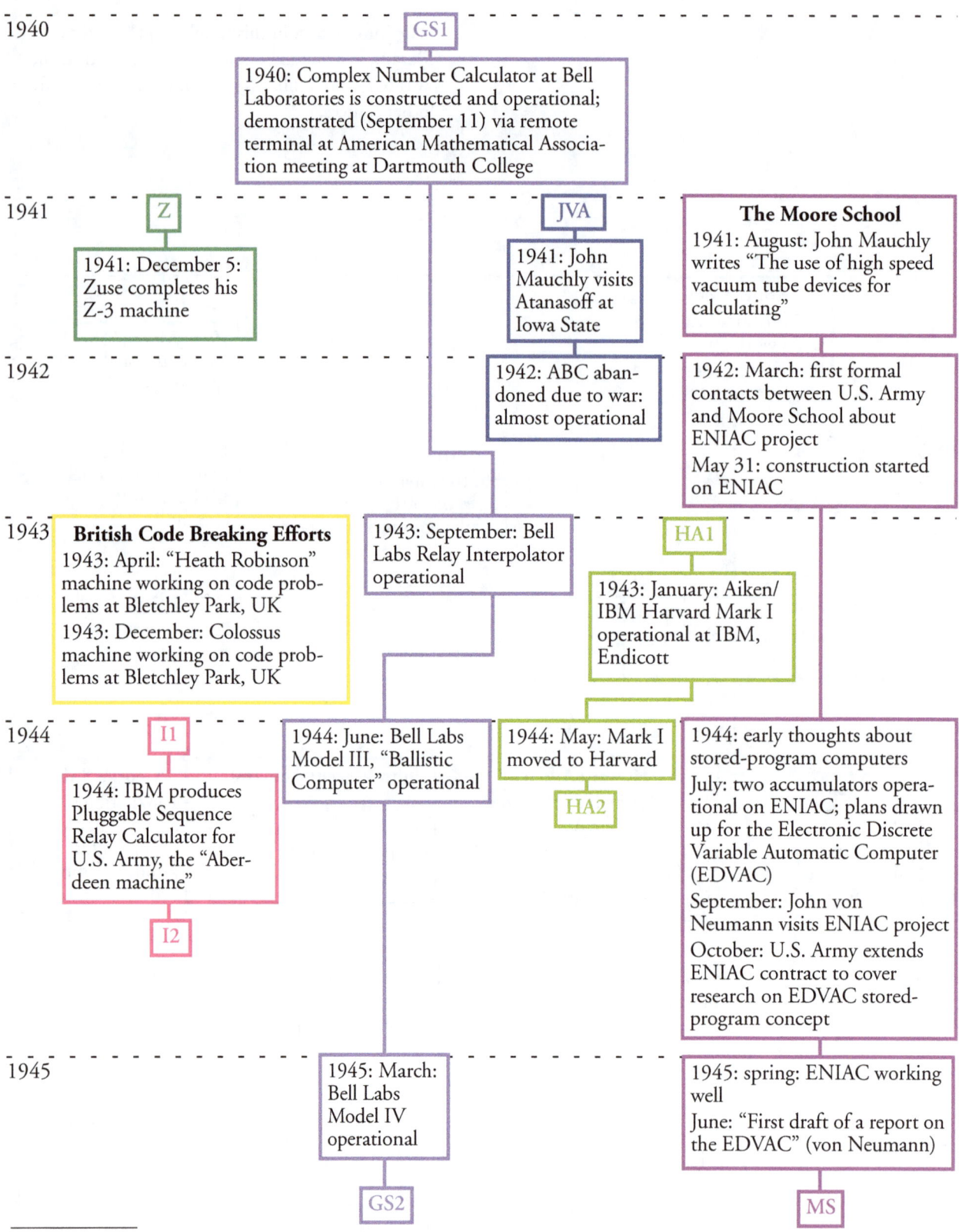

Note: For information on mechanical calculators, see the Special Issue of the *Annals of the History of Computing*, Volume 18, Number 3, *Women in Computing* (Fall 1996).

1946

Institute for Advanced Study
1946: March: von Neumann attempts to set up a computer project at the Institute for Advanced Study, Princeton, NJ
June 28: "Preliminary discussion of the logical design of an electronic computing instrument," by Arthur W. Burks, Herman H. Goldstine, and John von Neumann*

British Computer Efforts
1946: May: Maurice Wilkes sees a copy of the "First draft report"; Wilkes attends Moore School lectures
Alan Turing's designs for the ACE (Automatic Computing Engine) are well under way at National Physical Laboratory (NPL)
August: Wilkes considers building a computer at Cambridge University

GS2
1946: July: Bell Labs Model V operational at Aberdeen

MS
1946: March: Eckert and Mauchly leave Moore School and establish Electronic Control Company
July: Moore School lectures at University of Pennsylvania

1947

1947: January: Harry Huskey arrives at National Physical Laboratory, UK
Construction started on Electronic Delay Storage Automatic Computer (EDSAC) at Cambridge University

HA2
1947: July: Harvard Mark II operational

1947: March: delay line memory for EDVAC project working
ENIAC converted into elementary stored-program computer via the use of function tables†

1948

I2
1948: January: IBM unveils the Selective Sequence Electronic Calculator (SSEC)

1948: June 21: Manchester prototype in limited operation
May: EDSAC fully operational

Other Computer Projects
1948: Standards Eastern Automatic Computer (SEAC) project started at National Bureau of Standards (NBS)

1949

1949: Standards Western Automatic Computer (SWAC) started at the Institute for Numerical Analysis, NBS‡

1952

1952: Ordnance Variable Computer (ORDVAC) copy of the IAS machine operational at Aberdeen¶

---

* Copies of this report were included in the registration packets of attendees.
† Clippinger (1948) describes a strategy for "central programming" of the ENIAC using the function tables. Copies of this report were included in the registration packets of attendees.
‡ Harry Huskey joined the Institute for Numerical Analysis in December 1948 and started the INA computer construction project in January 1949; see Huskey et al (1997), Huskey (1997, 1980), and Rutland (1995).
¶ ORDVAC was built at the University of Illinois and was BRL's fastest computer during the 1950s (*Ballisticians*, vol. I, pp 73–74).

2. ENIAC: Development and Early Days

Harry Reed (chair):
I've been asked to make one announcement. As you all may notice, we've got television coverage, at least video coverage, of all the events here, and we are going out over a thing called the MBONE, which is the Internet slow TV system. People around the world can log in on their PCs and watch what's going on here today. This is one of the little marvels that Tim Bergin referred to earlier.

I'm Harry Reed. I came to BRL in 1950, and started working on the ENIAC and the preparation of firing tables. For many years, I'd heard about some of the people that are here today, some of whom I finally had a chance to meet at the 1996 ACM Conference in Philadelphia. It's my privilege today to have two real pioneers on this panel: **Herman Goldstine**[1] and **Harry Huskey**.[2] Herman was, as mentioned earlier, the project officer on the ENIAC project. Harry was at the University of Pennsylvania and worked on the ENIAC.

[1] See biography, p 5 (this volume).

[2] See Presenter Biographies, p 138 (this volume).

We are going to have a rather informal format; we're going to have a chat. I'm not sure how it's going to go, and I'm not sure what topics we're going to cover. But we're going to try to reflect on some of what happened in those days, get a little bit of the flavor of the times, and perhaps hear a few anecdotes. We will try to give you some idea of some of the things that led up to the development of the ENIAC and some feeling for the early days of the ENIAC.

Guys, I want to thank you both for being here. Herman, let's start with you. It was one of those fortuitous things, I guess. In 1936, you were at the University of Chicago, right?

Herman Goldstine:
That's right.

Harry Reed:
And that was rather significant, wasn't it?

Herman Goldstine:
Yes, it was! I was fortunate enough to be able to teach a course on exterior ballistics. I was very fortunate in being the assistant to a man named Gilbert Bliss, who had been here during the First World War; he thought it would be a good idea if we taught a course in exterior ballistics.[3] Unfortunately, Bliss developed heart trouble, and so I taught the course. This got me into a shape where I knew a lot about the subject. We finished the book!

[3] Bliss (1944).

And also, I was fortunate in having taken a master's degree in mathematical astronomy, and so I knew a fair amount about calculations. It was the natural thing for the Army to transfer me immediately to Lowry Field, in Denver, and then to Sacramento, California, as an Adjutant of a squadron. Fortunately again, Bliss got hold of Oswald Veblen,[4] who was the Chief Scientist in both the First and the Second Wars here at BRL, and they got me out of the Army Air Corps, and back here to Aberdeen.

Harry Reed:

That was a little unusual, actually, for someone to teach a course in exterior ballistics in a university, in the pre-war days, wasn't it?

Herman Goldstine:

Yes, it was.

Harry Reed:

I guess Bliss was really kind of enthusiastic about exterior ballistics.

Herman Goldstine:

He was. There was a group of men that came here including Oswald Veblen and Gilbert Bliss. Norbert Wiener was an enlisted man here in that period.[5] And there was a great interest by mathematicians in the work at BRL. Mr. Bliss was a young patriot, who decided that he really ought to equip young people to help in the war effort. That was my good fortune.

I'll tell you, when I got my travel orders at Sacramento to come to Aberdeen Proving Ground, they were signed by the Adjutant General of the United States Army, but I also had orders to be the Adjutant of a squadron in Sacramento. So I called the Commanding Officer in Sacramento for advice, and he said, "Well, who signed the orders to come to Aberdeen?"

I said, "It's the Adjutant General of the Army."

He said, "Well, he takes precedence over anybody here." [laughter]

So I said, "What should I do?"

He said, "Get in your automobile and start driving and don't ask any questions." [laughter]

So I did.

Along the way, I picked the route and got here, where I met Colonel [Paul] Gillon,[6] who was to be my Commanding Officer. Under him, talking about mathematicians from the First War, there was a Major Albert A. Bennett, who had been an officer here during the First War also.[7] So there was a group that knew a lot about computing here [at APG].

Harry Reed:

So then they sent you up to Philadelphia, right?

Herman Goldstine:

Yes, I was very fortunate in that Colonel Gillon and I somehow just clicked together. There was an empathy that developed, which persisted through the remainder of his lifetime. Even after the war ended, we would see the Gillons—not frequently, but once a year or so. At that time, he took me to Philadelphia, and it was clear that something needed to be done. Fortunately, he said, "You do it."

Harry Reed:

You had something like a hundred and some people pushing hand calculators.

[4] Goldstine (1993) discusses this period in great detail (ch 9), "Ballistics and the rise of the great mathematicians"; Oswald Veblen is introduced on page 77. According to *Ballisticians*, vol. I, p 1: "The Range Firing Section, under Major Oswald Veblen, prepared all firing tables (at that time called Range Tables), made mathematical analyses of ballistics problems, and conducted experiments to obtain information for increasing the range and accuracy of the projectiles."

[5] Norbert Wiener, one of the most eminent mathematicians of this century, served as a "computer" at APG in 1918 and 1919. His most well-known efforts are *Cybernetics* (1948) and *The Human Use of Human Beings* (1950). He served on the MIT faculty from 1919 to 1960, and died in 1964.

[6] See biography, pp 5–6, this volume.

[7] "Another man, active in ballistics both in World War I and II and a longtime professor of mathematics at Brown University, Albert A. Bennett, described what went on as 'wrenching the equations into a form that could be easily solved by very simple means.'" Goldstine (1993), p 74.

Is that right?

Herman Goldstine:

Yes. One of the important things about Philadelphia was that there were a number of colleges and universities in the area from which we could hire people. The word "people" in those days meant women, because the men were all taken into the draft. I had, I believe, maybe one man, John Holberton, who was my civilian aide.[8] He did the civilian things for the unit. For the rest, we hired women. We were very fortunate. We managed to get very competent young women from all the schools in the area, and even older women. We had some remarkable people. As you know, it all worked out very well.

Harry Reed:

The next session, in fact, is going to focus on some of those first women programmers. [to Harry Huskey] Let's see, we have Herman at the University of Pennsylvania, Harry, so what was going on with a guy by the name of Mauchly, for instance, who was starting to have some ideas about putting computers together. Can you tell us something about the environment at Penn up to that point?

[8] John Holberton attended the Commemoration; he is married to Frances Elizabeth (Betty) Snyder Holberton, one of the original six programmers. Betty participated in the Women Pioneers session (pp 38–49, this volume).

Harry Huskey:

They were well under way with the ENIAC project by the time I arrived on the scene. I came to Penn as an instructor in mathematics, and as an instructor my salary wasn't all that high, so I looked for extra activities. I heard that there were projects going on at the Moore School, where one might get a job. So I went over and applied. The ENIAC, of course, was a classified project, so I didn't even know what I was applying for, or what it was about.

After clearance, I was admitted through the locked gate, and here was this machine which was partly constructed. There was a lot of work going on. This was after the initial test of the accumulators. This is when I came on the scene.

You asked about Mauchly. [see sidebar] Certainly, his interest in this sort of thing was because of his research in meteorological computations. I think he looked upon the interest at Aberdeen Proving Ground as something that complemented his interest in meteorology. Of course, Eckert was the engineering expert. [see sidebar] He had worked on radar and so on. So between them, they worked up a proposal and submitted it to the Army, and in due course contracts were written and the machine was built.

Mauchly and Eckert

John William Mauchly received his degree in physics in 1932 from Johns Hopkins University. After a short tenure at Ursinus College, he joined the faculty of the Moore School of Electrical Engineering at the University of Pennsylvania. He is regarded as co-inventor of the electronic digital computer (with J. Presper Eckert). He married Kathleen McNulty, who was one of the six original ENIAC programmers, in 1948. Kay (now Kathleen McNulty Mauchly Antonelli) was a speaker in the Women Pioneers session. John Mauchly died on January 8, 1980. (For a retrospective on Mauchly's life, see Stern, 1980.)

John Presper Eckert was born in 1919 and took his BS and MS degrees from the Moore School, University of Pennsylvania, in 1941 and 1943. "Pres," as he was known, worked with John Mauchly on ideas for increasing the speed of computations. On his 24th birthday (April 9, 1943), the Moore School received the authority to begin the ENIAC project, for which he served as chief engineer. Eckert died on June 3, 1995. (For retrospectives on Eckert's life, see Lee, 1995a, pp 271–275; 1995b.)

Harry Reed:

One of the interesting things is that these things all kind of came together then, because for hundreds of years, people such as Charles Babbage were talking about building some sort of a calculating device, but it never quite culminated in anything until the wartime technology came along.

Harry Huskey:

I think there are two requirements: first, you have to have the technology to build appropriate components; and second, you have to have a need so that people will support the effort, financially and otherwise. Both of these things were certainly present at that time.

Harry Reed:

Do you mean radar development and things like that?

Harry Huskey:

Yes, like digital circuitry, for example.

Harry Reed:

[to Herman Goldstine] Ok, so anyway, Herman, you're at Penn and your young ladies are overloaded with trajectory calculations and so forth. And you bump into this guy, Mauchly, right?

Herman Goldstine:

That's right.

Harry Reed:

And you start talking …

Herman Goldstine:

It was a very interesting little group at the Moore School. We haven't talked about John Grist Brainerd yet.[9] He was the man who was the liaison for the Moore School with the Army. He was a very important person on the ENIAC project, and when we got to seriously talking, he became the head of the project. Another thing I'd like to mention was the fact that when we started, my first efforts had nothing to do with building a computer. I was occupied with hiring young women and supervising the construction of firing tables.

Brainerd formed a teaching team with my [first] wife Adele [see sidebar], Mary Mauchly (who was John Mauchly's first wife), and a splendid woman named Millie Kramer, whose husband was a great Assyriologist at the University of Pennsylvania. She is still alive, and a remarkable person.

We started right away with the training of our new people. At some point, when we ran short of trained women, we brought in a company of WACs [Women's Army Corps]. Our team trained them. I think there was a close connection between our bringing women into the forefront of the working community as normal employees, not just as ancillary or support personnel. I think that was an important accomplishment in its own right.

We, moreover, had a differential analyzer—a copy of the Bush machine—and a Moore School professor named Cornelius Wygandt, who was in charge of the analyzer for us. Pres Eckert and John Mauchly were around that machine a lot. In fact, Pres made a great invention. He replaced the mechanical torque amplifiers with some

[9] John Grist Brainerd was a lifelong faculty member and served as dean of the Moore School of Electrical Engineering, University of Pennsylvania, and was co-principal investigator for the ENIAC project.

Adele Katz Goldstine and stored-program machines

Among other contributions, Adele Goldstine pioneered an improved programming system for the ENIAC. "During 1947 von Neumann realized that the lack of a centralized control organ for the ENIAC was not an incurable deficiency. He suggested that the whole machine could be programmed into a somewhat primitive stored-program machine. He turned the task over to Adele Goldstine, who worked out such a system and passed it along to Richard Clippinger, who was then head of the computing Laboratory … and is also a mathematician of note … The system … provided the ENIAC programmer with a 51-order vocabulary. This was modified to 60 orders by Clippinger and then later to 92 orders." Goldstine (1993), pp 233–234.

Adele Goldstine wrote *Report on the ENIAC (Electronic Numerical Integrator and Computer), Technical Report 1* (2 volumes), Philadelphia, PA, 1 June 1946.

See also Clippinger (1948, 1949). Clippinger (1948) was provided to attendees.

Polaroid™ sheets, and made an electronic device that increased the reliability of those machines a great deal. It was things like that which helped to build my feeling of confidence that these young men, Pres Eckert and John Mauchly, were really people who understood computing.

Harry Reed:
And you started talking?

Herman Goldstine:
We started to talk and …

Harry Reed:
One thing led to another?

Herman Goldstine:
Yes, it did. If I may, I'd like to read you something my first wife wrote in her diary.[10] It was written in about 1962, and was her summary, for our two children, of how we spent the war years. It is simply told, so the children would have little difficulty understanding the complex story of our war years. The reader must therefore recognize that these few pages that I have excerpted were written for young children and yet are poignantly clear. It certainly is the most unbiased of the ENIAC records. It has not seen the light of day for many years, and I only now open up this part of my life for the benefit of historians. It's a very simple and elegant description of the relationships among the ENIAC designers as told by a woman who was a key worker, yet who had no need or desire to bias facts. This document was written after Adele knew she was stricken with a mortal disease and would be unable to tell her story of the ENIAC design and construction to her children when they grew up.

> … by now Daddy was working at the Moore School at the University of Pennsylvania to set up a computing station for Aberdeen and classes to train more computers under the auspices of the Engineering Sciences Management War Training Program. I got a teaching job in this program that fit me like a glove, since it involved teaching serious grown-up students who wanted to learn.
>
> During this period, Daddy had begun to speak to two engineers at the Moore School, Pres Eckert and John Mauchly, about building an electronic computer that could take over some of the calculating work of the Aberdeen lab. Daddy was already using the differential analyzer at the Moore School, which was a mechanical machine that could solve differential equations through representing quantities by lengths of rods and turns of cams … the idea these three men had was to build a digital machine that actually carried out arithmetic operations by electronic means. For several hundred years there have been gropings toward a digital machine, but these were mechanical in operation. At this point in the war, there was a tremendous growth in electronic technology that made it seem feasible to build a digital computer that could work with prodigious speed.
>
> … the engineers had begun work on the computer. Daddy had persuaded Army Ordnance to sponsor this work, and he was transferred back to Philadelphia to supervise the project for the Army, as well as to run the computation office at the University.
>
> Then I got a marvelous job at the Moore School which consisted

[10] Ellen Goldstine (Herman's second wife) sent a note to Paul Deitz in October 1996, saying, "While the ENIAC celebration was being planned in Philadelphia, I had copied the attached from Adele Goldstine's notebook. Thought you and Kay would like to read it. It's all so simply put."

of learning how the computer would work and writing a manual to instruct operators in the use of the machine. At first I thought I would never be able to understand the workings of the machine, since this involved a knowledge of electronics I didn't have at all. But gradually as I lived with the job, and Daddy and the engineers helped to explain matters to me, I got the subject under control. Then I began to understand the machine and had such masses of facts in my head, I couldn't bring myself to start writing. But this, too, I finally surmounted. I am very proud to have finished the job. It has even been printed by the Government Printing Office and listed by the Library of Congress.

… Daddy and I worked together days and often returned to work in the evening or had dinner with some of the engineers and then went back to the Moore School or one of our houses for more talk. Pres Eckert, the chief engineer, was a very clever young man and stimulating company. Grist Brainerd, who supervised the ENIAC project for the university and later became Dean of the Moore School, was another friend of ours.

As the ENIAC neared completion, Daddy interested John von Neumann in the idea of large-scale computers. When he told Pres Eckert that the great von Neumann was coming, Pres, who was not a mathematician, was not strongly impressed. Skeptically he told Daddy that he would see if V.N. asked a particular question that he considered crucial; then he would be impressed. Johnny passed the test.

[laughter and applause]

One of the other people who worked on this set of manuals was Harry Huskey.[11]

Harry Reed:
Right! [to Harry Huskey] Harry, some of the notes you gave me suggest how the ENIAC compared to what one thought of as the general-purpose computer, the Babbage machine, and stored-program machines. Would you put the ENIAC in some context with respect to this?

Harry Huskey:
As it was initially designed at the University of Pennsylvania, the programming was all by jumper connections from one unit to another. So changing a problem was a matter of removing these wires from the prior configuration and putting them back in a new configuration and testing to see if it worked. This might take days if it was a complicated program. So you can think about it as being a wired program machine. It was electrical in the sense that you could change the wiring, but once you set up the wiring, then it was fixed. For example, if you programmed a ballistic problem on it, it would take two or three days to set up, but then you could run trajectories in seconds, varying initial conditions and parameters.

Of course, it was really just a collection of accumulators, some arranged to do multiplication and some arranged to do division and so on.[12] You could hook the units up in any combination you liked. So, it was a general-purpose computer. This was in contrast to the British (Colossus) code breaking activities that were mentioned this morning.[13] So I think it was the first electronic general-purpose computer. Programming was wired programming, and it's only in the machines that come later, and particularly the EDVAC machine, that the stored-program

[11] Huskey (1946).

[12] The ENIAC consisted of 40 separate units: initiating unit, cycling unit, master programmer (two panels), three function tables (two panels each), 20 accumulators, divider and square rooter, three multipliers, constant transmitter (three panels), and a printer (three panels). In addition, the ENIAC used three portable function tables, an IBM card reader, and an IBM summary punch (Stern, 1981).

[13] Keynote address, pp 16, 22 (this volume).

concept was introduced. And that's a very important milestone in computer development.

Harry Reed:

The ENIAC had an intermediate version of programming [see sidebar] where you set the programs on the function table switches and the wiring was left alone. You didn't move the jumper cables anymore, but they were designed to accept two-digit codes from the function tables and then run the programs. So you almost had a stored-program machine, but you couldn't modify the program when you were running. The switches were set and that was it.

Harry Huskey:

That's right.

Harry Reed:

What was it like working on the ENIAC project?

Harry Huskey:

I was teaching full-time in the mathematics department, so this was extra work for me, and extra pay too! [laughter] It was very interesting learning about the concept and capability of this machine. Actually, before that, when I was in graduate school, I had thought about building a relay machine to do calculating. I decided there wasn't any use for this thing, that it wasn't practical, and so I never spent much effort on it. Here was this electronic version of a full-scale calculating machine, occupying a large room. It was exciting! In fact, one of the things that we worried a bit about was the effect of the rounding errors. Professor Rademacher in the Math Department had been asked to do a report.[14] So the first opportunity that I had, I asked if I could run a problem on the ENIAC. So I set up the integration of a very simple differential equation system to see what the rounding error would be in practice. It was an exciting time!

Harry Reed:

[to Herman Goldstine] Anyway, Herman, you and Mauchly and Brainerd, I guess, put together a proposal which you showed to the Army; is that right?

Herman Goldstine:

I think it was Eckert and Mauchly, with help from Brainerd, who put the proposal together. What I did was to get the idea across to them that if they could make a proposal, I felt confident I could sell it to Paul Gillon. And with Paul's help, Oswald Veblen was going to be a cinch. Veblen believed in people rather than in projects, and he had a lot of confidence that we would do it.

Harry Reed:

Do you have a little story about that one?

Herman Goldstine:

Yes. It's a nice story. I think it was on Pres Eckert's birthday[15] that we drove down from Philadelphia with a proposal, with Pres and John Mauchly in the back seat, writing away to get this thing put together. We got there, and I felt confident that it was to be a *fait accompli*, no matter what the University personnel were going to do. One had to go through these formalities, though,

---

> **"Intermediate programming"—converter code**
>
> The converter code is similar to the *Load* and *Store* machine code of most present-day central processing units. The ENIAC function tables consisted of about 3600 rotary switches. In the converter-code version of the ENIAC, these switches could be used to store machine instructions as well as numerical constants (often in tabular form). Pairs of switches were used to represent the approximately 100 orders, and these pairs were sampled in order of their position on the function tables, unless an instruction required the computations to move to another section of the tables. A converter was added to the ENIAC, and the computer was wired permanently so that these numbers could be converted into the approximate string of pulses. One set of orders moved numbers from accumulator 15 (the central register) to the other accumulators; another set moved numbers from the other accumulators to accumulator 15 (with addition). A variety of other orders carried out various arithmetic operations such as shifting and printing. Whereas the original ENIAC required a fortnight to be reprogrammed by rewiring, the new system required only a couple of hours for a programmer to set up a new program. (See Clippinger, 1949.)
>
> —Harry Reed

---

[14] According to Goldstine (1993), p 232: "Profs. Hans Rademacher and Harry Huskey did computations of tables of sines and cosines to study the way round-off errors develop in numerical calculations (15–18 April 1946)."

[15] It was Eckert's 24th birthday, April 9, 1943.

and there were Leslie Simon[16] and Oswald Veblen representing BRL and there was Brainerd with his two young men. The presentations went on and finally Veblen, who was sitting with his feet up on the table leaning back, bounced forward, stood up, and said, "Simon, give Goldstine the money." [laughter]

Harry Reed:
Just like that, huh?

Herman Goldstine:
Yes, I think it was kind of a letdown to Brainerd, who expected that it would be a big hard proposition. It took just a matter of a few weeks for Paul Gillon somehow to get the Philadelphia Ordnance District involved, and they wrote the contract. Away it went.

Harry Reed:
Veblen was quite a fellow.[17] He was from Princeton. During the war, he was chief scientist at BRL, I think, and helped pull together the scientific staff.[18] If you go look at some of the displays, you'll find Nobel Laureates and so forth.[19] A lot of the credit for gathering the group, I think, went to Oswald Veblen.

Herman Goldstine:
Well, Veblen was actually a part of Army Ordnance when it was located at Sandy Hook Proving Ground before it was moved here. I think he was a Major, and I know that he was busy leaning out of an airplane dropping bombs from his hands trying to see how this whole bombing thing would go during the First World War. He was a tremendous organizer. He was one of the men who organized American mathematics. There were three key leaders: Veblen at Princeton, George Birkhoff at Harvard, and Gilbert Bliss at Chicago; they ran American mathematics when it was a thing in its infancy. It's sort of remarkable; one thinks of mathematics as having been in existence in the United States for some time and that we were a totally civilized country. But in fact, just before my time, everybody who was going to be a "mathematician" went to Europe and got his Ph.D. abroad. So it was just in the 1920s and 1930s that American mathematics began to mature.

Curiously enough, with respect to the ENIAC project, I don't think there was anybody on that project who had ever heard of Babbage or any of the machines that were talked of in earlier times. Now Harry Huskey may have heard of Babbage, I don't know.

Harry Reed:
[to Harry Huskey] Did you know about Babbage before ENIAC?

Harry Huskey:
Not until afterwards.

Harry Reed:
Babbage never actually made this thing you called an *analytical machine*, did he? It was just a concept?

Harry Huskey:
He worked on parts of a "difference engine" and got so excited about the "analytical engine" that he stopped working on the difference engine.

Harry Reed:
But was there technology to do really what he wanted to do?

[16] At the time of this incident, Colonel Leslie Simon was Director of the Ballistic Research Laboratory (notes Harry Reed).

[17] "The other leader in the story of ballistics in the United States in World War I was Oswald Veblen (1880–1960) … After many years as a professor at Princeton, Veblen and Albert Einstein were appointed the first professors at the newly-founded Institute for Advanced Study, where he remained until his retirement." (Goldstine, 1993, p 77.)

[18] "Dr. Oswald Veblen … came back to the Laboratory as a consultant in April 1942, and proved to be one of the most successful recruiters of scientific talent." (*Ballisticians* (vol. I, pp 29–30). *Ballisticians* then provides numerous examples of scientists who were recruited and their institutional affiliations.

[19] There were a number of photographic displays at the commemoration. In addition, a handout on "Applying science and technology to military problems" was included in the registration packet. There was also a one-page flier, with a photo, identifying the members of BRL's Scientific Advisory Committee in 1940.

Harry Huskey:

It's kind of an interesting question. He proposed to build something involving a lot of gears operating in sequence. Now the clocks that were built at that time were very elegant mechanical devices, but did not have chains of gears like those envisioned by Babbage. So it would be interesting if somebody had really tried to make the calculator. They'd probably run into difficulties. Anyway, Babbage failed because of disagreements with his chief mechanical assistant, so it is hard to say. [see sidebar]

Herman Goldstine:

He had another difficulty: he had to get money from the government. The Prime Minister said, "It's going to be a long, cold day before I get up before the House of Commons and ask for thousands of pounds to build a 'wooden man' just to evaluate the formula $N^2 + N + 41$." [laughter]

But Babbage, to give him credit, was one of the important founders of operations research. In part, he was responsible for the introduction of the penny post. Before his time, people thought that the expense of postage had to do with the distance that the letter traveled. He did an analysis pointing out that almost all the expense of postage was incurred at the two termini. That resulted in a common post.

Harry Reed:

[to Harry Huskey] I'm not quite sure of the answers, but you had the chance to work with Alan Turing, legendary in the computing business. [see sidebar opposite] He too built a conceptual computing machine. What sort of a fellow was Alan Turing?

Harry Huskey:

A genius, I guess. John R. Womersley, who was superintendent of the Math Division and next above Turing, talked about how difficult it was to work with him, primarily because Turing was a peculiar mixture of impatience. If he felt you did something stupid, he had nothing to do with you. Typically he would never talk to newspaper people. [laughter]

On the other hand, if you had a serious problem that you were struggling with, then he would be very helpful. I spent a year working with him, and it was certainly a very pleasant experience.

Herman Goldstine:

He was a very stubborn man. Von Neumann and I had the idea that Gauss's method of elimination—which is a way of solving a system of linear equations—was probably the correct way to use on a computer. We had a mathematical proof, and Turing came over for a few weeks and worked with us. He had a somewhat different idea, and we never were able to get him to agree with what we said.

I should mention that as a graduate student, Turing got his Ph.D. at Princeton under Princeton logician Alonzo Church. Turing's thesis was essentially on a

---

Babbage

Charles Babbage was born in 1791 in Devonshire, England. A polymath, he is known as the "Father of Computing" for his work on his difference and analytical engines, neither of which he ever completed. (See Williams, 1997, ch 4, and Lee, 1995a, pp 51–64.)

According to the story, Babbage, who was a difficult person, argued with Samuel Clement, his chief mechanic. Because of their differences, Clement kept the machine tools that he had constructed to Babbage's designs (as he was allowed to do, under British law); he did, however, return Babbage's drawings.

His engines

In 1840, after reading about Babbage's ideas in the *Edinburgh Review*, a young Swede, Georg Scheutz, did build a difference engine. One of Scheutz's difference engines is in the Smithsonian Institution's *Information Age* exhibit in Washington, D.C. (See Lindgren, 1990.)

The Science Museum in South Kensington (London) sponsored a project to build a difference engine according to Babbage's plans; this work was completed in 1992 to commemorate the 200th anniversary of Babbage's birth. (See Swade, 1991.)

paper computer.[20] Johnny von Neumann's office was just a few doors away from Turing's, and Johnny followed everything that Turing did. There was a meeting of minds there from 1937 on. Von Neumann was so impressed with Turing that he wanted him to stay as his assistant. But Turing wanted to go back because he had a call from the Foreign Office to work at Bletchley.

Harry Reed:

You mentioned John von Neumann. There was a rather important historic meeting at the Aberdeen railroad station, wasn't there?

Herman Goldstine:

Yes, there was. Actually, I knew von Neumann but he didn't know me before that date. There had been a conference of the American Mathematical Society at the University of Michigan and I was the rapporteur.[21] Among the lecturers were Norbert Wiener, Johnny von Neumann, and a bunch of other very important people. I was a young man who had just recently got his Ph.D. So I had to take notes and write up the material for one of the mathematics journals. I was awestruck at von Neumann. He was just brilliant.

The other person I was awestruck by was Wiener because he gave such a lecture that I couldn't follow it. [laughter] I thought I would never get that summary for the journal done. At any rate, that's neither here nor there, but that's how I knew von Neumann and he didn't know me. Because all I was doing was sitting in the back of the room scribbling as fast as I could to try to take notes.

One day during the war, after attending a meeting here at APG, I went to the railroad station to go back to the Moore School. I saw Professor von Neumann standing on the railroad platform, all alone. I was an egotist and decided that I would go and talk to this famous man. Accordingly, I went over, and found him to be a polite, European gentleman, who felt it appropriate to be polite and to make conversation. But he was totally uninterested.

Then, gradually we began to talk about more things. Pretty soon he learned that we were building a machine that would do 300 multiplications a second, and suddenly he changed. [laughter]

He finally found the thing he had been looking for. I didn't know, of course, that he was a consultant to Los Alamos and had been doing everything in the world to get computing done. He had even worked at Harvard on the Mark I.[22] None of these things had been satisfactory.

So when he heard that this machine was going forward, he asked me how he could get involved, and I arranged it through Paul Gillon, so that he was immediately cleared to come. Every time he was in the east, he would be at

[20] Turing (1937).

[21] The purpose of a rapporteur at an academic meeting is to take notes on the speakers and write a summary of their remarks; in some instances, the rapporteur may direct questions to the speakers or may give a short summary at the end of the session.

Bletchley Park

The British government's Code and Cypher School was located just outside London in Bletchley Park. It was here that an electromechanical device, known as the *Heath Robinson*, was constructed to assist in deciphering code; later a number of electronic special-purpose computers, the *Colossus machines,* were built. Since this work is still covered under the British Official Secrets Act, many of the details—such as Alan Turing's contributions—are unknown. (See Williams, 1997, pp 291–294.)

Turing

Alan Mathison Turing (b. London, June 23, 1912) is recognized as the creator of the concept of the "universal machine," described in his 1937 paper. Turing's "theoretical computer" is known as a "Turing machine."

Alan Turing left his code-breaking efforts at Bletchley Park and joined the staff at the National Physical Laboratory (analogous to the U.S. National Bureau of Standards) in the fall of 1945. He immediately began a project to design an Automatic Computing Engine (ACE).

Another project to build a computer, later called the Manchester Mark I, was started at Manchester University in July 1946, and was in limited operation in June 1948. Turing joined the Manchester computer project in September 1948. After many design changes, and assistance from Harry Huskey, construction started on a modified version, known as Pilot ACE, in early 1949; this machine became operational on May 10, 1950. (See Williams, 1997, pp 321–344.)

Turing died on June 7, 1954, in Manchester. (See Lee, 1995a, pp 670–678.)

---

[22] See Bergin lecture and timeline (pp 12–23, this volume) and Goldstine (1993), p 118.

the Moore School, at least once a week. That had great consequences, because by the summer of 1944, the ENIAC consisted of two accumulators and some other ancillary gear. The two accumulators were feeding each other and were calculating a very simple sine function or something of that sort.[23] It was very clear that the success of the ENIAC was practically assured. The only thing that remained was the manufacturing of additional units.

The question was, "How would the engineering group keep busy?" With everybody being restless, we all said, "What can we do to make a better machine? Our ENIAC has got 18,000 vacuum tubes in it, and it's going to be a monstrosity." Its programming is practically zero, as Harry Huskey has pointed out. You could change from one problem to another, but it was a matter of days of manual labor. So we said, "We've got to get rid of that."

We began to talk about how we could build the computer of our dreams. We had more or less weekly meetings. Johnny von Neumann joined into that little club. It was a remarkable experience. The main characters were Johnny von Neumann, Eckert, Mauchly, Art Burks, me, and maybe a few others. And the conversations were heated and often irrelevant, back and forth on all sorts of topics: the technologies that could be used and the ideas that should be embodied in the machine. Out of all of this hammering and changing, and tugging back and forth, people expressed their ideas. Sometimes, they were talked out of those ideas, and later on it turned out that some of those ideas were accepted. It was just a free exchange with much freedom for everybody to express themselves.

Johnny von Neumann went off to Los Alamos for the summer as he always did, and he wrote me a series of letters. Those letters were essentially the thing called the "First draft of a report on the EDVAC." I bashed those letters together into a document without any footnote references to who was responsible for what. It formed a blueprint for the engineers and people to use.

Then, it somehow took off in a peculiar way. People began to talk in spite of classification; people began to talk about this new idea, and letters kept pouring into the Ordnance Office asking for permission to have a copy of this report. And pretty soon, we had distributed a few hundred. Everybody in American and British scientific circles began to get copies and understand how important this was. [see sidebar]

About this time, Paul Gillon and I decided that we ought to get some people over from abroad to get the idea of the computer out to the world—as much as we could. I picked a man whom I thought would be a very good person to bring over; that was a man named Douglas Hartree, who was a mathematical physicist then at Manchester University. He had built a differential analyzer out of a Meccano set.[24] He was interested in air flow over airplane wings. So Paul Gillon got permission from the government to bring him over, and he programmed a big problem. Kay Mauchly [then Kay McNulty] was assigned the task of being his programmer. Hartree and McNulty, with perhaps some help from me, got that thing going as an early example of how the computer

[23] The ENIAC can be thought of as 40 separate units, 20 of which were accumulators. Thus, getting two accumulators to work would have been a critical proof of concept.

The "first draft report"

Herman Goldstine notes that "Johnny's idea and mine was to take his beautiful analysis and synthesis of what we had discussed as a first step in reaching a final text. I did not take the time to attribute ... to each individual but lumped it all into what I viewed as a first draft, and put his name on it. I believed that only a dozen copies would appear; in fact, hundreds did."

Harry Reed points out that "there has been, and still is, controversy over the degree to which von Neumann was responsible for the development of shared memory machines. Dr. Goldstine credits von Neumann with the seminal role. Another school of thought credits Eckert, who claims to have had the idea for internal programming long before von Neumann." (See Eckert, 1988, interview.)

In the light of this controversy, it is interesting to note a passage from Adele Goldstine's diary that follows the excerpt given on pp 28–29: "During the last few months of work on the ENIAC, von Neumann, Daddy and Pres Eckert began formulating ideas for a superior computer with central control, the EDVAC."

[24] A Meccano set is a child's toy much like the Erector sets sold in the United States. D. R. Hartree and A. Porter built a working differential analyzer based on the work of Vannevar Bush at MIT.

should run. He received, while he was in the States, an offer to be a professor at Cambridge University, which he accepted. He took documents from us like the "First draft report" and got Maurice Wilkes interested. Maurice attended the class, which Tim Bergin mentioned, in 1946.[25] Out of that grew that first machine called the EDSAC, which was a successful copy, essentially, of the EDVAC.[26]

Harry Reed:

[to Harry Huskey] Harry, were you mixed up with the EDVAC at all, or were you just an ENIAC person?

Harry Huskey:

I worked on the EDVAC before I left in June of 1946. In fact, during that spring, Eckert and Mauchly had quit because of disagreement on patent rights and commercial development. Herman Goldstine and Art Burks went to Princeton. So at that stage of the game, I was the senior person, although I was only part time. In fact they offered me a job of running the EDVAC project but they didn't clear it first with J. R. Kline, who was chairman of the Math Department. He wasn't about to let the Moore School hire somebody from the Mathematics Department. [laughter] He said no. So I was mad, and I resigned. [laughter] I worked on it there awhile.

Harry Reed:

Kind of a cantankerous machine, wasn't it?

Harry Huskey:

Not at the stage I worked on. I was just doing diagrams of how it might work. Later on, there were problems as far as the memory in particular. In fact, it was probably worth mentioning that Wilkes was successful in getting his machine going before the EDVAC was completed, partly because he operated at half the frequency that it was proposed to run the memory lines on the EDVAC. They were supposed to run at a megacycle [1 MHz], a million pulses per second, and Wilkes settled for 500,000, which makes it a lot easier.

Harry Reed:

Actually the ENIAC was always advertised as operating at 100 kHz. But we found that if you turned it up much above 70 kHz, you were headed for trouble. In fact, we only ran it at 100 kHz early in the week to see if everything was working all right, because it would develop more errors if we kept operating it that way. We'd sit and turn the clock down a little bit, and things worked a lot better. Pretty finicky machine. People here, maybe a lot of people, in the audience probably have never seen a vacuum tube.

Harry Huskey:

There are a few vacuum tubes over there in the display case.

Harry Reed:

Tim Bergin brought some. You think about it, you used to have television sets with a dozen vacuum tubes, and keeping them running for a couple of months was a sensation. The fact that you had 18,000 of these cantankerous things in the machine was a monument to engineering persistence, I think.

Harry Huskey:

When there was a problem, it took maybe two days to discover which tube was not functioning. It was actually good engineering and the fact that the tubes were burned in for 100 hours before ever being used; that reduced the number

---

[25] In the summer of 1946, a lecture series on the "Theory and Techniques for Design of Electronic Computers" was held at the Moore School of Electrical Engineering of the University of Pennsylvania (the "Moore School lectures"). The lectures, covering a wide variety of topics on computing, were delivered by faculty members as well as other members of the small but growing computing community. Maurice Wilkes attended some of the lectures.

[26] There were three projects in the UK: Wilkes' efforts to build the Electronic Delay Storage Automatic Calculator (EDSAC) at Cambridge University, the Mark I at Manchester University, and the Pilot ACE at the National Physical Laboratory.

of failures. So, that's really one of the significant points about the ENIAC, that it showed that a very complex electronic device could be made to run reliably enough to be worthwhile.

Harry Reed:

Eckert was really the driving force behind that accomplishment, wasn't he?

Herman Goldstine:

He noticed that if you left the filaments burning all the time, it made a tremendous difference. The thing couldn't possibly have worked had it not been for Pres Eckert's understanding of how to run equipment at below standard ratings to increase reliability. At the beginning, Paul Gillon and I decided we would try to get opinions from the NDRC, which was mentioned earlier by Tim Bergin.[27] We went to the electrical engineering group at MIT, consisting largely of protegés of Vannevar Bush. In the first place, they thought analog computing was the way to go. They said digital computing is "for the birds, everything is analog, and 18,000 vacuum tubes is preposterous. There ain't such an animal ever been built and it will never work." So that was the learned opinion of those people.

Harry Reed:

Be kind to MIT. [laughter]

Herman Goldstine:

The person who turned them around was Jay Forrester.[28] Under his leadership, they did a magnificent job from then on. The next group was the Applied Mathematics Panel of the NDRC. They were the people who said, "Well, we don't know whether 18,000 vacuum tubes is too many or not; the thing we know is there ain't such a thing as a problem which would take 300 multiplications per second." [laughter]

In fact—Tim Bergin mentioned George Stibitz in his lecture[29]—it was Stibitz who was largely instrumental in taking that point of view. He had the idea that if you took a couple of his relay machines and put them together and let them run day and night, that would do all the computing that Aberdeen needed. So somebody at BRL got cold feet during the war while the ENIAC was being developed, and ordered two Stibitz machines.

There was a nice young mathematician named Franz Alt, a Viennese, who was in charge of running those two computers here. It turned out that they were more unreliable than the ENIAC by a considerable amount. They didn't run day and night, they were always in trouble, and in the end, it turned out that instead of the vacuum tube being the unreliable element, it was the mechanical parts which were the unreliable thing.

Harry Reed:

The IBM cards, for instance, which we used to feed in data would swell with moisture because of excess humidity.

Herman Goldstine:

That was one of the great things, because we air-conditioned the computer room. [laughter]

Harry Reed:

Right! The ENIAC room and the room below it, which had IBM equipment, were the only two rooms in the whole of BRL that had air-conditioning.

[27] The National Defense Research Committee (NDRC) was created in 1940 to provide advice on weapons research. Partly in response to criticism that its focus was too narrow, President Roosevelt established the Office of Scientific Research and Development (OSRD) by executive order, which then incorporated the NDRC. The NDRC did a report on the potential of the proposed ENIAC project, which was not favorable. (Stern, 1981, pp 16–23.)

[28] Jay Forrester was the technical leader of Project Whirlwind at MIT. This project started in 1943, when the U.S. Navy needed an airplane stability and control analyzer. After initially considering using analog techniques, the project focused on digital techniques once Forrester learned of the ENIAC project. The Whirlwind project and the computer that resulted from it were significant developments in the history of computing. See Redmond and Smith (1980).

[29] See Bergin lecture and timeline (pp 14, 21–23, this volume) and Lee (1995a), pp 640–644.

Herman Goldstine:

Yep! And anybody who was smart in the computing field said that they had to have equipment in a cool room, and therefore had to have air-conditioning. [laughter]

Harry Reed:

Well guys, I think we're just about at the end of our time. I want to thank both of you. Anybody who wants to, I'm sure, may catch up with you and ask you for some of your reminiscences. Any last words before we adjourn this session?

I'd certainly like to thank both of you. It's been a great pleasure. I met Herman finally after Jimmy Prevas[30] and other people kept telling me about you. I finally met you last January, I guess. And I finally caught up with Harry Huskey last night. One of the great pleasures of this whole celebration has been meeting you guys.

Why don't we adjourn then? Thank you both again. [applause]

[30] Chief of the Firing Tables Branch, BRL, in the 1940s and 1950s.

3. Women Pioneers

Jill Smith (chair):

This session is on women pioneers. As many of you have already heard this morning, "computers" were the women at that time. We have many of them here today and we'd like to recognize them. What I thought I would do is to give them fairly brief introductions, because in the next hour I'd like you to hear mostly from them—and not from me—about what it was like working here during that time, and about their contributions.

First of all I'd like to introduce *Lila Todd Butler*, who graduated from Temple University in 1941, with a degree in mathematics. She was the only female mathematician in a class of 1600. She was employed first by the engineering department at DuPont; later, in March of 1942, Lila joined BRL at Aberdeen Proving Ground. She was one of the original people sent to Philadelphia to work on the differential analyzer, and was a supervisor along with Willa Wyatt Sigmund of the various shifts that ran the calculations.

Lila was transferred back to BRL in 1945, somewhat before the ENIAC arrived here, and was a supervisor of mathematicians. For the women in the audience, she's also a mother and took a short maternity leave from 1947 to 1951 and then came back to work in 1951 and worked for another 28 years here at BRL. Lila is one of the two women on this stage that were here when I arrived in 1977. She retired in 1979, after a career in which she worked with the ENIAC, the EDVAC, the ORDVAC, and BRLESC. She played a significant role in the development of FORAST, a machine language. [see sidebar]

Mrs. *Francis Elizabeth Snyder Holberton*, known as Betty, had a 43-year career in computing. She started her mathematics study in the George School in Bucks County, Pennsylvania, and earned a Bachelor of Arts degree in English and journalism. However, she wanted to start in mathematics and was told that girls really didn't study mathematics in college. [laughter] She was told forcibly enough that she switched her major to journalism. However, she did come back to mathematics, originally starting with the *Farm Journal* magazine in the economic statistics section. By 1942, Betty had moved to the BRL Unit at the University of Pennsylvania, working as both a "computer" and a supervisor. From 1945 to 1947, she was here with ENIAC, as an ENIAC programmer, and then left

---

FORAST

"Before 1960, essentially all programming at BRL was done by having the programmers translate their assembly language into the actual numeric code required by the computer. In July 1959, Glen A. Beck and Lloyd W. Campbell, BRL, proposed to simplify programming by combining an assembly program and formula translation into one routine which allowed symbolic addresses and mnemonic language to be used rather than the final machine code ... In less than a year, the simplified language and translator program FORAST (Formula and Assembly Translator) had been devised and used on the ORDVAC. This language, much easier to program, allowed the programmer to write actual machine orders in symbolic assembly language, some arithmetic formulas written in a manner similar to conventional mathematical notation, and English words for high level statements instructing the machine."

—*Ballisticians in War and Peace*, vol. II, p 25

in 1947 to go with the Electronic Control Company, which was later [renamed] the Eckert-Mauchly Computer Corporation.[1] She was there until 1953.

From 1953 to 1966, she was a supervisor of advanced programming at the Applied Math Laboratory at the David Taylor Model Basin, which is a U.S. Navy facility. In 1966, she left to become a supervisor and mathematician at the Institute for Computer Science and Technology at the National Bureau of Standards, where she stayed until 1983. Betty is known for her work on sort generators and many other areas, and has been cited by Dr. Grace Hopper as one of the best programmers that she had known.

Holberton:
I'll refute that. [laughter]

Jill Smith:
Well, you can straighten us all out!

Kathleen Mauchly Antonelli is another woman pioneer. When I first started reading about her accomplishments, I thought surely Kay was not also a mother, but I found out in reading her biography that she has two daughters that she had during the period while she worked continuously.

Kay started her career in mathematics after graduating from the Chestnut Hill College for Women in 1942. Again, she was one of three mathematicians to graduate in a class of 92 women. In July of 1942, she was employed by APG at the Moore School of Electrical Engineering at the University of Pennsylvania. In a note to me, she said that she started here as an "SP-4"—an SP-4 is a "subprofessional level 4"—even though she had her degree in mathematics at the time. She still recalls her salary, which was $1620 a year. [laughter]

Antonelli:
That's right!

Jill Smith:
In December of 1946, she moved back to APG as one of the original six ENIAC programmers to come to APG and helped the ENIAC adjust to its new home until 1948, when she left to marry John Mauchly.

Homé McAllister Reitwiesner graduated from Randolph Macon Women's College in Lynchburg, Virginia, with a degree in mathematics in 1946. She reported to work at BRL in July of that same year, and was computing the firing tables. She was a BRL programmer in the fifties, and mentioned that they had three different number bases in which they had to work: the ENIAC was base 10, the EDVAC was base 8, and the ORDVAC was base 16. So, as she switched between the machines, she needed to recall just what base she was working in. In 1951, she married George Reitwiesner, and in 1954 she took her first maternity leave; she came back to work again until 1955, when she left government service.

Viola Woodward is the other person that I recall from when I arrived here in 1977. Viola came to BRL in 1948. I asked her to come today, because she spans many of our machines. She's worked on the ENIAC, the EDVAC, the ORDVAC, and the BRLESC. She was chief of our ORDVAC section for a long while and also worked as a supervisor and computer programmer. She retired in 1978, after a 30-year career, and then returned, as many do, consulting for another three and a half years.

Also we have *Betty Jean Jennings Bartik*. Betty Jean was one of the first original five people chosen to program the ENIAC. She started working here in 1945.

[1] In March, 1946, John Mauchly and Pres Eckert left the University of Pennsylvania to start their own company, the Electronic Control Company, the first commercial organization devoted to building computers. In late September 1946, ECC signed a study contract with the National Bureau of Standards (on behalf of the Census Bureau) to build a computer. This contract was amended on May 24, 1947; at this time the computer was identified as the UNIVAC (Universal Automatic Computer). In December 1947, ECC was renamed the Eckert-Mauchly Computer Company (EMCC). (See Williams, 1997, pp 358–365.)

She worked on many of the firing table calculations and also on the UNIVAC. She was here at APG for a year and eventually left to go with the Eckert-Mauchly Computer Company.

What I'd like to do now is turn the program over to these ladies, and ask them, in turn, to tell us what it was like to be working at that time and about their contributions. I'd like to start with Lila.

Lila Todd Butler:

I came to work at the Proving Ground in 1942. At that time, there were no living accommodations available for single people around here. Major Gillon told me they planned to open a branch in Philadelphia. So I was lucky enough to be chosen. Six of us went to Philadelphia, and after two months, only two of us remained: Willa Wyatt and me. Then, John Holberton was sent up with several more people and we started forming sections. At the time we handled the differential analyzer and a firing table section. For 16 hours a day we used the facilities, so therefore we were each on for eight hours. At that time, computing firing tables was the only work performed.

Then they started to expand, and they hired more people and we moved to a row house near the University of Pennsylvania, where six sections were eventually formed. At the beginning, they hired college graduates with majors in mathematics, and then they hired college graduates without majors in mathematics and gave them training on the desk calculator—which was what was principally used to compute the firing tables, once we got the trajectories from the differential analyzer. When they could no longer get college graduates, they started hiring students with good mathematical backgrounds, right out of high school, and that proved to be very efficient.

Eventually we moved to the fraternity house, because we needed more room, and then expanded to around 80 people, most of whom were females. We had a few men. And Willa and I continued to handle the firing tables, but we expanded into other fields.

At the time when we were first hired, we were SP-4s because the administration didn't believe that women should have professional ratings. During this time, Dr. Dorrit Hoffleit, who was from Harvard, finally convinced them that this should be changed, but it was several years till they established the P-ratings. So two or three of us got P-3s. But it was due to Dr. Hoffleit that the women were given professional ratings.

After the war, the supervisors of these sections were led to believe that they would be given a chance to work on the ENIAC, but it was already established, so we were sent back to the Proving Ground. At that time, I supervised about 15 mathematicians. Then I left to go on maternity leave.

The first person from the Proving Ground who was transferred to the ENIAC was "Wink" or Winifred Jonas. She continued to work on the ENIAC until she resigned.

When I came back from maternity leave, I went to work on the ENIAC. At that time, the EDVAC was being completed, and it was being transferred to the Proving Ground. It wasn't in operational condition. John Gregory was the main engineer that spearheaded all of our electronic work, and he got it in operational order.

Following the EDVAC, there was the ORDVAC I and the ORDVAC II. EDVAC was octal and the others were hexadecimal.[2] At that time, we had no automatic programming. When they developed the BRLESC, John Gregory and Lloyd Campbell worked together in establishing the first FORAST compiler. I programmed something in FORTRAN and also in FORAST; it was a camera orientation for Dr. [Helmut] Schmidt. It took about half as long with the FORAST as it did with FORTRAN. But because FORAST was a government project and didn't have commercial backing, it wasn't well recognized. But it was far superior to FORTRAN at that time.

In the early days of the Computing Laboratory, they had ENIAC, EDVAC, and ORDVAC sections. Later, programming sections were established to program for all the laboratories. Then, BRL decided each laboratory would have its own programmers, and the Computing Lab was disbanded. Our programmers were sent to the different computing labs. It wasn't long before the labs were contracting their programs out. I was in the Systems Analysis Group, and we were besieged with all these programs that they had problems with. So, although the Lab expanded and everything, it was much more practical to do the work in-house because you could work with the sponsor directly.

After the BRLESC I and BRLESC II, APG rented a commercial machine from CDC (Control Data Corporation), and we went through all the problems of getting it into operation.[3] At that time, over in the Human Engineering Lab, they had a machine which they needed help on, so I was detailed over there part-time. It was one on which you simulated different war conditions and all. It was similar to what you do with electronic games on computers today, but we didn't have that on our facility over in BRL. But it was very interesting to work with then.

I don't know whether any of you knew Dr. Helmut Schmidt, but he was the only one from von Braun's group that worked at BRL.[4] I was fortunate enough to be able to do his programs. I did the one-camera, the two-camera, and the strip-triangulation orientations, and that was sort of the forerunner of the more advanced work that NASA now does.

I worked at the Proving Ground in the Systems Analysis Group till I retired in 1979. It was most interesting work, and the most interesting part was the fact that you actually got to work on the software that made the computer operate. Today, most people talk about computers from the operational view rather than the programming point of view.

Jill Smith:

Thank you, Lila. Next, we will hear from Francis Elizabeth Snyder Holberton, known as Betty.

Francis Elizabeth Snyder Holberton:

I was originally supposed to major in mathematics. The first semester, I had to run from the hockey field down the Schuylkill River to my class at the University of Pennsylvania, and every single morning for a whole semester, the professor said, "You women should be at home raising children." [laughter] The next semester, I had the same professor for calculus. So I switched to something I could get an education in, and they allowed every woman to go into any class if you majored in journalism. So I took that because I wanted to get an education. So that's the story behind that.

[2] Octal is base 8 (0, 1, 2, 3, 4, 5, 6, 7), and hexadecimal is base 16 (0, 1, 2, 3, 4, 5, 6, 7, 8, 9, A, B, C, D, E, F).

[3] According to *Ballisticians,* vol. II, p 24: "The competitive procurement resulted in a contract award late in 1976 to Control Data Corporation, of Minneapolis, Minnesota, and Vector General, Inc., of Woodland Hills, California. Control Data Corporation was to provide the central facility consisting of two major processors: A CDC CYBER 170/173 … and a CDC CYBER 70/76 … Vector General would provide four additional remote graphics terminals and all interfaces with the central site."

[4] Wernher von Braun was considered the foremost rocket engineer in the world. Born in Wirrsitz, Germany, in 1912, von Braun played a major role in developing the V-2 rocket. In 1945, von Braun led a group of German scientists who surrendered to the United States Army. In 1954, the Army assigned von Braun and his team to the Redstone Arsenal in Huntsville, Alabama. Von Braun became a U.S. citizen in 1955. (*The World Book Encyclopedia.*)

I have wanted to know, to this day, why I was ever hired here because I never was a mathematician in my whole life. [laughter] I didn't even know how to do integration, to tell you the truth. I asked Dr. Goldstine, "Why in the world did you ever hire me?" That's one thing I never figured out, because I never claimed to be a mathematician.

Anyway, how I got started at Aberdeen was that I was gung ho for what happened in World War II, and I wanted to do my duty. So I switched from working at the *Farm Journal,* where I was raising a whole bunch of mess with some surveys and what not, and I took a job with Aberdeen in Philadelphia. So I stayed there and did trajectories like everybody else did. Then I got selected to work on the ENIAC. I don't know why; I was never interviewed. So that was another thing that was peculiar, but it made my career anyway, so it was worthwhile.

So I stayed in computers all my life, because I was so excited about the whole thing. I just couldn't believe that they wouldn't survive. I wanted them to survive, so I made sure I was in the field of what I called "human engineering" and today they call "user friendly" software development. I was interested in whether operators, programmers, and engineers could run the machine, and if they got into trouble, could we get them out—and all that kind of thing. I was just working for other people, not for myself at all.

So, when the Vietnam War came, I was at Carderock, at the David Taylor Model Basin. I just couldn't stand the Vietnam War, so I switched from military to civilian employment. I joined the Bureau of Standards, really for the one reason that I wanted to wind up my career there, because my grandfather had been the person who proposed a Bureau of Standards, back in 1884. It took until 1906 to get the Bureau of Standards, so I wanted to be there. My grandfather is a footnote in history. I tried to keep my whole career rather quiet because I was most interested in getting things done for other people.

I wrote the whole book. There was nothing like Windows then. The book had to do with all of our routines that ran the ENIAC, as well as debugging and whatnot. And I sent that out to all 46 UNIVAC sites in industry just because I thought somebody could use some help. And I wanted to help people. I did wind up at the Bureau of Standards, and I got on the FORTRAN Committee and stayed there most of my life.[5] I was on the COBOL Committee when they introduced that language. I never believed in COBOL; it's too wordy! [laughter] But my daughter is programming in it for the Fairfax County Government. And when she was two years old, she used to run around the house yelling "Oddball, softball, COBOL," making all kinds of fun of what I was doing. [laughter] So now she's programming in the language and doing very well.

Jill Smith:
Thank you, Betty. As Betty mentioned, she was both on the COBOL development committee and, while at the National Bureau of Standards, on both the international and the national standards committees for FORTRAN, and has made many contributions. I must say we do consider you a computer scientist and mathematician.

[We will now hear from] Kathleen McNulty Mauchly Antonelli.

[5] FORTRAN (formula translator) was a scientific computer language developed by John Backus and his associates at IBM, introduced in 1954. When the Department of Defense saw a need for a commercial equivalent of FORTRAN, it called together a committee that in 1959 introduced COBOL (Common Business-Oriented Language). Each of these languages had a committee to standardize the language, on which Betty Holberton served.

 **Kathleen McNulty Mauchly Antonelli:**
I brought with me today my original hiring paper from the War Department. This little document says a lot about the changes in our life today. It says I was hired on July 15, 1942, designation: "assistant computer." The grade was "SP-4" and the salary was $1620 per annum. Now, I think, a programmer can get $1620 per week. The other interesting thing when I look back at this document is that it says *race: white* and *sex: female*. I wonder if the hiring documents nowadays still say the same thing?

I was one of the first few people that were hired in Philadelphia in 1942, and my immediate boss was Lila Todd. After a few weeks there, learning how to calculate a trajectory, I was assigned to the differential analyzer, which was at that time, or until it was finally taken away, housed in a room in the basement of the Moore School. Now this was the only room in all of the Moore school that was air-conditioned. And as Dr. Goldstine referred to it today, they cared more about the machines being taken care of than they did that the people were able to work in such conditions. But the fact that we were in an air-conditioned room meant that most of the high-level talking that had to go on during the summertime went on in the analyzer room.

It was just shortly after I came there, in July of 1942, that Mauchly evidently wrote his original proposal for an ENIAC. He would sometimes tell us that instead of having to sit there hour after hour, grinding out these trajectories on the differential analyzer, "Wouldn't it be great if there was something that could do this in 20 seconds?" He had dreams, and we just thought he was a little bit crazy. But I stayed there all during the war.

When the war was over, I was one of the five women originally chosen to learn to be a programmer for the ENIAC. Well, at that time, in May of 1945, we had never even seen the ENIAC, because it was a project that was going on behind closed doors marked "Secret" or some level that we were not able to go to see. But the first thing that Aberdeen did for us was to send us to the Aberdeen Proving Ground to learn all about IBM machines—which we did.

We came back from there, right around VJ Day, and we were told that now we had to learn all about the ENIAC, if we were going to learn how to be operators—what we were told we were going to be. However, at that time, no manuals had yet been written, and we were given all the blueprints, the wiring diagrams, and the block diagrams, and we were told we could follow the circuits and find out what was going on. Well, thank God, the ENIAC was not yet finished at that time, and all the engineers were still around and very available and very helpful to us. Dr. Arthur Burks was the one who was assigned to teach us all about how an accumulator worked. Now, an accumulator was sort of a basic unit of the ENIAC, and there were 20 of them. If you learned how one worked, you learned how 20 different units of the machine operated.

So we sat down with our great big block diagrams and our wiring diagrams, and we did learn a little bit about what every tube did inside that machine. Then, we were to learn, or teach ourselves, I suppose, how to program a trajectory so it would fit on this machine. Well, nicely enough, those designers and the Aberdeen Proving Ground working together had built the machine so that it was really a great thing for solving trajectory problems. It had everything there ready to do that. So that was not a hard job. But on the very first day we ever saw the ENIAC itself, a problem was already being put on and we were to help. This was something entirely foreign to us—the feasibility of the H-bomb. Dr. Goldstine and his wife [Adele] were there, and they had to help the scientists from Los Alamos make up the punched cards which we inserted in the front. They also gave us directions as to how we were to set the switches. Our job was to help set the switches for a program that was already designed.

Well, after a while we learned pretty much how to troubleshoot all kinds of problems. Once the Army saw that the machine was really working, they decided that they would advertise it. We had a big public demonstration on February 15, 1946. After that, we stayed with the machine. There were still little troubles boiling up and things, and there were problems that we were helping other people to solve.

In December of 1946, the ENIAC was finally moved back to the home which had been built for it down here at Aberdeen Proving Ground. I was one of the programmers who came with it. I stayed here and helped the ENIAC as it was being reassembled, and finally left in 1948 to marry John Mauchly. That didn't take me away from computers; it just involved me much more deeply, because even if you didn't work at them all day, you had them for supper, and all night. [laughter] I never went back to work in computers, but I never got very far away from them either.

Jill Smith:

Thank you. Next we'd like to hear from Homé McAllister Reitwiesner.

Homé McAllister Reitwiesner:

I was another one that worked under Lila when I first came in July 1946. I hand computed solutions to problems, in the building behind BRL in the nice hot summer, and learned, from the bottom up, how hand computing gives you a firing table. Then, after I was there a couple of months, they said, "We want you on the IBM." They took me screaming and hollering, because I said, "I'm happy here, I'm happy here. Why should I have to go to a machine?" [laughter] I got down to the IBM, and fell in love with it. A couple of months later they said, "You know everything we need you to know about the IBM; you're going to the ENIAC." [I said,] "Oh, no, no, no, I want to stay here." Well, that was another good move. They moved me several more times after that, and I always went kicking and screaming.

I ended up on the ENIAC. One of the first things I did was to help follow through on switches for some changes that had been made. I never programmed under the original system. Soon thereafter, the converter code [see sidebar, p 30] was brought in—100 different two-digit numbers which we coded by. Then we set the machines, all the switches and all the wires, to a common place and we just used it that way. I worked a long time up there. I did a lot of funny little problems.

One of the other co-workers was George Reitwiesner. He was trying to prove to the engineers that they had done a good job, and that the machine would run longer than the two or three seconds or minutes that other people were telling them that it was doing. They kept saying, "It won't run, it won't run!" And he said, "Yes, it will! It will run for long times." So he finally convinced somebody to let him put on what he called "Slow Moses." He would put the cards into the machine in the evening, and take them out in the morning. He also ran π to 2556+ digits and e. And then von Neumann fell in love with those and wanted to use them as random digits. So von Neumann asked for $1/e$. George happened to be working at Harvard that summer, getting his degree, and so he sent me the material on what to do to change computing e to $1/e$, and we ran it overnight and we proved the machine would hold up.

Then von Neumann stood over me as I multiplied e times $1/e$, doing all the rounding. I can still see him as I'm leaning over the tabulator watching the cards print up. He wouldn't let me put the pointer through the holes. He had to see all those nines on that piece of paper. [laughter] He was so fascinated. That was one of the fun things I was doing.

I worked on the weather problem. They were integrating in two different directions. You'd put the cards in, and then you'd take them out and tabulate them.[6] Then you'd have to run them through the sorter to sort them in the other direction, and run them through the ENIAC again—and keep integrating for xy and then yx, or whatever the dimensions were. We got it down to a science on the night shift especially. We were able to compute 24 hours worth of weather in 25 hours. [laughter] I think they do a little better now.

They were testing on the ENIAC because they were planning to put the problems on a different machine that was much faster (the EDVAC). I mean we had to use part of the accumulators as numbers, but it was lots of fun. You'd sleep for a few minutes and all of a sudden it would be ready and you'd run it through the tabulator, run it through the sorter, and run it back in again.

In her introduction, Jill mentioned that we had coding in decimal and binary. I had a desk calculator in base eight. It was a Monroe, and if anything ever went wrong with it, the guy wouldn't work on it unless I was right there to show him how I could make it fail. Then he would work on it and fix it—because he didn't understand how the binary system became the octal system or how it worked at all.

I married George in 1951. We were doing our checkbooks one night, and I had been working in octal all day, and I was able to do what I was supposed to do, but all of a sudden when I was putting the checks in order, I pulled up and handed him two checks and said, "I don't know what to do with these." They were checks numbered "1018" and "1019."[7] [laughter] He never let me live it down!

We had problems with cleaning personnel. We would come in the morning, and look all the way around the bottom of the ENIAC. If a plug was sitting in a place that didn't have the same kind of dirt pattern as the others, we would know that a cleaning person had knocked it out and just put it near a nearby plug. [laughter] We spent hours trying to find out what was wrong one day and we discovered that cleaning personnel had moved one of the plugs. After that we checked every morning. [laughter] We didn't learn it from you all, [referring to a comment made from the audience, presumably by an engineer] though we should have.

I think it was von Neumann, wasn't it, that had an accident with a tree on the way up to Aberdeen? If it wasn't he, it was somebody like him. He told the story that he was driving along and the trees were in perfect order, and all of a sudden, one tree moved out into the street and he hit it. [laughter]

I ran the night shift for Dr. Richard F. Clippinger and Dr. Bernard Dimsdale. We were running air-flow problems around a wing or whatever—it was an airflow problem. We ran on the night shift, and that was fun because his wife would cook lunch for us. We would work on building his house in the daytime, eat the lunch that she had made us, and then we'd all go back to our own places. I went

[6] The ENIAC had no output devices, so all output was punched into cards and then printed (or "listed") on an IBM punched card unit (or "electric accounting machine"—EAM) called a tabulator.

[7] In octal, the symbols 8 and 9 do not occur.

back to the dorm and he went back to his house. Then we'd work 11 to 7 and go out and build his house on Robin Hood Road. [laughter] Lots of fun.

I was working on another problem, and all of a sudden it went completely haywire. Now, we didn't have floating point. We had to figure out where everything was supposed to go, and how big the numbers would be. All of a sudden, the people from White Sands—I think it was White Sands or some place like that—said, "Oh, it went all the way up to 99 and went above." So we had to change all the decimal points all the way through, because the trajectory that they were doing had gone so much higher than they expected this particular projectile to go. Floating point is much better. [laughter]

Jill Smith:

Thank you, Homé. Next is Betty Jean Jennings Bartik, and I believe I missed mentioning that her degree in mathematics is from Northwest Missouri. I was wondering how she got to Aberdeen from Missouri, actually.

Betty Jean Jennings Bartik:

I am much later than these other people. I came in 1945. Actually I graduated in December. At that time, most math majors were men, and as Betty Holberton said, they didn't encourage women to become math majors, although I was one. So they were always trying to recruit me to teach, because they needed math teachers. I had applied for a job at Aberdeen, and I wanted to get the hell out of Missouri! [laughter] My father was a school teacher, and he would come home every day and tell me that this other district was wanting me to come teach. I kept saying, "No, I'm waiting." So, finally they sent me a telegram saying that I was hired and to come as quickly as possible. Well, I caught the midnight train to Philadelphia. [laughter] I had never even thought of coming to Philadelphia. I thought of going to Chicago, New York, or San Francisco, but Philadelphia—I couldn't even imagine what it looked like.

Well, anyway, I got here and I also worked for Lila. We were doing these calculations, and I realized this was pretty boring. I had also taken classes from Adele, and if you ever wanted to see an interesting woman, you should have seen Adele Goldstine. Anyway, I'll talk about her later.

They just sent around announcements that said that anybody who wanted to apply for a job on a new computer should apply. Well, I didn't have any idea what it was, but it was sure going to be better than running all those Monroe calculators. So I applied, and guess who interviewed me? He's sitting right here on the front seat, Dr. Goldstine. I was also interviewed by Dr. Cunningham. I'm going to tell you the kind of questions he asked me. [laughter] Believe me, if you think this man knew what he was doing, I'm going to disabuse you of that idea right away. [laughter]

He said to me, "What do you think about electricity?"

I said, "I've had a course in physics; I know $E = IR$."

He said, "No, I don't mean that. I mean, are you *afraid* of it?" [laughter] So I said, no, I wasn't afraid of it.

He said, "Well, this is going to mean you're going to pull plugs and set switches." I said I didn't think it was going to bother me.

So anyway, I was hired as the second alternate. There were five selected and I was the second alternate. I thought, "Well, that's the end of that!"

But on Friday, they called me in and said, "Can you be ready to go to Aberdeen on Monday?" I didn't know a thing about Aberdeen and I had an apartment in Philadelphia. At that time apartments were very hard to find; housing was very slim in Philadelphia.

What happened was that the first person had an apartment in Philadelphia and she didn't want to go to Aberdeen, because Aberdeen was considered a "hell hole." [laughter] So anyway, she didn't take the job. So the second person was on vacation, and they called her and said, "You were selected. Come back and go to Aberdeen on Monday." Well, nobody wanted to cut short a vacation to go to Aberdeen on Monday, so she turned it down. So I said, "Gee, I'd be delighted." [laughter]

Let me tell you what it was like working on the ENIAC and being a part of this. I thought I'd died and went to heaven, I really did. It was the most exciting thing that you can imagine, because from the very beginning, the people that we talked to, and who trained us, had the vision and inspiration of where this was going to lead eventually. And we talked about it constantly.

Also we worked with John Mauchly, who was always trying to persuade us to think of things beyond the trajectory. He was always concerned with applications. And Pres [Eckert], at this time, I never talked to him at all. I was scared to death of him! [laughter] Absolutely! Furthermore, he didn't think programmers amounted to much anyway. I think it was only later, when I worked for him, that he was absolutely wonderful. But at that time I did not think so.

Anyway, I worked, of course, with Adele Goldstine, and then, when the ENIAC was moving to Aberdeen, I was getting married, so I did not go. But Dick Clippinger[8] at the Wind Tunnel had problems that he couldn't get on the ENIAC, because they were too big, and also, Dr. Dederick, who was head of BRL, wouldn't give him any programmers.[9] So Dick saw a loose programmer, and he said, "How about you setting up a group at the University of Pennsylvania and I'll write a contract to program for me?" Well, that suited me fine. So he did that, and I hired four programmers. We were the ones that worked with Dr. Clippinger, von Neumann, Adele, Dr. Giese,[10] and Dr. A. Galbraith to turn the ENIAC into a stored-program computer.[11]

But anyway, let me tell you, it was wonderful, wonderful, working at that time, when the people came from all over the world to see the ENIAC. Is the press still here? [laughter] Anyway, one of the worst things about it were the stories that were written about the ENIAC. They were just absolutely terrible.

One of the nicest things about this period was that people came from all over the world, because they understood what an important machine the ENIAC was. We met some of the greatest minds of that era. That was fun; it was really fun. Thank you.

Jill Smith:

Our next speaker is Viola Woodward. Viola actually worked on all the machines that I mentioned earlier. She retired in 1978.

Viola Woodward:

I didn't give Jill too much of my background, but I think with everybody else plugging their colleges, I should at least say that I graduated from the University of Cincinnati, in mathematics, back in 1942. Then I also took my teaching degree there, in another year, and then I joined the Navy after

[8] Clippinger (1948) (included in commemorative packet).

[9] Dr. L. S. Dederick served as an Associate Director of BRL from 1938 to 1953; Dr. Robert Kent also served as Associate Director of BRL from 1938 to 1956. (*Ballisticians*, vol. I, p 12.)

[10] Dr. John H. Giese served as Chief of the Computing Laboratory from 1959 to 1968 and as Chief of the Applied Mathematics Division from 1968 to 1974, when he retired. Dr. Giese was a speaker in Session 4.

[11] Clippinger (1948) contains an overview of this effort and identifies the participants.

teaching for a year. I didn't want to teach after that. In fact, I told one of my Navy chums, I could finally pass a school without shuddering. [laughter] I do have something in common with Betty Holberton. I was stationed at David Taylor Model Basin during my whole Navy career of two years plus. But then, I thought, if I want to work in mathematics and I don't want to teach, I better get back into higher mathematics, since I'd been away from it for four years. And with the help of the GI bill,[12] I applied to Stanford University, in California, and was accepted.

[12] A Veterans Administration program under which people who served honorably in the military services could receive monthly stipends for college-level studies.

I spent a year out there getting my master's in mathematics. At the end of that time, computers were still almost unknown. You occasionally read a little reference to an "electronic brain" someplace, but you just didn't realize computers existed in the sense that we do today. Stanford had a very good placement bureau, but when I went to them to find out what my job opportunities were, they said they had no jobs. They said they had the list of about five places where you could apply, like the Glenn L. Martin Company and the General Electric Corporation. Someone said, "But we also have a letter from a Dr. Dederick at Aberdeen Proving Ground, who would like any math graduates to write to him." So he was one of the people I wrote to. He wrote back and offered me a job on the ENIAC and wrote me a very nice letter about electronic computers, which made it sound very interesting.

I came to Aberdeen in March of 1948, and I went to work for Mrs. Young for a month, learning to compute a trajectory, which I'd never done. And then I worked on the differential analyzer, including changing gears and gear boxes and all of that mechanical stuff. Eventually I got to the ENIAC because, during the time I worked on the analyzer, they were putting the converter code on the ENIAC, and they weren't doing too much else except checking that out. So I worked a little time on the ENIAC. When they had the contract out for the ORDVAC, we all took a course in ORDVAC programming. Dr. Clippinger and Dr. Bernard Dimsdale said, "You're going to Illinois; you're going to be in the ORDVAC section." My career on the ENIAC wasn't very long, but I remember many night shifts working with Clippinger, working with Bill Carter, and working with Dr. Giese on exterior ballistic problems. Then, from there, I went on to be chief at the ORDVAC section.

Eventually, when there were separate machines, we realized that programmers could program on any computer—they just had to know how to make it work. We divided the sections into individual interest areas, and all the programmers in each of these sections programmed up for all the machines—so they were most familiar with the problems and would run them on whichever machine was available.

Of course, the big change from the ENIAC to machines like the EDVAC and the ORDVAC, was that, suddenly, you didn't have this long preparation time—where you got on the machine and stayed on it until your program was all finished. You could go ahead and read in a program on the ORDVAC. We eventually had—what did we call it, Homé? We had a system where you came down a half an hour before lunch, and you could bring your program and get three minutes or five minutes on the machine to find the next mistake and go back and correct it. That was a big step forward.

But I always said I'm very glad they invented computers just in time for me, because I sure didn't want to teach. [laughter] And I was very happy when they wrote to me to accept me at Stanford and they said, "We're sorry to inform you that, although we like our graduate students to teach courses, we don't have any teaching positions available." [laughter]

I did work, not only on the differential analyzer, but on the ENIAC and the ORDVAC. I didn't do any programs on the EDVAC. We did use it for a while.

I was also director of a class. When we got to the point where we could handle big quantities of input/output, the Army was interested in training all their people in the Payroll Section to use computers. Computers were going to do all the payroll and all those boring, repetitive jobs that people had to do. So, Aberdeen was the logical choice, since we already had three very different machines, and we had programmers programming for all of them. So somehow, I ended up as the director of the courses for about five years, I think. We taught people from all the Ordnance Districts all over the country the basic principles of computing. I think maybe George and Homé Reitwiesner were the ones that designed the synthetic program—now it would be called a compiler—that we put on the EDVAC. This was a three-address decimal system, which the people that were taking this four-week course could use to actually run a program on the machine. That was a big step forward.

Anyway, I retired in 1978, 30 years almost to the day. I came the 29th of March and retired the 6th of April, 30 years later. Then Dr. Ceslovas Masaitis wanted me to finish what I was working on, and he kept extending the time and extending the time, and when he finally retired, I said, "That's it; I'm not going to do it anymore. I've got other irons in the fire." While I like computers, and thoroughly enjoyed my work with them, I was through with computers and I don't have one. [laughter]

Jill Smith:

I'd like the audience to join me in thanking all these women for sharing a part of their life and the excitement that they felt. They are truly pioneers to all of us. I would say, especially for the women in the audience, that they broke many barriers, and that they made it easier for many of us to follow. I would point out that in the audience you will also meet more people that have the blue ribbons that designate them as pioneers, and I would ask you all to get to know them and learn about them. One of the things they didn't mention was that these women were working six days a week, on two shifts (the day shift and the night shift) throughout the war, with only two holidays—Christmas and the Fourth of July. So I think that we all should thank them for their efforts and for the information they've brought to us today. [applause]

4. Digital Computing at BRL: 1938–1969

John Gregory:
Thank you for attending the second session of historical remembrances. You are about to go back 50 years into the dark ages of the analog world, and we still use analog technology today. You're going to witness the efforts of digital computer pioneers to bring us into the digital world.

This session is devoted to covering the earliest digital computers purchased, developed, and operated at the home of computers, the Ballistic Research Laboratories, Aberdeen Proving Ground, now called the Army Research Lab. For our session, each speaker will allow five minutes for questions and answers at the end of the presentation, and I will moderate the time with an analog stop watch and a gong. [laughter]

As digital computer pioneers, we had to convince the (then) analog world that digital electronic systems are superior to analog electronic systems. It was a formidable task at that particular time. I'm John Gregory, the organizer and moderator for our session, and I started my work here at Aberdeen by changing tubes for Joe Cherney, a pioneer on the ENIAC. I supervised putting the EDVAC into operation and some improvements, and I supervised the design and development and operation of BRLESC I while I was at Army Ballistic Research Laboratories. I then went on to manage extensive design application work at Westinghouse Electronic Systems Operations in Baltimore and applying digital computers to weapons systems, space systems, intelligence systems, and commercial applications.

Our distinguished computer pioneer speakers are as follows: Dr. **Martin H. Weik**, developer and publisher of the earliest digital computing surveys and consultant/teacher for digital computer design, standards, and later for electro-optical sensors for weapons systems. In 1961, the *Journal of the American Ordnance Association* published Marty's "The ENIAC story."[1] Marty invented the famous computing tree, which is on display there, and here's a sample of it.[2]

Our next speaker is Mr. **William Barkuloo**, who cut his teeth on ENIAC, EDVAC, ORDVAC, BRLESC I, BRLESC II, and the Heterogeneous Element Processor (HEP),[3] and went on to consult on every computer used in the Army Research Lab Computing Center, now called the Major Shared Resource Center (MSRC).

The speaker after him will be **Don Merritt**, who did engineering design work on the BRLESC I and BRLESC II[4] computers, as well as engineering for operation of every computer at the Army Research Lab Computer Center. He will present BRLESC I and BRLESC II and the early digital technology contributions by the Army.

---

[1] A reprint of Weik (1961) was contained in the registration packet for the commemoration.

[2] See pp 52–53.

[3] The world's first massively parallel supercomputer.

[4] BRLESC (pron. "burlesque") stands for "BRL Electronic Scientific Computer."

Mr. Bill Barkuloo will then talk about the HEP parallel computer used for Army scientific computing.

Mr. **Mike Romanelli** supervised the earliest software programmers and engineers, who performed major technical and scientific program calculations during the Ballistic Research Laboratories' pioneer days, as well as many recent Army applications. Mike will address "pioneer software technology."

Then, Mr. **Barkley Fritz**, who pioneered the use of scientific computing programs on the ENIAC, will present the various applications that were run on the ENIAC. Barkley also wrote a paper about this.[5] One of the significant features of the paper was an appendix of the major programs run on ENIAC. From BRL, Barkley went to Westinghouse, where he managed mathematical analysis and software programs for many major weapons and sensor programs. He then joined the Computer and Information Science Department at the University of Delaware. Today he will present some of those major ENIAC application programs.

[5] Fritz (1994).

And our last, but not least, speaker will be Dr. **John Giese**, who was a Director of the Ballistic Research Lab Computing Laboratory, which solved scientific problems for Army laboratories, as well as outside government agencies. Dr. Giese will address computing applications analysis and some historical solutions of Army and other agencies' science and technology programs.

Historically, the Army's Ballistic Research Laboratories did more than just introduce digital computers to the world. It also funded the first digital technology developments for areas like high-speed ferrite core memories, high-speed printers (two types: impact and chemical), the first disc storage devices, synchronous drums, software technology, and system simulation and modeling of weapons systems—and even oil-well modeling. Much of the Army's history in the digital computing field has been lost, and today we hope to recall some of it through the remembrances of these computer pioneers.

Our first speaker is computer pioneer Dr. Marty Weik.

1939–1954: ENIAC and the First Computer Survey

Martin Weik:

Thank you very much, John. John was my role model. When I first got here to Aberdeen Proving Ground, I watched him and learned a lot. In fact, I learned practically everything I knew about digital computers initially, from John Gregory. Actually I'm going to tell you three stories, although the program says two. The first story is about how I got to Aberdeen Proving Ground.

If you travel Route 40 West far enough you get to Junction City, Kansas, and Ft. Riley. That's where I was, in the middle of the Korean War. I was an Infantry Captain at that time, and I wore the "crossed rifles" on my lapel. I took Route 40 East, and three days later, I arrived at Aberdeen Proving Ground on Route 40, only I wore the insignia of an Ordnance Captain. And that little piece of magic was performed by Colonel Alden B. Taber, who was then the Director of the Ballistic Research Laboratories, and that's how I got to Aberdeen Proving Ground.

The reason I'm on the program first is because I'm going to talk about the ENIAC story. As John mentioned, there was an article in *Ordnance* magazine entitled "The ENIAC story."[6] I really didn't write that story, because I got

[6] Weik (1961).

most of the material from Herman Goldstine, Dr. Mauchly, J. Presper Eckert, and all those good people who I spoke to at that time. They gave me material to put in the article, so all I did really was edit the material, rather than author the article.

The ENIAC story begins way back in 1938 or 1939, when the University of Pennsylvania had a "brain trust" made up of a lot of good people. Among them were some people at the Moore School of Electrical Engineering. They had the larger of the Bush differential analyzers there, so a contract was let by BRL for performing calculations. And, at that time, the contract was the responsibility of a Lieutenant Paul N. Gillon, who was in charge of ballistic computations for the Ordnance Department. In numerous discussions with Dean Harold Pender and Professor J. G. Brainerd, these three people finally put together a kind of a concept, which would be called ENIAC. They got Eckert and Mauchly to put together the written concept, and they proceeded down to the Chief of the Ordnance Department and tried to sell the idea—which was successful.

The assistant to Captain Gillon was Lieutenant Herman Goldstine, who came to the project with a lot more than just his lieutenant's commission. He was also a Ph.D. in mathematics, from the University of Chicago.

By 1943, Captain Goldstine and Prof. Brainerd brought to Captain Gillon an outline of the ENIAC concept. The outline was prepared by Dr. John W. Mauchly and J. Presper Eckert, Jr. It called for a high-speed computation device for computing ballistic trajectories. On June 5, 1943, a contract for six months in the amount of $61,700 called for the following, and this I quote from the contract: "Research and development of an electronic numerical integrator and computer and delivery of a report thereon." That was the contract!

There were nine more supplements to that contract, totaling $486,804.22—you could say roughly a half million dollars. A pilot model was first built at the University of Pennsylvania's Moore School, and it was subsequently moved to Aberdeen Proving Ground. At the time of construction at the Moore School, Mr. Eckert was the chief engineer, and Dr. Mauchly provided the principal consultancy for the project.

Captain Goldstine, at the time, was the resident supervisor for the Ordnance Department. He added a lot to the project too, with his mathematical assistance. Of course, the work was done by many people, not just the ones I mentioned. The first cycling unit went into operation in June of 1944, about the time of the Normandy landing. Finally, the assembly was completed in the fall of 1945. At that time, the machine only weighed 30 tons, had 19,000

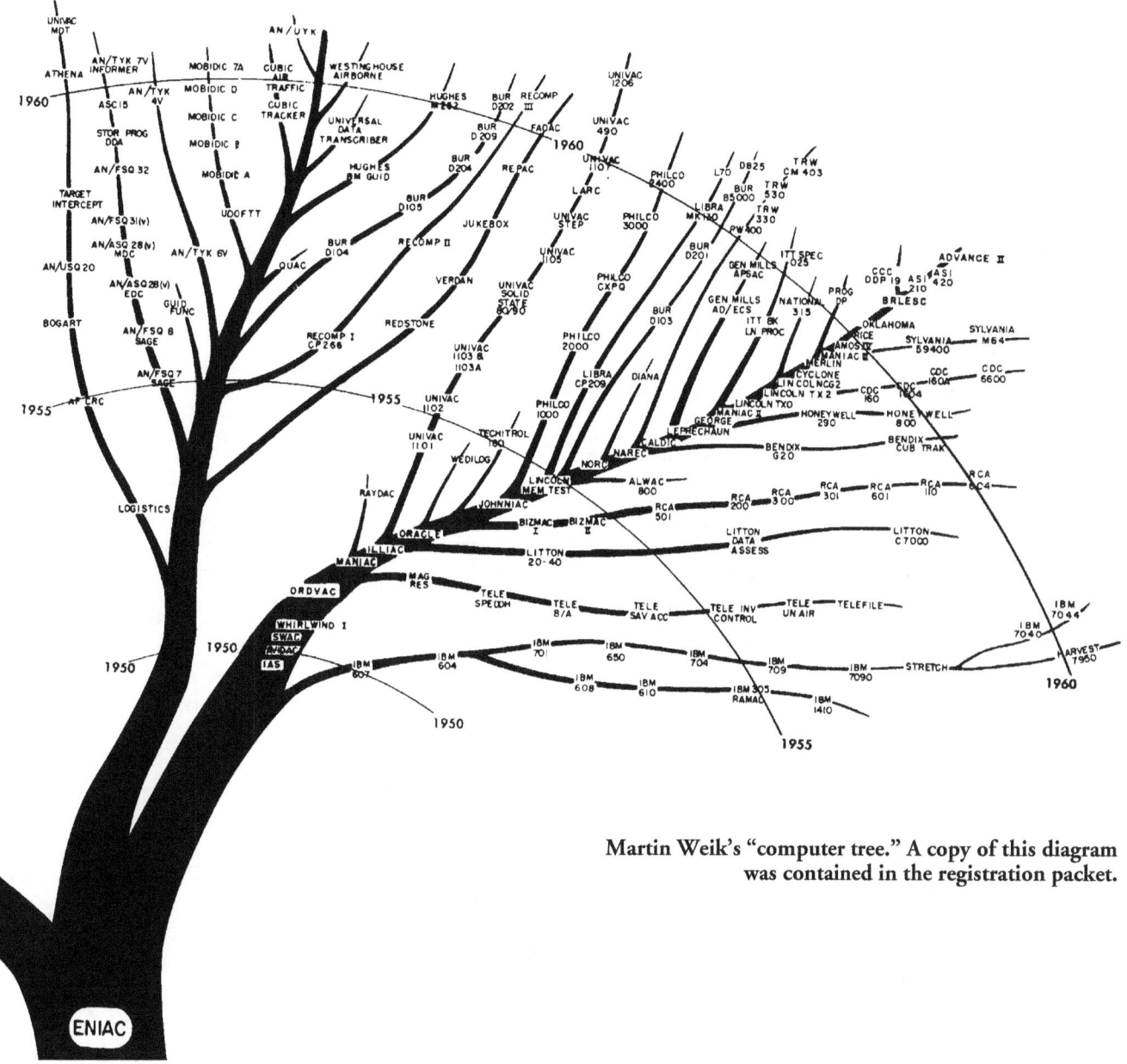

Martin Weik's "computer tree." A copy of this diagram was contained in the registration packet.

tubes, 1500 relays, as well as hundreds of thousands of resistors, capacitors, and inductors. It was quite a monster! You'll get more detail on the machine from Mr. Billy Barkuloo and Don Merritt in a little while.

The formal dedication took place on February 15, 1946, at the Moore School. That's 50 years ago, and this is the 50th anniversary of the operation of the machine. The first unit arrived at Aberdeen Proving Ground in January 1947. It could multiply two 10-digit decimal numbers in 2.6 ms. One time, someone told me that we didn't have a requirement to compute that fast in the Army, and therefore, we really didn't need the machine! There was opposition, too. The division and square root calculations took 25 ms, which was pretty fast. Then it was dismantled, and moved to Aberdeen Proving Ground, where, in

August 1947, it was placed in full operation. Applications are going to be talked about by Dr. Giese.

At the Proving Ground, we added a lot of features. You know when the machine arrived, it had 20 accumulators and not much else—a square rooter and a divider, and that's about it. The input/output was extremely slow. They finally got punch card machines.

There's a story about the punch card machines we attached to ENIAC at that time. Some IBM engineers were at the Proving Ground looking after our punch card machinery, and we had a 407 Calculator/Tabulator and a few other pieces of IBM punched card equipment—sorters, collators, and so on. One of the engineers was called into one of the rooms, and we said, "We have something to show you here."

There was nothing in the room but a card reader and a card punch. He said, "Well, I know these machines. What am I looking at?"

All of a sudden one of the card readers started up and started reading cards like mad and quit. Then there was silence.

A couple minutes later, the card punch started up, and he said, "Well, what's going on? Nobody pushed the actuator button; there's nobody in here operating these punch card machines. What's happening?"

We said, "Well, the *computer* called for some data, and it read it, accepted the data, did computations, and printed out the results."

The IBM guy said, "Computer, what's that?"

So IBM at that time didn't have much but typewriters and punch card machinery.

Then the IBM guy passed on a remark; he said, "There might be a commercial application to this machine." [laughter]

Okay, ENIAC was a workhorse for quite a while from 1949 to 1952, and was actually a leader and all, but then EDVAC and ORDVAC took over, and other machines came along. They moved my office inside the ENIAC room, and it was nice and cool in there too. [laughter] I had a little Special Systems Section at that time, and a couple of military and civilians. We did computer research projects with our desks inside the ENIAC machine itself. It was good floor space and, besides, it was air-conditioned, which not everyone had in the laboratories at that time. ENIAC was finally retired at 11:45 pm on October 2, 1955.

Some units were preserved. The U.S. Military Academy got an accumulator. A piece went to the Smithsonian; I don't know if any of you have seen it there. I understand a piece went to the museum in Munich, Germany, but I'm not quite sure. Maybe someone here knows about that endeavor. I understand they did get a piece too at that time. Well, so much for the ENIAC, and this early history; that's why I'm on first, to tell this 1939–1954 story.

Now, in regard to the computer surveys, the problem with the surveys was we wanted to get data on a lot of machines that were available, either about to be built, being built, or being applied. There was little information about experience on computers and applications on computers, so we thought it would be a good idea to find out all about all the computers that existed in the world at that time. So, we came out with the idea to survey all the computers. Now, in order to get data from industry, you had to do two things: you had to have a "carrot" and you had to have a "stick."

Well, the "stick" was to get a *Report Control Symbol*, which would require the respondents to answer our questionnaire. So we came up with a questionnaire, and we sent it out to everybody. Of course Dr. Giese insisted that all the letters of transmittal be original letters. Well, you couldn't get out hundreds of original letters. In those days, we only had typewriters, and it was impossible to get someone to sit down and type the same old letters.

So Mrs. Ermalee McCauley came along with an idea.[7] We had a Flexowriter.[8] She did a tape with the body of the letter on it and programmed it to stop where the address goes, so she spent her days watching the machine and entering the addresses, and we got the letters out with a transmittal. That was the "stick"—to get the Report Control Number and require industry to respond.

Okay, what was the "carrot"? The "carrot" was that we were going to give respondents a copy of the completed survey. Dr. Giese said in his letter: "If you respond to this survey, you're going to get a copy." Of course, we got tremendous response. Anybody who gets a questionnaire like this, doesn't want to respond—but with the carrot and the stick, we got a lot of responses.

But the problem was, how could we describe a *computer*? In those days, the early days in 1951 to '52, nobody knew a really good way to describe a computer, so we had to come up with one. Well, you know there's always five parts to a computer: input, output, arithmetic, control, and storage units. So that was pretty easy. But we had to go further than that. So we came up with a questionnaire that had all these things in it: the name of the manufacturer, the name of the computer, the operating agencies that operated the computer, the general system description, the numerical system description, the arithmetic unit descriptions, the storage, the input, the output, the number of circuit elements, the features and factors, manufacturing costs, personnel requirements, reliability, and all that. So, getting the questionnaires out, and getting them in the mail, was fine.

There were four surveys. The third survey got to be so heavy and so large that we had to do the fourth survey just as a supplement. We didn't include all the computers of the past, which we did in the third survey, of which we printed 2500 copies. When it came from Raritan Arsenal,[9] the tractor trailer truck was so loaded, we couldn't put them in the building. We didn't have space. So, we put all the address capabilities and people out on the tailgate of the truck! These surveys were mailed to something like 2000 people who we promised would get a copy, which was the "carrot."

My time is up; thank you very much. [applause] It was really fine to have all of you here, and to see all you people, and I certainly was delighted to have had the chance to speak. Thank you. [applause]

EDVAC, ORDVAC

William Barkuloo:
Well, folks, I guess I'm next. I started work at BRL in April of 1951. I was a young kid then, and I had hair. [laughter] I retired in September of 1985, and I was a person who felt privileged that I had been a part of computing history here at BRL.

[7] At that time, Secretary to Dr. Giese, Chief of the BRL Computer Laboratory. She subsequently became his Administrative Assistant, and Dr. Weik became his Technical Assistant.

[8] The Flexowriter was a paper-tape driven typewriter produced by the Freiden Company. An operator could punch tapes with alphabetic characters, numbers, and special characters, as well as certain control characters that let the operator type in material. The operator could then instruct the machine to continue typing the material on the paper tape.

[9] U.S. Army arsenal on the Raritan River near New Brunswick, New Jersey.

My uncle, who worked here at the Proving Ground, congratulated me when he found out I went to work at the Proving Ground. He said, "I hadn't been able to locate you; where are you working?" I said, "Unc, I'm working at BRL." He expressed his concern. He said, "Bill, couldn't you find employment somewhere else? Those people at BRL are nuts." [laughter] Believe me, that was the opinion of the outer perimeter of people.

> **How a core memory element works**
>
> A "core" memory element was a small amount of magnetic material formed in the shape of a toroid (a doughnut). When sufficient current was passed through a winding in one direction, the core became saturated in one direction, and if sufficient current was passed through the winding in the other direction, the core became saturated in the other direction. The saturated state of the core can be detected by a *read* winding, and thus a series of such cores could be used to store data (numbers in binary form)—where cores saturated in one direction represented a "1," and cores saturated in the opposite direction represented a "0." The material used to make the cores' memory elements was one of a number of ferromagnetic (iron-containing) compounds.

The ENIAC, as you've heard quite a few times, was a decimal machine that had 18,000 tubes. The ENIAC was cooled with outside air (no air-conditioning) and consumed 175 kW of power. ENIAC's memory was three function tables (manual switches), each with 104 words. Tomorrow you'll see what a function table looks like, if you haven't already seen one. That memory was sort of a static memory. You set the switches and they remained set for the entire time you were running a problem. Input/output was by IBM cards. The speed of the ENIAC was controlled by an adjustable 100-kilocycle [kHz] clock. Maintenance was performed every Sunday night with the objective of having the machine run as close to 100 kilocycles as possible. During the week, as tubes aged, the clock was decreased to keep problems running.

I was not assigned to the ENIAC, but at times helped ENIAC engineers and mathematicians. This included pulling tubes, changing "grasshopper" fuses during machine failures. There were huge panels of grasshopper fuses, and during failures it seemed as though the majority of the fuses would blow and have to be replaced—sometimes more than once. We assisted the mathematicians by setting switches on the function tables, and verified their settings.

I remember that one person spent almost full time stamping dates on tubes. There were two ladies in the tube room, and they worked full time "burning in" new tubes, [with filaments on and bias voltage on the cathodes] testing these tubes after they were burned in, and also testing tubes that had been taken out of the machine and put back in for recycling.[10] Originally there were only ENIAC tubes, but eventually there were EDVAC, ORDVAC, and BRLESC I tubes also to test.

Of the many improvements to the ENIAC, the most impressive, to me, was the addition of 100 words of core memory. There were 4100 cores of molypermalloy material, each approximately the size of a quarter. [see sidebar] This was the first use in the industry of core memories, and the cycle time was really great—it was less than 200 µs, which was the add-time of the ENIAC.

The EDVAC arrived at BRL in 1949. It had serial synchronous logic, a one megacycle [MHz] clock.[11] It had 44-bit words and a four-address system. You took the first 10 bits of the word and operated on it with the second 10 bits; then put the result where the third 10 bits specified; and then went to where the fourth set of 10 bits told you to go to find the next instruction. The last four bits were the order types. The EDVAC, with a 10-bit address, could only address 1024 words.[12] The EDVAC had a 1024-word acoustical memory. That is like 2 KB in today's world, if you talk about kilobytes.

The memory was a mercury tank memory, where RF packet signals hit an

[10] One of the engineering decisions attributed to Pres Eckert is that he required all vacuum tubes to be turned on for a period of time, so that weak tubes could have time to fail during a test period, rather than failing when in the ENIAC. This practice, later adopted across the fledgling computer industry, was a major reason for the ENIAC's good performance record.

[11] See Stern (1981), pp 94 and 95, for EDVAC specifications.

[12] Computers use the binary system, which has only two elements: 0 and 1. The number of unique combinations of binary numbers 10 elements wide (e.g., 0101010101) is 2^{10} or 1024.

X-cut crystal, created an acoustical sound wave (which went down the column of mercury), and hit another X-cut crystal, transferring it back into an RF packet again, and then the signal was recirculated. The time of recirculation was 384 μs. The fastest access to that memory was 48 μs and the slowest was 384. We had paper tape input/output. The original paper tape operated at 2.5 words per second.

There's quite a few things that were added to the EDVAC, even before it had become a real production machine. We had a fast teletype paper tape reader, and in Marty's article, he said it was 78 words per second. I don't know how fast that son of a gun was, but we had tape rolled up on a reel with a screwdriver through it, and when it started reading, it spewed tape out for a good six or seven feet before it ever started falling to the floor. [laughter] It was really great because you got things in the machine in a hurry. There was only one problem: the reader just spewed it out on the floor. Now you had to go back and roll it back up. [laughter] We never did solve the handling capabilities of that paper tape, but nobody ever came up with a faster paper tape reader.

Eventually, EDVAC had an IBM card reader and punch system attached. EDVAC had a synchronous parallel drum. When it came around, it tossed out all 48 bits in parallel. Synchronization was achieved by using an eddy-current brake. The surface of the drum was nickel-plated.

Another feature that was added to the arithmetic unit was a floating point arithmetic unit. I believe it was Homé Reitwiesner that mentioned [in the morning session] that floating point was the only way to go. The EDVAC had it, and also had magnetic tapes.

The ORDVAC arrived at BRL in 1952. It had parallel asynchronous logic with 40-bit words, two instructions per word. It was a fixed-point machine. It had adjustable filament voltage, and the technicians who were operating the machine had their own little secret way of setting the filaments, because they knew that such and such a problem operated better with the filament set at a particular level. So whether it was superstition or not, I don't know, but that's the way they operated.

The ORDVAC's memory [a Williams-tube electrostatic memory] had 40 three-inch cathode ray tubes, one for each bit of a word. The rectangular raster on each tube contained 1024 dots—the same bit position for 1024 words. This particular memory was very satisfactory memory, so long as we had good tubes. The corners of the raster presented problems due to the curvature of the face of the tube and the unevenness of the phosphorus coating. The Williams tube memory had a refresh cycle to prevent loss of bits.

I spent two years in the Navy (1955–1957), stationed at the Naval Research Laboratory (NRL), in Washington, D.C., supporting their computer, called NAREC. NAREC was a later version of the ORDVAC, and its Williams tube memory had three tubes representing each bit of each word. The bits on each of the redundant tubes were scattered so that a corner bit would be "on" on only one of the three tubes. They averaged the total current for each bit to determine a "one" or a "zero." NRL's memory was more reliable than APG's, but they had another problem. The Naval Research Lab had a 100-inch radar unit mounted on the roof of a building close to the building housing the NAREC. The radar was used to bounce signals off the moon. Whenever the radar was activated, the data in the NAREC was destroyed.

Later, ORDVAC replaced the Williams tube electrostatic memory with a 4096-word core memory. ORDVAC with two 20-bit instructions per word was able to dedicate 12 bits for addressing memory. The cycle time for the core memory was 15 μs. Other features of the ORDVAC were a paper tape reader/punch, an IBM card reader/punch, a serial magnetic drum, and later, a transistorized arithmetic unit.

John Gregory mentioned earlier that there were several other things that were accomplished at BRL during the early days of computing. A high-speed impact printer and a high-speed chemical printer were developed. BRL put "seed money" into a company in New Jersey to develop ferrite material. The first use we made of this ferrite material was making "cup cores" so we could hand wind our own pulse transformers. Another use was to make a core memory, which then could be made smaller and faster than what we had with the ENIAC. It was similar to the type that went into the core memory of the ORDVAC.

At this point, I'm probably out of time or very, very close to it. The three machines I mentioned were really the backbone here at BRL. They did yeoman-type duty. Their production schedules kept going up, up, and up! They were very reliable machines. That is what allowed us to go on and create the two machines that Don Merritt will talk about. Thank you. [applause]

BRLESC I and II

Donald F. Merritt:

Well, I first arrived at BRL in January of 1961, as a 19-year-old electrical engineering co-op student from Drexel.[13] After graduation, I started work at BRL as an electronics engineer in the Computing Laboratory. Except for two years on active duty with the Army Ordnance Corps, I've been here ever since. When I arrived in 1961, BRLESC was nearing completion on floor space that had previously been occupied by the ENIAC. BRLESC was designed and built by the engineers, scientists, and technicians of the BRL Computing Lab. It was the first of two large-scale, high-speed digital computers that were built in-house. When the second machine was built, it was named BRLESC II, and the original BRLESC became known as BRLESC I.

[13] Drexel Institute of Technology, now Drexel University in Philadelphia.

BRLESC was built with synchronous vacuum tube logic and used a 1-MHz five-phase clock. BRLESC had a complex instruction set. As an example of the level of the instructions, the instruction set included the first hardware implementation of a polynomial-multiply instruction. Instructions had three addresses and were 68 bits long. Each address consisted of a 14-bit fixed address, plus six bits that specified one of 63 index registers. The index registers were really a 63-word by 16-bit magnetic core memory.

Numeric words were also 68 bits long for both fixed and floating-point formats. This allowed BRLESC to compute solutions at a level of precision that was not possible in most other high-speed computers of the day without resorting to slow, multiple-precision arithmetic.

Here are some examples of the speed of the arithmetic unit. These are excluding memory access time:

fixed-point add or subtract	1 μs
fixed or floating multiply	20 μs
fixed or floating divide	60 μs
floating add or subtract	3 μs

The original main memory was 4096 words by 72 bits of magnetic core for the 1-μs cycle time.

BRLESC was designed to take advantage of concurrent operations whenever possible. It had many special instructions that could be executed while the arithmetic unit was working on an instruction. It had five input/output trunks, where each trunk was an independent unit that processed one input/output instruction, and all five trunks could be operating simultaneously.

The design of BRLESC began in 1957, with the intention of pushing the state of the art as much as possible. The designers had a 1-μs adder designed and wanted to use a 1-μs core memory. For comparison, ORDVAC's core memory at that time had a cycle time of 24 μs. When BRL put out a request for proposals for a 1-μs memory, there were no responses. Finally, a best-effort R&D contract was let to Telemeter Magnetics for the 63-word by 16-bit index memory and the 4096-word by 72-bit main memory, both with 1-μs cycle times. This contract resulted in the world's first 1-μs core memory.

BRLESC became operational in November of 1961. At that time, it was the world's fastest computer. It ran eight times faster than the most prevalent IBM machine then on the market. The CDC 6600 was the first machine to run faster than BRLESC, and it was not available until after 1964.

Improvements continued to be made to BRLESC throughout its lifetime. The first improvement was the addition of more memory. BRL's R&D contract for the 1-μs core memory allowed the technical problems involved to be solved, and resulted in a market where there were several companies offering much larger 1-μs memories at much lower prices. BRL bought 48K words of 1-μs core memory for BRLESC at the same price as the original 4096 words.

Other improvements included the addition of standard half-inch tape drives. A disk system that used IBM 2311 or Bryant 1100 disk drives was designed and built. Improvements were also made that increased the reliability of BRLESC. The vacuum tubes and pulse transformers on the logic-gate boards were replaced with a small "daughter" board containing a few transistors. This also saved the cost of replacing the tubes, which was about $25,000 a year.

Work started on BRLESC II around 1966. Again, this machine was designed and built by the engineers, scientists, and technicians of the Computing Laboratory. The intention was to build a reliable solid-state computer that would run about 200 times faster than the ORDVAC, which it was scheduled to replace. BRLESC II was built using asynchronous, complementary transistor, integrated-circuit logic. Like the ORDVAC, BRLESC II was a single-address machine. Instructions could be either short, with 16 bits and an 8-bit address, or long, with 32 bits and a 20-bit address. The word size was 68 bits, and one word could store two, three, or four instructions. Numeric words were 64 bits plus sign for integer, fixed-point, and floating-point formats.

Another 48K words of 72-bit, 1-μs core memory was purchased for BRLESC II in 1966. The memory was identical to the BRLESC I's memory and brought the total available memory up to 96K words. A digital crossbar switch was designed and built by Computing Laboratory personnel so that the 96K words of memory could be manually switched in 16K-word blocks to either machine. Here are some examples of the speed of the arithmetic unit. These are average times including memory access time:

    integer add or subtract   1.45 μs
    fixed-point add or subtract   1.45 μs

fixed or floating multiply	14.4 μs
fixed or floating divide	22.8 μs
floating add or subtract	3 μs

BRLESC II was also designed to take advantage of concurrent operations whenever possible. It had four independent I/O trunks that could be operating simultaneously. After the completion of BRLESC II, work started on the design and construction of a new arithmetic and control unit for BRLESC I in 1968. The integrated circuits used in BRLESC II were used in the design of this unit. The unit was synchronous and used a 10-MHz four-phase clock and dual carry/save adders. Here are some examples of the speed of the new arithmetic unit; these are excluding memory access time:

fixed-point add or subtract	300 ns
fixed or floating multiply	2 μs
fixed or floating divide	1 μs

BRLESC I and BRLESC II were the last BRL-designed and -developed computers. BRLESC I was shut down April 3, 1978, after 16 years of round-the-clock operation. BRLESC II was shut down July 1, 1978. They served BRL and the Army well. BRL's work on these machines also made many contributions to the computer industry, such as the first 1-μs adder, the first 1-μs core memory, the first complex instruction set computer, and the first hardware implementation of a polynomial multiply instruction. Thank you very much. [applause]

HEP

William Barkuloo:

Well, folks, I'm back again. In the mid 1970s, BRL was recruited by the Army to participate in a program to encourage the analog computer manufacturers to develop an analog computer without patch panels. One proposal was for a complete digital approach to analog computing. BRL was chosen to pursue this proposal. The company that submitted this was a small company whose name was Denelcor, Inc., located in Denver, Colorado. A prototype was built that exhibited promise, not in the analog world, but as a scalar, parallel processor. The Heterogeneous Element Processor (HEP) evolved, over a period of time, into the first large-scale parallel processor available.

As with most new architectures, software was a problem. HEP had a lot of memory, real nice features, the processors were pipelined, all of our function units were pipelined, the machine operated—if you had eight processes operating, in parallel, within each processor—at maximum speed. BRL HEP had four different main processors; they likewise operated in parallel. But, as with most new architectures, software was a problem. Denelcor tried a lot of things, and none of it seemed to really work. BRL's Mike Muuss, who is in the back, and his cohorts came to the rescue and installed a Unix operating system on the HEP.[14] This was no small task. Unfortunately, many of the parallel processing problems uncovered by the HEP still exist today.

The HEP, after it was delivered to BRL, had possibly as much opposition as it did support. We had the four-processor module. We had a megaword[15] of program memory distributed across the four units. We had 2 megawords [64-bit words] of global data memory. We had a switch, which was a method to communicate from these processors to different banks of data memory or to the input/output cache that HEP also had. Everything worked well with Unix and TCP/IP[16] protocol; it was relatively successful.

---

[14] Michael John (Mike) Muuss was a member of the Program Committee for the commemoration sessions. See also *Ballisticians,* vol. III, pp 14–15, for a discussion of the HEP.

[15] A million words.

[16] TCP/IP stands for transmission control protocol/internet protocol, which was the protocol used to transfer information between elements in the HEP.

Some of the features of this contract would improve manufacturing techniques of IC [integrated circuit] boards, allowing trace impedances to be constant over the entire board. The way big boards were made at that time resulted in all sorts of ripples in the board, which had to be smoothed, to keep a constant impedance of traces. This allowed the density to be pushed to over 250 ICs per board. When we first started out, nobody could put over 100. We forced supercomputer companies to use Unix, which was very important. We developed a software program to simulate wave shapes and the timing of signals, which resulted in better designed boards.

We used scoreboarding techniques on each dataword. Each dataword had a control. The rules were if an instruction wanted to write data into a dataword, it must be "empty." If not, the instruction was turned away until it was empty. The instruction stored its data in the dataword and set the dataword to "full." If an instruction wanted to read a dataword, it must be full. If not, the instruction was turned away. If the dataword was full, the instruction was allowed to read the dataword and set the dataword to empty. So the HEP was able to synchronize on one dataword within the 2-megaword memory. With the register memory of each processor, the scoreboarding was different, employing "full," "empty," and "reserved." *Reserved* was for anticipated write instructions.

We developed a high-speed switching network, which was a packet-switching network with three nodes of full duplex. We had collisions (two or three messages trying to go to the same destination), but somebody always got the right-of-way to go. The other guys [messages] were sent in a nonoptimal path to their destination—the losers had their "age" increased. Messages with the greatest "age" were given priority. This is a method of making sure that everybody got serviced on the switch.

In conclusion, I feel that BRL, and now ARL, has been on the crest of the wave always looking forward, developing new ideas and techniques, and making the past 50 years of computing successful. All of you pioneers out there in the audience, take heart! The younger generation is on this crest of the wave looking forward to the next half century of computing. Thank you. [applause]

Software

Michael J. (Mike) Romanelli:

I feel fortunate and privileged to be here today to speak to you on the development of software for the BRL machines. I'll essentially be referring to the means by which we communicated with the computing machines, that is, the computers. I direct my remarks to those of you who are not familiar with what began many years ago.

I'll tell you at the outset, it will be practically impossible to restrict my remarks exclusively to software, since hardware and software were so inextricably connected in those days, particularly with regard to machine language coding. Further, historical developments in software generally followed progressive improvements in hardware. The developments eventually led to communication by way of high-level languages, independent of machines. I will comment on a few of these improvements and corresponding developments in some of the software.

Initially, programming for ENIAC required the setting of a large number of dials and switches, and cable rewiring of the variable circuits. A significant earlier improvement did not require the use of cable wiring. Basically, communication with the machines began with absolute machine language consisting of *numbers only*. The decimal number system was used on ENIAC, and the binary, octal, and sexadecimal[17] number systems on EDVAC, ORDVAC, and BRLESC. Next followed the introduction of *symbolic machine language*, consisting of numbers, alphabetic characters, and some mathematical symbols, and some special characters. [see sidebar] Eventually, the higher level languages admitted formula expressions, mathematical expressions, and English-word statements. FORAST (a formula and assembly translator) and FORTRAN (a formula translator) were two high-level languages used on the BRL machines.

[17] The 16 symbols of the sexadecimal number system are 0, 1, 2, 3, 4, 5, 6, 7, 8, 9, K, S, N, J, F, and L. The symbols K, S, N, J, F, and L may have been taken from the Baudot or Western Union teletype code (note courtesy of Mike Romanelli).

We began by learning the language that the machine understood. We called this primitive language *machine code*, or absolute machine language. We were not very comfortable with the numeric machine codes, since they bore no resemblance to meaningful communication. Further, the machines had relatively small vocabularies, restricted to elementary arithmetic operations, comparison and recording of numbers, and some elementary control operations. Fifty of the 60 ENIAC operations simply provided for moving numbers. The instruction set for EDVAC consisted of 12 operations! There were four bits, which allowed for 16 different combinations, but four were unused. Now, if we could express the solution of a problem as a combination of the basic operations in numerical language that the machine understood, *hopefully*, the machine would obey and carry out the detailed numerical instructions and produce desired solutions!

To develop the pre-planned instructions, we used a "crutch," because a sheet full of numbers was far from expressive of a problem being solved. To retain some association to the problem, we used an intermediate language whose symbols had more meaning than the code numbers. For example, the plus symbol (+) was far more meaningful than the number "2"! Hence, we first coded in the symbolic language using *symbols* for operations and *symbols* for the data used in the operations. We then manually *translated* or coded the *operation symbols* and the *data symbols* into the specific numerical absolute machine language. This translation was not difficult, but was obviously subject to human error.

This translation later became the major function of symbolic assembly language. To simplify this procedure, coding forms were designed with columns to accommodate the symbolic language and adjacent columns to accommodate the numerical absolute machine language. Before the symbolic code was written, *flowcharts* were drawn to display an overall method of solution.[18] For testing the programs on the machines, we prepared test runs using desk calculators, such as Monroes, Marchants, Friedens, and even a special octal desk calculator to check the results of binary operations.

> **Machine language**
>
> Early machine functions were identified by numbers; this made the coding of problems difficult because the code was simply a listing of numbers (as *operations* and as the *data* to be operated on). The substitution of symbols, such as "A" or "+" for add, and "S" or "–" for "subtract," made coding much simpler; however, these symbols had to be translated into their numeric equivalents before the program was submitted to the computer. A major advantage for symbolic programming systems occurred when the programmer was looking for errors (i.e., "debugging" the code) or later when the program was maintained over long periods of time.
>
> **FORTRAN and FORAST**
>
> FORTRAN is considered the first "high-level language"; it was developed by IBM under the direction of John Backus, and introduced in 1954. FORTRAN's brevity and algebraic syntax made it easy for mathematicians, engineers, and a wide range of scientists to learn and use FORTRAN, thus significantly increasing the number of people who could program a computer. Mike Romanelli adds: "FORAST was somewhat richer than FORTRAN in that a programmer could intersperse, in the high-level language program, symbolic or absolute machine language instructions of ORDVAC or BRLESC, giving the experienced programmer full access to the power of the computer."

[18] Flowcharts take the idea of using symbols to another level of abstraction. In flowcharting, the programmer uses graphic symbols (rectangles, diamonds, and circles) to identify operations such as "read a number" or "add a number to a register"; arrows (, , ,) are used to indicate the order in which the operations are to be performed.

To get the program onto the ENIAC, the dials/switches of the function table were manually set to correspond to numerical code written on the coding forms. For EDVAC and ORDVAC, the numerical codes were recorded on teletype paper tape. Later, the codes were recorded on punch cards.

A severe coding restriction was a requirement that all data representations in the machine and the results of all arithmetic operations had to be less than one.[19] This requirement was removed when read/write memory was provided on EDVAC and ORDVAC, accommodating subroutines that performed the floating-point operations.[20] EDVAC and ORDVAC initially had 1024 words of read/write memory; ENIAC had 20 such words.

It should be noted that the ENIAC function tables and the *JK switches* [see sidebar] that accommodated two 10-digit constants would appropriately be classified today as ROM (read-only memory). The seeds of symbolic language, and even higher level languages, can be found in an early Clippinger report,[21] from 1948, on ENIAC coding:

"2_l" meant accumulator number 2, "listen";

"5_t" meant accumulator number 5, "talk";

"Pr" meant punch a card; [see sidebar] and

"Rd" meant "read" the numbers from the punched card in the card reader and store the numbers in specified registers of the ENIAC.

READ and PRINT statements were standard expressions in FORAST and FORTRAN.

I noted above that the read/write memory on EDVAC and ORDVAC provided space for floating-point subroutines. Another important asset of the read/write memory was the ability to have the computer operate on instructions as though they were data. Memory addresses within the instructions could thus be modified for subsequent operations, providing an effective means of processing streams of data (i.e., vectors and matrices, which were stored in uniformly spaced memory locations). This feature was also used in diagnostic test programs, wherein the diagnostic test program automatically moved itself throughout the entire memory. This was what was known as "leapfrog."

The use of the binary number system on EDVAC, ORDVAC, and BRLESC required a conversion of decimal input data to binary, and the reconversion of the binary data to decimal output. Specially designed subroutines were coded to carry out these essential processes. A library of subroutines was developed that included the commonly used mathematical functions and other service routines. The subroutines themselves were coded as complete entities, easily relocated in main programs, to any area of memory, by transcribers or assemblers. A "code-checker" routine provided a means of monitoring any portion (or all) of a given program, yielding numerical output

[19] The problems suitable for computation at this time ran the gamut from astronomy, with extremely large values, to microscopy, with extremely small values. Since the computers of this period were primitive, an additional burden of the numerical analyst or programmer was to "map" the solution space to the limitations of the computer, usually requiring that all values be less than one. After computation, the numerical analyst or programmer would translate the solution into the appropriate numerical range.

[20] All decimal numbers can be broken into two components: 2,220,000 would be represented as 2.22×10^6 or 1,000,000; fractions are indicated by the use of a negative value: e.g., 0.00025 would be represented as 2.5×10^{-4}.

[21] Reprints of Clippinger (1948) were provided to attendees.

JK switches

The J and K were two read-only memory registers. They could be "hand set" before the running of a program—in the same manner as the function tables. They were used to accommodate two 10-digit constants needed in the solution of a problem. When we finished setting the switches on the function tables, a familiar admonition of one of the programmers was "Don't forget to set 'JK.'" They were somewhat isolated from the function tables and easily forgotten!

Interpreting punched cards

"Pr" (from "print") really meant to punch a card; the interpretation of what was punched in the card was performed by an off-line machine called an interpreter. This machine printed near the top edge of the card the numbers that were punched in the columns of the card. Punched cards could be fed into another off-line machine, a card printer, which printed on paper the numbers that corresponded to the punches in the columns of the card. The numbers punched in the card were taken from specified registers of ENIAC.

—Mike Romanelli

results for detailed comparison with hand calculations.[22]

Let me take you back to "BC-C"—before code-checker—and relate to you a process or "paper trail" in software development. First of all, we received the statement of a problem on paper: for example, a set of differential equations. Second, we selected a numerical method to obtain a solution. We used classical numerical methods such as Heun, Adams, Cowell, Simpson, or Runge-Kutta. Bear in mind that the ultimate solution had to be reduced and expressed as a sequence of machine-coded operations. And, incidentally, as has been stated, all quantities had to be scaled so that the machine representations were less than one in absolute value. For commonly required trigonometric and other mathematical single-value functions of a single variable, we often use truncated power series (i.e., a resulting polynomial readily expressed arithmetically). Next, we drew a flowchart (some more paper) to exhibit the overall plan and solution, and followed this by writing the symbolic code and corresponding machine code, and committed those to paper.

Finally, using a teletypewriter, we typed and obtained perforated tape containing the absolute machine language that we had written on the coding forms. We were now ready to approach the machine with our folder of paper and the precious paper tape. After we manually set a read tape instruction into the computer and put the paper tape in a tape reader, the machine read and recorded our program in memory. We directed the machine to the first instruction in our code, and the machine was off and running.

Alas, after what seemed like a fraction of a second, the machine halted, and the "exceed-capacity" light informed us that the machine did not know how to divide by zero! Noting where this mishap had occurred, we began anew, stopping at predetermined points in the program to compare machine results with our hand calculations.

We eventually found the source of the error. The machine, as directed by our code, had performed a subtraction instead of an addition, resulting in a denominator with value zero. This was a fruitful session. To correct this error, we retrieved one piece of circular confetti from the disposal bin of the teletypewriter. We inserted this less than $\frac{1}{8}$-in.-diameter circular piece of paper into a particular hole of the original paper tape. We covered this patch with Scotch tape, thereby changing the binary three to a binary two, or changing the incorrect subtract code to the correct addition code. We were prepared for another trial. After a series of such trials, we eventually corrected the errors, and the program was ready for production.

Let me digress, briefly, to describe what was termed a "closed-shop" operation. Laboratory scientists would submit problems of interest to applied mathematicians in the Computing Lab. The applied mathematician would present a solution, or suggest a method of solution, to a programmer. The programmer would code, check, and run (or have a technician run) a program on the computer. The results were presented to the applied math analysts for review and subsequently presented to the lab scientist, who subsequently reinitiated a cycle of runs, changes, and reruns. Later, with the publication of programming reports and regularly scheduled Ballistic Institute courses on programming, math analysts and most of the programmers were reassigned throughout BRL. A small group of programmers was retained in the Computing Lab for the development and maintenance of the software operating systems. Thus began the transition to an "open shop," where many of the

[22] Note the careful approach used: the machine results were always compared against test calculations performed on mechanical calculators; once the program had been verified as operating correctly, then other values could be used.

scientists in BRL, AMSAA, and HEL[23] learned how to program and use the BRL machines.

[23] AMSAA, Army Materiel Systems Analysis Agency; HEL, Human Engineering Laboratory.

Let me now return to the development of FORAST, the high-level Formula and Assembly Translator language. Hardware improvements to ORDVAC included a 4096-word magnetic core memory, card reader, and a magnetic drum. Core memory replaced the 1024-word electrostatic CRT memory. BRLESC had a 4096-word magnetic core memory, card reader, high-speed magnetic tape input/output, and an enriched instruction vocabulary. It had a three-address code, 63 index registers, built-in floating-point operations, a look-ahead feature with some concurrent operations, and a flexibility in mathematical operations that included 16 different kinds of addition and subtraction.

In short, the hardware improvements provided more speed and more space relative to the constrained space and speed of the predecessors. The compilers accepted mathematical formulas made up of alphabetic symbols and symbolic operation characters, English word statements for various types of controls, and formatted input/output statements for labeled, printed, or plotted outputs.

Compilers converted the formulas and English word statements into absolute machine language for "LOAD and GO" operations. During a compiling process, FORAST detected and printed grammatical errors.[24] There usually were many! The variety of errors detected during the running of the program was also provided as output for the programmer. A programmer could intersperse the symbolic or absolute machine language of ORDVAC or BRLESC with formula and English word statements. Hence, the language was rich enough to accommodate the novice or journeyman and allow the experienced programmer the full power of the computers. The simplicity, flexibility, generality, and attributes of the language and the machines are well documented in BRL reports.

[24] The compiler did a "syntax check" and was capable of finding such errors as misspelled operators, but it could not find *logical* errors, i.e., errors in the program itself.

Let me now conclude with an "IF" statement; pardon the pun. "IF" statements were admissible conditional control statements in FORAST and FORTRAN. If I had a video camera way back then, I could have shown you a multicolor page of a firing table produced by multiple passes on a high-speed printer that was ready for publication. I could have shown you a multicolor anatomical cross section of the human body, which was the output of a wound-ballistics application. I could have shown you the sociability of EDVAC engaged in playing a game of NIM! I could have shown you, and you could have seen and heard, the patriotic, mannerly, and talented character of ORDVAC playing out the tune to "My Country 'Tis of Thee" for a group of Boy Scouts on tour of the computing facility, and that same ORDVAC at the end of that tour playing out the tune to "So Long, It's Been Good to Know You!"

Finally, if someone asks you, "What is FORTRAN?" tell them it's a formula translator, the standard scientific computer language, or better yet, tell them Mike [Romanelli] said it was a diluted dialect of FORAST! Thank you. [applause]

ENIAC Put to Work

Barkley Fritz

I'm going to take you back to February 17, 1951, the day I talked to the President of the United States for 10 minutes, when President Harry Truman was doing his inspection of the Aberdeen Proving Ground, as Commander-in-Chief.

I had a planned briefing of 10 minutes, which was what I've been given today, and on the same subject: "ENIAC put to work." What did ENIAC do anyway? The President came walking in the room and said to me, "I'm Harry Truman," and threw out his hand like this. I said, "I'm Barkley Fritz. Pleased to meet you, Mr. President." My planned briefing and demonstration of ENIAC turned into a conversation, as the President asked a number of questions. That Saturday morning meeting took place in the ENIAC room in Building 328, which is still standing and in use a short distance from where we are today.

He was one of the many presidents who had served in the armed forces before he became president. As Captain Harry S. Truman, he had headed an Army battalion during World War I in France, as a field artillery officer. Now as President and Commander-in-Chief, he apparently remembered using firing tables and showed an interest in ENIAC's role in generating such tables.

We had a trajectory running, and he could see the lights. He was very fascinated by this, asked a lot of questions, and we talked. Then he said, "What about these hydrogen bomb calculations you've been running?" I wasn't really prepared to talk about the hydrogen bomb. I'd worked night shift on it but I didn't really know anything about it. I said, "Yes, we've been doing some work on that," or words to that effect. Two years or so later, when he gave his State of the Union address, I happened to hear him on the radio say, "I'm announcing to the world today that the United States has developed the hydrogen bomb."

Well, I said 1951 was a big year for me. Besides talking to the President, I had the opportunity to speak to the Association for Computing Machinery at their annual meeting in Detroit, Michigan. At that meeting, I had a paper, "The ENIAC, A five year operating survey."[25] For five years, from the end of 1945—when the hydrogen bomb calculations were done by the group from Los Alamos at the University of Pennsylvania—to the beginning of 1951, ENIAC had been solving problems.

[25] Fritz (1951).

During my 7 years here, ending in April 1955, I was a member of a group of civil service employees in John Holberton's branch, who performed and used ENIAC as a problem solver. I authored or co-authored 14 papers covering numerical techniques and applications of the BRL computers. Another 200 papers and other publications were written by other users of the several computers available here at Aberdeen.

During ENIAC's 10 years of successful operation at the University of Pennsylvania and here at BRL, about 100 problems were programmed and discussed in the published records of ENIAC's use. Seventy of these problems originated within BRL, while the remaining 30 came from users representing other U.S. government agencies, private organizations, and universities.

Truman visits ENIAC, 1951.

I had an opportunity to outline that in the paper that John Gregory referred to earlier.[26] I was teaching computer science at the University of Delaware, and I was allowed to take a sabbatical leave. So I wrote this paper. You may want to take a quick look at the last four pages, which are an appendix listing the various problems that were solved on ENIAC. The APG organizations which used the ENIAC during this time were the Computing Laboratory, Exterior Ballistics Laboratory, Interior Ballistics Laboratory, Terminal Ballistics Laboratory, Ordnance Engineering Laboratory, Ballistics Measurements Laboratory, and the Surveillance Laboratory. The following outside organizations also used ENIAC: Atomic Energy Commission, U.S. Bureau of Mines, University of Cambridge, University of Pennsylvania, Institute for Advanced Study, MIT, and the University of Michigan. In addition, Armour Research Institute and the General Electric Company also used ENIAC to analyze problems.

[26] A reprint of Fritz (1994) was included in the attendees' packets.

A problem, as I put it in a paper, is defined "as a machine program or group of machine programs related to a subject under investigation or a particular mission to be accomplished."

In the language of a later day, ENIAC was a *scientific* computer, and essentially all the problems it solved involved numerical calculations related to a mathematical model of some scientific problem. Hence it is appropriate to classify these applications, at least initially, by the type of mathematics involved.

ENIAC had been originally designed to solve trajectory problems, which were important steps in producing firing tables. Mathematically, the path of a shell is modeled by a small system of nonlinear ordinary differential equations. It is therefore not surprising that over 50 of ENIAC's problems involved the numerical integration of ordinary differential equations. ENIAC was particularly good at this. It was fast (200 to 1000 times faster than any other previous device) and if single-step numerical integration techniques were used, these problems did not place an undue strain on ENIAC's limited memory.

About 20 of the remaining applications involved solving small systems of algebraic equations involving matrix operations. Another 20 problems were essentially either systems of hyperbolic partial differential equations or a single partial differential equation of the parabolic type. The remaining 10 categories of ENIAC problems included a few integral equations, the first computer use of the *Monte Carlo* technique, and several number-theoretic computations.

Okay, what are some of these problems? Well, you've heard about a number of them. Doug Hartree, from Cambridge University in the UK, was a real top scientist. He used the ENIAC to examine compressible laminar boundary layer flow problems. What Kay Mauchly Antonelli did in working with him gave real big international attention to ENIAC, because this problem was too big for ENIAC. Certainly, the hydrogen bomb calculations done for the Atomic Energy Commission were important, although it was essentially operating as a mechanical multiplier—in the sense that cards went in and out. The weather forecasting that you've heard about was done for the Institute of Advanced Study.

It is interesting to note that it seems like you always find a problem that your computer can't solve: the problem is too big; it requires too much speed or more memory than you have. However, we can define things and set up problems that are too big for the tools at hand, and that provides *progress*, and that's important.

Keep in mind that the announcements made at the dedication of ENIAC mentioned that the ENIAC was to be made available by the Army to everybody. Universities were encouraged to bring in problems such as those Homé mentioned, the calculation of π, e, and so on. The ENIAC was so fast that if you had a program that would run, you probably could get some time. We would squeeze it in on Labor Day weekend or whatever.

I certainly want you to know there's a lot of names in the appendix to the paper [Fritz, 1994] of people who wrote papers about the ENIAC applications. In fact, I want to mention that John Giese, Herman Goldstine, Harry Huskey, Homé McAllister Reitwiesner, Harry Reed, and George Trimble, who are here today, are associated with papers about programs that were run on ENIAC. The group that I worked with when I came here was headed by John Holberton, who's also here today.

My time is up. Thank you all for being here. I've enjoyed it. I'm 72 and I hope to come back to the 60th anniversary, which we will celebrate hopefully in 10 years.

We have time for questions.

Unknown questioner:

What was your favorite application for the ENIAC out of your big list?

Barkley Fritz:

One I liked which hasn't been mentioned was work that was done for the Bureau of Mines in explosives. It was done by a man by the name of Stuart R. Brinkley. Stuart Brinkley had both hands blown off in an experiment that resulted in an explosion. He was a brilliant man and was using mechanical hands when Mike Romanelli and I worked with him. He programmed ENIAC better than I could at the time, but that isn't really much of a compliment! Anyway, he was good at it. There he was, using a computer to do mathematical modeling of problems that he'd previously been solving in a testing lab. [applause]

Applications

John Giese:

What can I say to you in 10 minutes about the computer-assisted accomplishments of hundreds of people over a period of over 50 years? Generalities about sources of information, recollections of early estimates of the nation's needs for computers, and descriptions of simple but important examples that won't take too long to explain.

Information for the period 1938 to 1992 is recorded in a three-volume history, *Ballisticians in War and Peace*.[27] A skimpier set of topics is contained in an article "Ballistics calculations" in the first edition of the *Encyclopedia of Computer Science and Technology*.[28]

Since the information superhighway has become an item of high-level national policy, it might be amusing to recall early estimates of the prospective market for computers. The author of a recent book on complexity theory has mentioned that the product-planning department of IBM spent the entire year of 1950 insisting that the market for computers would never amount to more than about 18 computers nationwide.[29] [laughter] I have a vague memory that at about the same time someone estimated the Army's needs at about seven.

[27] *Ballisticians* [various authors].
[28] Belzer, Holzman, and Kent (1975).

[29] Waldrop (1992), p 155.

[laughter]

Last week, John Gregory mentioned another example of a dim vision of the future. He told me that one of the first chiefs of our Computing Laboratory responded to an assertion that we needed another computer by saying: "What's wrong with the ones we already have?" [laughter] But since many of the rest of us also did not foresee that 50 years later, millions of American households would contain tremendous computer power and stunning printing virtuosity, further cheap shots at the myopia of others are unjustified! [laughter]

Let us consider some anecdotes. I've carefully, and probably mistakenly, made these all very anonymous. Soon after the ENIAC had been modified and installed here, the Computing Laboratory was asked to devise a program to determine optimum flight plans for some aircraft. With mathematical models of the propulsion and controls of the systems supplied by the client, the equations that governed the motion of aircraft, rocket shells, and astronomical objects are conceptually the same. They have quite a few common features. The analyst assigned to this problem, an astronomer, decided to treat it as a problem in the calculus of variations with suitable constraints. Eventually he briefed his programmer in meticulous detail.

Sometime later after she had written and debugged most of her program, the programmer found the flight path was going underground! [laughter] As Mike Romanelli told me at the time, "Well, just impose another constraint that says flights occur above ground and above water levels." [laughter] What happened to the eventually completed project? Perhaps the Air Force used it to check or improve programs from other sources. An account of the analyst's formulation was published in the *Quarterly of Applied Mathematics*.[30]

[30] Garfinkle (1951).

Next consider a post-ENIAC computing problem anecdote. Many of the problems submitted to the Computing Laboratory came from the Weapons System Laboratory, or its successor, the Army Materiel Systems Analysis Activity (AMSAA). Sometime in the mid-1960s, someone in AMSAA needed to determine a way to disable a target without excessive damage. This client decided to solve his problem by using an overkill function that depended on many parameters, such as the number of types of weapons available and the numbers of each type used and so forth. The problem was reduced to finding those combinations of parameters that minimized the value of the overkill function. Because the client wanted the answer, or answers, as soon as possible, he and our programmer agreed to solve their problem by "brute force": that is, by evaluating the overkill function for every permissible combination of parameters, a process that took about seven and one-half hours of computer time.

About a week later, our programmer was told by our client that the desired minimum should be determined for a *much larger range* of parameters! When our programmer found that treatment by the "brute force" approach would require the order of a thousand years of processing, he went across the hall to ask one of our problem analysts for help. The analyst said, "I just returned from a course of Richard Bellman's about this kind of problem. Come back in an hour and I'll tell you how to handle it." The problem that took seven and one-half hours could now be solved in 30 seconds. The problem that might have required a millennium could now be solved in about a half an hour.

At the end of an afternoon of serious accounts of the development and use of electronic computers, let me tell you an item of historic triviality that might be entitled, "The Skeptic Hoist by his Own Petard." When I arrived at BRL, in May 1946, the ENIAC had been tentatively assigned to the Ordnance Engineering Laboratory. Its chief, Dr. T. E. Sterne, was a brilliant, strongly opinionated, caustically critical individual, who constantly scoffed at and disputed forecasts of the future importance and potentialities of automatic computers. Not surprisingly, the ENIAC was soon assigned to a newly established Computing Laboratory with Dr. L. S. Dederick as its Chief. As time passed, Stern's iconoclastic attitude toward the value of computers in scientific and engineering research was not noticeably softened. [laughter]

In 1953, W. B. Fritz, of the ENIAC branch, gave a survey and lecture entitled "Five Years Operating Experience on the ENIAC," in which he enumerated the problems that had been solved on that machine and gave sharp abstracts of the less familiar applications. At the end of his lecture, he made the customary offer to answer questions. At his first row seat, Sterne noisily knocked his pipe's ashes into a metal ashtray, solemnly cleared his throat, and insolently demanded, "Tell me, Mr. Fritz, for what and how many problems has the ENIAC been used that could have been solved better by simpler and less expensive means?" Fritz was inspired to blurt the perfectly deadpan reply, "I don't remember what problems have been solved on the ENIAC for *your* laboratory, Dr. Sterne." [laughter and applause] The audience burst into roars of laughter, dominated by Sterne's own guffaws. [laughter and applause]

I'm supposed to be prepared to answer questions but I'm not sure I'll be able to answer them.

Barkley Fritz:

I really worked hours thinking of a reply for that question; sheer luck was not involved!

John Giese:

I'll amend my speech.

Jean Bartik:

John, my name is Jean Bartik, and I worked with you when we converted the ENIAC into a stored-program computer. Remember those trips we used to take to Princeton with Dick Clippinger, and you and Adele? It struck me at that time that you were sort of a skeptic. I'd like for you to reminisce how you felt when we were taking those trips to Princeton.

John Giese:

I have no memory that I was opposed to the development.[31] [laughter] With regard to skepticism, in other talks that I have given, I've done Dick Clippinger an injustice, by saying that the idea to develop the 99-order code for the ENIAC was to be attributed to John von Neumann. Dick wrote to me some time ago, to say that von Neumann's role was that of an interested consultant, and the genesis of the idea came from Dick.

How did I feel about his efforts? He was my boss; he's a free agent—if he does things that make sense, I don't have to complain. That may not be the kind of answer you wanted, but you didn't have to be clairvoyant to decide that changing the ENIAC from a device that was programmed by using plug boards and rewiring stupid machines, so to speak, every time you changed problems was a good thing. Without the changes, there's no way computers would ever have been anything but a rich nation's playthings.

[31] Dr. Giese commented later, "This is another example of my own myopia. I went to work with Clippinger on supersonic flow calculations. I did not realize at the time that turning the ENIAC into a stored-program machine was of vastly greater importance."

John Gregory:

Thank you, Dr. Giese. Marty Weik would like to make a few comments before we end the session, and then I'll end it.

Martin Weik:

I just wanted to comment. You recall that I mentioned that Mrs. Ermalee McCauley helped me get out those original transmittal letters for the computer survey using the Flexowriter and the paper tape. What I failed to mention was that Violet J. Confer—is she here in the audience? Violet, would you stand up please?—Violet J. Confer organized the material, the data, that came in as a result of the survey and actually had to type the survey by hand on a typewriter. I think she deserves a round of applause for that. [applause]

There's one other little story that I'd like to tell you about how BRLESC got its name. One day Dr. Giese said, "The computer is ready and operating, and we should invite the Commanding General, Aberdeen Proving Ground, to come over and look at it, and give him a briefing, description, and demonstration of its performance." The Commanding General came over a few days later, on his regular schedule. He looked at the machine, listened to the presentation, and was very much impressed. On the way out of the door he said, "What is this big sign across the top of the machine, *Brachistochrone*? What is that? I can't even pronounce it; I can't even spell it. What is it supposed to mean?"

Well, we went into a description about the shortest time between two points and so on. It didn't satisfy him! He said, "I want a better name. I want a more sexy name than that." He stormed out of the building with his adjutant.

Well, Mrs. McCauley and I got together, and we decided, "We've got to get a better name than that for the General." We came up with a lot of words like *automatic, digital, computer, Ballistic Research Lab, electronic, scientific,* and *binary*. All these words were spinning around, and all of a sudden it popped right out to us: Ballistic Research Laboratory Electronic Scientific Computer [BRLESC].

We said, "Let's try that!"

"The commanding general would never buy it, too *sexy*, too far, too much. How could he justify that to Washington D.C.?"— i.e., calling an Army computer by such a name.

We said, "Let's try it anyway."

So we called the adjutant, told the adjutant, "We've got a name—it's called BRLESC!"

"It is? Is it b-u-r-l-e-s-q-u-e?"

"No, no, no, B-R-L-E-S-C, Ballistic Research Laboratory Electronic Scientific Computer!"

"I'll try it on the General," he said.

I hung up the phone, and two minutes later [the adjutant called and said:] "That's it! It's BRLESC!" [laughter and applause]

There's another little story I'd like to tell if I just have about another minute. Anyway, I left the Proving Ground in about 1964, went down to DC and worked in the U.S. Army Office of the Chief of Research and Development (OCRD). A few years later, I became the chief of a division and I had to give a briefing about the scientific and technical information program that I headed.

It had to do with distributing funds for applications to computer organizations around the country. We had several programs in that regard.

Well, I gave the pitch, defending my program, and Lieutenant General Dick [32] was sitting right there in the audience. He said, "Mr. Weik, what in the world … why are we spending all this money for all these information systems, all these computers? What do we need them for, anyway?"

[32] U.S. Army Chief of Research and Development in 1969.

Well, I was stuck with the question, so I just blurted it out—I didn't know why I said it, but I said—"General Dick, if you want to manage your R&D program from a platform of ignorance, then do so." [laughter]

There was a hush in the audience, and nobody said anything. There's this three-star general and I'm by myself. [laughter] A hush goes over the audience and everybody goes, "Oooooh." [laughter]

And I thought to myself, maybe I said the wrong thing. And I got scared stiff.

All of a sudden, General Dick gets up and he says, "You've got your money." The whole $7M I asked for.

Of course, a lot of people got disturbed because I got what I wanted but they didn't all get what they wanted. But I got it for the computer.

Thank you. [applause]

John Gregory:
Mike Romanelli would like to make a few comments, since we've got a few minutes.

Mike Romanelli:
I wanted to comment that I never met anybody with more of a knack for words, than my boss here, Dr. Giese! I remember one of my first assignments when he said, "You've got to write a report so that people can understand!" He assigned Dr. Lesser and me to write a report on how to program for the ORDVAC.

The other comment I wanted to make is that I know of no other discipline that has so many acronyms. I can take you back to one when we were first putting out requests for proposals and we were faced with Army regulations. One of them was abbreviated with the acronym *AIDS* for "Army Information Data Systems."

Later, with regard to programming, you've heard of languages like BASIC, COBOL, Pascal, Unix. I remember when I was in high school, the grading system recognized that if you were great and you did good, you got an *A*. But then, there were so many people who were "a little above," that in order to denote the difference between *A* and somebody "a little bit above," they wrote *A+*. I know that you have heard of a new computer language called *C*, that has been replaced with *C+*. There's another one that replaced that one, and that one is *C++*. There's even a newer one that is called *J++*! The *J* stands for *Java*, so it's *Java++*. I've seen these recently in an issue of *Software Development,* in 1996, where one of the authors complained that the compiler was too slow and the screen scroll was too slow. I suspect that maybe, in the next issue—maybe not this year, maybe next year—you'll see an acronym that says *–J++*. And that is going to denote *decaffeinated* Java! [laughter and applause]

John Gregory:
Thank you, Mike.

John Harrison:

Mike, since you talked about acronyms, [do you] recall that who it was that invented the letters for the sexadecimal system as "King-Size Numbers Just For Laughs"?

Mike Romanelli:

I really don't know the author of that, I think it might have been Viola Woodward or one of her cohorts. I also remember another little story. While I'm up here I'll tell you. Viola told you that, at one time, she was the Chief of the ORDVAC Section, and she also reminded you that getting access to the machine was at a premium. Just before the end of the day, they would have what was called "scramble." You lined up, first come first served, and you got a crack at the machine. You might have found an error in a little short session. And at noon time, when everybody wanted to go and have their bridge games, Viola would go passing by each of the programming rooms and ask, "Does anybody have anything for the ORDVAC for lunch today?" One young man pulled open his desk drawer, reached in, took out a little packet, held it above his head, and said, "I've got an extra cheese sandwich." [laughter]

John Gregory:

The *analog* gong doesn't apply to me, I was just informed. There were many more pioneer accomplishments, and you pioneers should be real proud of the great contributions you've made to the digital computer and scientific fields. The Army, BRL in its day, produced the first digital computer and also the fastest computer of the early 1960 era, on budgets that were cost effective. We encourage all you pioneers to document your work, and capture the earliest digital computer efforts of the century. I would like to mention, in addition to all the pioneer names mentioned, a Mr. Richard L. Snyder, who worked on the earliest television, designed power amplifier tubes, light amplifier tubes, designed most of the EDVAC circuitry, and the first pulse circuitry and pulse switching power supply, which is in prevalent use today. He designed the first synchronous drum and was the brains behind the technology research for digital systems at BRL. He re-used WWII radar technology to assemble EDVAC.

I would also pay tribute to Professor Dan Slotnik, who suggested a low-cost personal computer usage back in the latter 1950s, but whose idea was rejected by one of the big companies as being very impractical. Dan Slotnik also pioneered the parallel processing computer architecture for mesh calculations and weather forecasting. Parallel architectures are used two ways—ORDVAC had a parallel operation versus a serial operation for EDVAC—but parallel in this new term means using multiple computers working together interchanging information to get greater speeds as well as greater efficiencies.

Finally, I want to recognize "Mr. Joe ENIAC," Joe Cherney, who showed up a few days ago. We would have put him on the agenda, because he's done a significant amount in the pioneering fields of the ENIAC and its operation. Thank you all. [applause]

5. The Early Computer Industry

Tim Bergin:
This is the closing panel for the day. When the committee got together to talk about how we wanted to wrap up the day, the thought was entertained that we would look at "the industry." I can't add all that well, but my best guess is that we've got close to 150 years of experience on this panel. I would like to have each speaker share some thoughts about the growth of the computer industry, and where appropriate, tell us what happened after they left BRL, i.e., what happened in places other than Aberdeen?

The first person on our panel was to be Harry Huskey, who did not feel good at lunch and has been taken to the hospital for observation. The news I have is that he's doing quite well. So I asked two colleagues to join us, **John Gregory**, who chaired the previous panel, and Mr. **Armand Adams** of Sperry Rand, who befriended me a number of months ago by giving me the UNIVAC I module that's in the display case. Indeed, when the photographer from Expert Events went to return the artifacts he had borrowed from Armand for the ACM Conference in Philadelphia, Armand was kind enough to say, "Give them to that nice young professor." So Armand, about four minutes ago, very kindly agreed to join us! Of course **Barkley Fritz** needs no introduction, and neither does **Herman Goldstine**.

What I'd like to say to John Gregory is, "When you left here and went to Westinghouse, *what was the industry like,* and what recollections do you have about *how the industry grew,* and the *kind of management in the industry* at that point in time?"

John Gregory:
The reason I left BRL to go to industry, and in particular to Westinghouse, was that we were in the era where the Secretary of Defense, Robert McNamara, was talked into reducing the DoD funds for government research and development, as well as the government operation and production of computers. Industry pushed him to do this. And by the way, we're going through a similar cycle with all the present downsizing, in which myriads of logistics and similar work are being pushed out of the government into industry. So it was that era when they started to cut back in DoD, the leader in the computer field at that time, and reduce the funds to government organizations like BRL, as well as leading universities. So the technology leadership for computers shifted into industry.

But then in industry, as I recall, the Remington Rand Corporation was way ahead with a superior machine, in terms of being able to program it and use it, versus the one-address machine of IBM. But because of the simplicity of the IBM machine, they were able to produce it, whereas Remington Rand had difficulty producing the UNIVAC I. So IBM sort of ran off with the market.

I went to Westinghouse, because they wanted to use digital computers in weapons systems. So I helped them develop the digital design group, which was already in rudimentary existence, but also added software technology, which I feel is a lost art today. We were able, through various different techniques, to re-use software between major weapons programs. As an example, for the F4 aircraft, we were able to convert an analog weapons system to a digital weapons system and get it flying in about nine months. This was with militarized hardware. The reason for this was that as we worked on different program developments in terms of interfaces between hardware modules and interfaces between software modules, we designed the operating system so that you could pull out a block of software and insert a different block of software without having major impact on the rest of the software. It's an art that we're just beginning to get back to.

And in order to accomplish all that, you needed automatic tools for the generation, development, and testing of software. So over a number of years, we've been trying to get those kinds of automatic programs running with great difficulty. Millions of dollars have been put into it. The industry has only recently begun to accomplish those kinds of things. So, from a leadership standpoint, industry led the advances, especially in the weapons area, that pushed the technology and reduced the ENIAC down to chips, but with significant government funding. The Japanese started to run off with the semiconductor fields, and a few people in the government had the foresight to fund a program called VHSIC, which stood for "very-high-speed integrated circuit" technology. This was able to shrink the lines and spaces between the transistors to the point where we're able to get literally hundreds of thousands of gates on a chip. Only because of this effort did U.S. industry get ahead of the Japanese again.

In the signal processing area, industry was way ahead of the majority of the users in the defense sector. For example, a programmable signal processor used by one of the intelligence agencies could run hundreds of times faster on specific signal processing programs than a Control Data 6600. And we used specialized processors in weapons programs, as an adjunct to a general-purpose computer which did all the major decisions. The signal processor just did the repetitive functions for various different fast Fourier transforms, filters, and things of that sort. So today, the field is starting to combine signal processing with general-purpose computing, including special-purpose parallel processors. However, we still need to develop the automation tools that lower the costs of developing software on parallel processors.

Tim Bergin:

Thank you, John. Barkley Fritz also left BRL and also went to Westinghouse. Since he and I have corresponded for a while, I have some insight into some of his career, and I know that he had a number of challenging management assignments after leaving BRL. So Barkley, perhaps you might want to comment on some of the *management challenges* in the early industrial days.

Barkley Fritz:

I want to follow up a little bit on what John has been saying, because it will help put this in perspective. We were both in the same general area. I left BRL six years before John did: I left in 1955 and he left in 1961. I was involved in engineering activities at Westinghouse for six years. I regard Westinghouse, especially at the Baltimore Defense and Space Center at Friendship International Airport [now BWI], as having been in the forefront in computing in a lot of ways with respect to the kinds of things that John was referring to. Essentially Westinghouse was quite a viable organization and did some very useful things for the military over this period of time.

Dan Slotnick joined Westinghouse in the late 1950s and organized an excellent group including John Gregory and some other very fine engineers who worked together and developed some of the early parallel computing concepts. Slotnick came out of the Herman Goldstine–John von Neumann–Princeton operation.

Eventually, Dan took the results of his work from Westinghouse to the University of Illinois and built the ILLIAC IV, a parallel large-scale computer at the University of Illinois.[1] He did this after Westinghouse had procured patents on a number of these ideas. I was involved in pushing the SOLOMON paper, not very much else. But I did help make sure that Westinghouse got patent credit for the work done by Dan and John while at Westinghouse.

Westinghouse had decided—after having the patent rights to build SOLOMON—that it really didn't have the funds to go into renting computers.[2] At least one customer was willing to fund SOLOMON but wanted to rent the finished product. Dan Slotnick's group then broke up.[3]

In any event, getting now to the question that Tim asked, I indicated earlier that I felt myself ready to leave Aberdeen for two reasons: first, I wasn't really interested in designing and building one-of-a-kind new machines, such as the BRLESC, but rather in *using* computers, i.e., formulation of mathematical models, numerical analyses, and programming.

The other reason I left Aberdeen was that I wasn't really happy with being a manager. As a Branch Chief at Aberdeen, I was responsible for as many as 80 people, and worrying about how they fit in to various things. I had headed the Branch for the ENIAC, and when John Giese went off to the University of Wisconsin for a sabbatical, I was left in charge of a lot of Ph.D.s. I didn't really like management, especially trying to manage a Saul Gorn and some of those

---

[1] Slotnick (1982) and MacKenzie (1991).

[2] IBM quickly took the lead in the fledgling computer industry and continued its policy of *renting* computers rather than selling them, as it had done with its punched card accounting systems; this put pressure on other manufacturers (who were not as well capitalized) to rent their computers rather than sell them.

[3] "Slotnick developed the concept of the processor array from his time with von Neumann. Whereas von Neumann could not accept the concept, Slotnick developed the idea into the SOLOMON scheme, which eventually evolved into the ILLIAC IV at the University of Illinois. However, funding restrictions only permitted the construction of a small portion of Slotnick's scheme." (Lee, 1995a, pp 636–637).

people, who had their own ideas about what they wanted to do and knew more about the research subject that they were involved in than I did.[4] However, getting to Westinghouse and doing some things that I was capable of doing, such as formulating models for engineering problems, modeling new concepts for computers on existing systems, hiring the first black woman programmer, and so on, were pleasing to me.

During that period, we installed a succession of computers (an IBM 650 and an IBM 704, for those of you who are familiar with the IBM equipment of that time period). Finally, an IBM 7090 followed by an IBM 7094, along with a UNIVAC 1107 and a UNIVAC 1108, were installed. I was chairman of a committee in late 1960, which was made up of concerned managers. I was an "Advisory Engineer" at the time. The objective of the committee was (1) to evaluate Westinghouse's computer needs for the future and make a study of the kind of equipment needed, and (2) basically to look at the question of whether engineering and business data processing could be put together in a single computer center. My answer was, "Yes, it can be done, but it will be hard to do!" I presented the concepts for a plan for doing it and got stuck—as I look back on it now—going back into management again. I accepted the opportunity after turning it down a couple of times. Remember, I left Aberdeen because I didn't want to manage people.

The reason I didn't want to do it was that I really didn't feel qualified to do it. But we did create a single data center because the group felt strongly that they wanted to make it work, and having obtained the backing of top management, it was destined to be a success. We put together a system of using a single multidivision computer complex, and made the computer language FORTRAN with "callable COBOL," if you will. (COBOL didn't exist at that time, but the kind of things we did would later be reflected in the COBOL language.[5]) We created a single system, so that the same compiler, a FORTRAN compiler, could take a program from the engineering departments, from the people that were modeling new computers, and from space applications as well as business and accounting applications, and put them on the same computer. We also entered programs through *remote job entry terminals*. In addition, we provided access to a GE time sharing service for some of the applications that needed very fast response. After all, we couldn't have too many people interrupting the payroll or the monthly reports!

What my group accomplished at Westinghouse-Baltimore pretty much became a way of life, i.e., a single center. I later went on to Westinghouse Headquarters and did a little damage up there along the same lines.

Westinghouse, like a number of other companies that I could mention, tended to get ahead of the game in some new developments and then back off before it ever got profitable. Later on, Westinghouse decided that it might be a good idea—partly on my recommendation—to offer software for sale. Westinghouse had developed an awful lot of good software that could do things that large corporations needed to do. For example, Westinghouse had the capabilities, in the late 1950s and early 1960s, that you have today with your checking account, where you can, for a modest fee, have any surplus at the end of the day turned into overnight deposits bearing interest. Well, Westinghouse did that for all its cash flow back in those days, using on-line, real-time UNIVAC

[4] Saul Gorn participated in the Army's computer development efforts at Wright Field (Ohio), and following WWII, he worked as a staff mathematician in the Aircraft Radiation Laboratory. He then served as a mathematics advisor at BRL at the time that the ENIAC was relocated from the University of Pennsylvania. Saul Gorn died February 22, 1992 in Philadelphia. (See Lee, 1995a, pp 342–348.)

[5] Westinghouse created a system known as "BEEF," which stood for *Business Enriched Engineering FORTRAN,* in which common business processes, such as payroll and personnel accounting, were coded into callable FORTRAN routines. (Bergin interview, Norman Moraff, College Park, Maryland, May 20, 1998; Moraff worked for Barkley Fritz on this project.)

490 and 494 computers. They had a tele-computer center for doing that, and we were investing their cash balances in such a way that they always had their surplus invested. Westinghouse at the time had lots of money, which disappeared shortly after I left. [laughter] I didn't spend very much of it while I was there, I guess.

But in any event, Westinghouse has relatively good control over its computing use throughout its separate divisions, where the division manager has profit-center responsibility but also has certain headquarters-mandated requirements. It's a well-run organization, except that it's now selling off everything left of what they had when John and I were working for Westinghouse. Westinghouse broadcasting, I guess, is all that's really left.

Then I went to a shipyard, Sun Ship in Chester, Pennsylvania, and worked there. This was a very thankless sort of a job, in an industry where foreign governments were subsidizing their industry, and the United States, with some modest exceptions, was willing to go out of ship building because of its labor intensity and so on. Work is still being done in a few U.S. shipyards, e.g., Newport News. The United States today has no shipbuilding capacity. I guess when we need naval and merchant vessels the next time, we're going to get most of our ships from Newport News, or we'll have the Japanese or the Swedes build them for us.

But in any event, the shipyard went under. I went to a consulting firm that was building ships for the Middle East—wooden ships—and I put in design techniques using interactive computing as had been done at Sun Ship.

After they went under, the University of Delaware decided that I had enough experience in running companies to the ground that they offered me a job in administration and teaching in the Computer Science Department. Perhaps they were thinking about wanting to go out of business! But in seven years before retirement in 1989, I couldn't quite put them out of business. Delaware is thriving. In fact, it has a new contract with the Department of the Army doing research on the use of computer chips to support the individual soldier. I heard about that on TV, when I happened to catch the 11 o'clock news.

In any event, if you're not loose and you're not ready to respond to change, find another field to get into. I'm not sure that I can name a field that's appropriate for the long pull, but computing is a heck of a lot more fun than a lot of other things you can do.

Tim Bergin:
Thank you, Barkley. Herman, if you can just share a couple of thoughts about what happened when you left the IAS project, and your thoughts about the industry in the late fifties.

Herman Goldstine:
Could I go back a little earlier?

Tim Bergin:
Herman, you have the microphone. You can do whatever you want!

Herman Goldstine:
What I wanted to tell you about were my interests, and the interest of Colonel Paul N. Gillon and Johnny von Neumann, in computing. Our interest in computing continued after the war, and we had a part in the internationalization of the computer. I thought this topic might be interesting, since many of you are maybe unaware of how all this came about.

The first group of people who came to the United States to learn about computer developments, apart from the English, were the Swedes. The Swedish government sent a man named Stig Ekelöf to come to see whether the Swedish government should build a computer.[6] I showed him the ENIAC, since that was the only operating machine. He and I went through a long day discussing the ENIAC and its development. The Swedes, of course, had a lot of money because they had been neutral during the war and had been selling large amounts of materiel to the Germans. He told me that if he reported back to the government that they should go into the computing field, his recommendation would have a big effect. We went over the thing in detail. When he got back home, he wrote me a charming letter and said our discussion reminded him of the story of the elderly English lady who went to the lecture to hear about the electric light, which was a new phenomenon. The little old lady listened and said she understood everything. The only problem, she said, was a minor one: "How does the oil flow through those wires in the tubes?" [light bulbs] [laughter] He said, he was in that same boat, so would I write a report for him that he could turn in to the government?

On the basis of that, three or four Swedish engineers came to the United States, one to the Institute for Advanced Study, one to Harvard, and one, I think, somewhere else.[7] Each of them studied for about a year and then went back to Sweden. Computers were built there. Out of that resulted an early emergence of computing in the Nordic countries.

The next thing that happened was that there was a lot of interest in the other countries of Europe. An organization which was then more popular than it is now, called UNESCO,[8] had a great idea. Their thought was that the electronic computer was a thing like an atomic power plant: they're very expensive, so you can only have a few cyclotrons, and you should build national or supernational laboratories. So UNESCO sponsored a conference at which the United States was not an active member but did participate as an observer.[9] I represented the United States government. The question to be answered was, "Should UNESCO set up an international computation center for the world, at least the European, Asiatic, and African worlds?" That meeting was successful, and they decided it was a good idea. A consultation took place, and as a result of that, UNESCO had another conference to decide where the machine should be placed.[10] Three countries bid actively on this project: Holland, Switzerland, and Italy. UNESCO, for some obscure reason, asked me to make the choice. It was a very complicated problem because all three countries were doing very good work. Well, the basis on which I made the decision was that the Italians pushed me harder than anybody else! [laughter]

[6] Goldstine (1993) has an appendix that discusses the early developments in Europe; Swedish efforts are on pp 349–352; Ekelöf visited in mid-1946.

[7] According to Goldstine (1993, p 350), the four men were Carl-Erik Fröberg, who spent his time at the Institute for Advanced Study; Göran Kjellberg, who spent a year at Harvard with Howard Aiken's project; Gösta Neovius, who sent time at the Massachusetts Institute of Technology; and Erik Stemme, who visited RCA, Princeton, and the Institute for Advanced Study.

[8] United Nations Educational, Scientific, and Cultural Organization (UNESCO).

[9] This conference was in Paris, in May 1951 (Goldstine, 1993, p 324).

[10] This conference was in Paris, in November 1951 (Goldstine, 1993, p 324).

A man named Mauro Picone was the first head of the International Computation Center. After he left, the Swedes took over, and more or less ran the Center in Rome. By that time, everybody had his own computer, and the Center was not a very great success.

At the time of the UNESCO meetings, the Danish government was very poor. A man named Richard Petersen had wanted to get money from UNESCO to build a differential analyzer. And I'm happy to say that my part was to prevent him from doing that. I got the Danish people to do something more intelligent. Out of that grew, in European terms, a very important computing community under a couple of men. One, Peter Naur, was an important figure in software,[11] and a man named Niels Ivar Bech was an important person in their hardware developments, which prospered for awhile, but gradually died out.[12]

Now, I'd like to go forward with you to other times. Von Neumann had, by this time, reached a point where his importance was realized by the United States government (in a larger sense than it had been in the past). This was due in part to the fact that Admiral Louis Strauss was the Chairman of the Board of the Institute for Advanced Study. Strauss was a man who was not scientifically trained, but had tremendous admiration for scientists, and in particular for Johnny, whom he regarded as the ultimate scientist. He got von Neumann to become a member of the Atomic Energy Commission. So Johnny left the immediate little institute which we had set up, and he was off to Washington to be advisor to great people like President Dwight D. Eisenhower.

But while he was working away at the Atomic Energy Commission, he did something for computing that was very fundamental. I think very few people appreciate it. He and I had a conference, and we decided that the thing that the AEC could do to push things forward was to give a *biggish* hunk of money to each of two companies—one to the Sperry Rand people, and the other to IBM—to build the biggest, most powerful computers that could be built. This resulted in the LARC on Sperry Rand's part, and Stretch on IBM's part.[13] The result of these research efforts was very important. In the case of IBM, the Stretch didn't quite reach the proportions or the speeds that Mr. Thomas Watson, Jr., [then president of IBM] wanted. In fact, however, it did such a tremendous job of advancing technology, that computers from there on—at least on the IBM side—were enormously improved. I suspect it had a comparable effect at Sperry.

Paul Gillon, in the meantime, did not lose his interest in these things either. When he left BRL, among the other things that he did was that he established what was then called the Office of Ordnance Research at Duke University. This organization, I think, is now called the Army Research Office. Jag Chandra, who was an important member of that organization, was here earlier today, I believe. At any rate, one of the things it did was to start an applied mathematics department, at a place that was chosen by competition. After spirited bidding by the big universities, the University of Wisconsin took over and started an Applied Mathematics Department under Rudolph Langer. This organization had ill luck during the Vietnam difficulties, when overzealous kids dynamited it. [applause]

---

[11] Peter Naur was active in the definition of the ALGOL and ALGOL68 languages. Naur also served as co-editor of the first *Report of the NATO Conference on Software Engineering*, Scientific Affairs Division, January 1969.

[12] See Lee (1995a), pp 74–76.

[13] In 1955, IBM was switching from the 701-702 line of computers to the 704-705 series. With support from the Los Alamos Scientific Laboratory of the AEC, IBM instituted a project to build a computer that would be 100 times as powerful as anything yet made. Although IBM formally called the machine the IBM 7030, it has always been known as Stretch—since it was intended to "stretch" the existing capabilities of computers. At the same time that IBM was working on the Stretch, UNIVAC received support from the Livermore Radiation Laboratory of the AEC to build the LARC (Livermore Atomic Research Computer). Both machines pioneered techniques used in later computers. (Wil-

Tim Bergin:

Thank you very much, Herman. Finally, Armand Adams will tell us a little bit about what it was like at Remington Rand.

Armand Adams:

I would like to start out by saying that I do have some ties to the Ordnance Corps. I did work for the Ordnance Corps for 10 years, from 1942 to 1952. I worked at another facility which has been closed, the Frankford Arsenal, in Philadelphia. I worked in the Antiaircraft Fire Control Laboratory at Frankford Arsenal. I was responsible for the electrical systems associated with the antiaircraft guns that were being produced at that time, namely the 40-, 90-, and 120-mm guns. I did a lot of work at Aberdeen Proving Ground over that 10-year period, because this was the nearest place that we could do test firing. In addition, I did work at Camp Davis in North Carolina, which was also a larger firing range, and then ultimately the antiaircraft fire control function was moved to Ft. Bliss, Texas, and I also did some work out there. So I do have some roots in the Ordnance Corps. I left the government in 1952, and formed a small company with two other gentleman, which ultimately was purchased by Beckman Instruments.

I have another interesting story, which is a sidelight on the computer industry. Many people ask, "Why is Silicon Valley in the San Francisco area of California?" The reason it is, is mainly because of the efforts of Dr. Arnold Beckman. William Shockley, Walter Brattain, and John Bardeen were the three inventors of the transistor. They all retired from Bell Labs. Dr. Beckman was making money at Beckman Instruments and looking for places to invest it—this was an example of *private sector* investment. He believed that the transistor had tremendous potential, and offered Dr. Shockley the chance to come to California and run an operation that would mass produce transistors.

Through an odd set of circumstances, I happened to be in California at that time, and was supposed to meet with Dr. Beckman. I went up to his office and his secretary said, "Gee, he'll be here, Mr. Adams, go in, sit down, and make yourself at home." A few minutes later another man came in, and the secretary said, "This is Dr. Shockley, he's going to wait with you, because he also has an appointment with Dr. Beckman." Well, Dr. Beckman never arrived during the next hour, so both of us left. However, I had an interesting chat with Dr. Shockley, and of course, he was telling me how they were going to mass produce the transistor and transistor circuits, and that they were going to package them automatically. They would come off the production line with a price tag on them. The only problem was, he didn't like Southern California. He was from Stanford, and he wanted to be up in the San Francisco area. So he agreed to go with Dr. Beckman but in San Francisco. So that was the beginning of what's now called Silicon Valley, and is another example of private enterprise coming into the field, and realizing the potential of computers, transistorized circuits, and other solid-state electronic devices other than vacuum tubes.

But after that, I didn't want to move to California. My two partners went out there. One is deceased; the other is still running a small electronic company and still lives there. I'm happy back in Pennsylvania. I went to work for Sperry Rand shortly after the merger of Remington Rand and the Sperry Corporation. This formed a new corporation, Sperry Rand. As most of you know, the chairman of the board was General Douglas MacArthur. Two other interesting people that I met at this time were Harry Vickers and James Rand, who was sort of at the end of his career as an industrialist.

I went to work for Sperry Rand in 1957. I was hired as the Administrative Assistant to a man by the name of Jim Weiner, even though I'm an electrical engineer by profession. Jim Weiner is in some of the pictures back there [in the exhibit] from the days of ENIAC and BINAC. I believe he came out of the middle west, probably the University of Chicago or somewhere in that area. He was one of the pioneers in the picture of BINAC, which again was built by Eckert and Mauchly, as the Eckert-Mauchly Computer Company (EMCC).

We were in a fairly big building on 19th and Allegheny in Philadelphia. Now, 19th and Allegheny, even back in the middle fifties, was not exactly the most desirable neighborhood to work in and live in. Harry Vickers, who had become the CEO of Sperry Rand, looked at the problems that UNIVAC was having recruiting at the various large colleges like MIT and Cal Tech. He said, "You know, you induce a bright young engineer to come in and look at these facilities at 19th and Allegheny, and they aren't exactly going to come rushing back. As a matter of fact, they may never come back; they may go to IBM or some other company in the industry." So he authorized the expenditure of $5M, in 1959, for a new laboratory in Bluebell, Pennsylvania, which is the current headquarters of the UNISYS Corporation, the successor corporation to Remington Rand and the Burroughs Corporation. And $5M, in that period, was quite a large investment, even for the president of a large company such as Sperry Rand, when you look at profitability and all that, particularly for a relatively *new* endeavor like digital computers.

Sperry Rand at this time was still maintaining some 50 UNIVAC I's, which had been built and delivered, and was in the process of mass producing another 50 UNIVAC II's, for most of which they had commitments from customers. So that was a big investment on the part of an industrialist—who, again, was a brilliant man in his own field. Harry Vickers was the founder of the Vickers Company, which was a leader in the field of hydraulics and hydraulic controls. Hydraulics have been compared to the digital computer in the sense that where a computer amplifies the power of your mind, hydraulics amplified the power of your muscles. He invented power steering; and this was the big thing that made the Vickers corporation successful. The steering mechanism in nearly every car today is hydraulically activated.

Anyway, Vickers invested the money in the new building, and his stockholders and some of the people said this was not a prudent investment. Remington Rand wasn't the most profitable corporation in this period of time, but Mr. Vickers had the foresight to see the potential of the computer. He said, "If we are going to compete in the industry, we've got to have a more appealing place for the bright young people that are coming in the future to design our computers." So he made this investment.

It so happened that the man I worked for was another pioneer in the field of digital computation, a gentleman by the name of Jeffrey Chuan Chu. Mr. Chu was a brilliant computer scientist. He came out of the middle west also,

I believe from the Chicago, Illinois, area. A wonderful man. He was at the ACM 50th Anniversary Celebration in Philadelphia. I expected that he might be here but he isn't here.

My whole purpose here is to show that there was faith in the future of the computer. There was faith in the growth of the industry, even though as some of you in the audience probably remember the old saying around the industry, in the late fifties and early sixties, that the computer industry was known as "IBM and the Seven Dwarfs."[14] As a matter of fact, some of the smarter journalists even had identification tags for the seven dwarfs, i.e., which one was "Happy," which one was "Sleepy," etc. *Fortune* had a good article about that at one time. Again, in the general industry—outside of the military, outside of defense work, and outside of the federal government—there was a great deal of interest, and there was a great deal of movement forward in the period of the sixties and of course into the seventies and eighties.

Another very important factor in the growth of the industry was the growth of computer user associations. One of the things that industry realized was that the users actually had a better knowledge of how to use the computer for various tasks that the company needed to accomplish. The computer manufacturer couldn't be the expert in the insurance industry, couldn't be the expert in the financial industry, couldn't be the expert in manufacturing, or couldn't be the expert in many other industrial endeavors. They might be very expert in the computer—how to build it and so on—but not in how you could use it in your business in a profitable way. The computer users associations became a very important factor in the *growth* of the computer industry. I personally feel that they were responsible for a great many improvements, particularly in the development and improvement of programs for the computers.[15]

Barkley Fritz:
I'll make this real quick, but I think one of the things to remember is the important role of the professional societies (such as the IEEE Computer Society (IEEE-CS) and the Association for Computing Machinery (ACM)) and the user groups. I'm not sure how popular the user groups still are, but I think that many of the people in the field who have been successful are people who have gotten themselves known and who have interacted with people from other companies by participating in professional and user group meetings.

Tim Bergin:
Did you want to say one more thing, Herman?

Herman Goldstine:
I would like to say just a word, since Chaun Chu's name came up. When we built the ENIAC, a man named Arthur Burks, who's now at the University of Michigan, built the multiplier and he had an assistant, a man who built the divider and square-rooter. That assistant was Chaun Chu. So I just wanted to add to that.

Joe Cherney [from audience]:
I would like to make one comment, which is just a little bit different. My name is Joe Cherney. I worked on the ENIAC for three years. Subsequently, I went to work in industry for North American to work on avionics and space systems.

---

liams, 1997, pp 391–396.)

[14] At that time, eight companies dominated the computer industry: Burroughs, Control Data Corp. (CDC), GE, Honeywell, IBM, National Cash Register (NCR), RCA, and Univac. The word "BUNCH" was also used as a mnemonic, referring to Burroughs, Univac, NCR, CDC, and Honeywell.

[15] User groups, such as *GUIDE* and *SHARE* for IBM (commercial and scientific) users and *AUUA* and *USE* for UNIVAC (scientific and commercial) users promoted the sharing of methods, programs (routines), and

I have been intimately involved in the development of five digital computers. One of the things that came out of the ENIAC, which hasn't been given a lot of recognition, was the fact that it demonstrated in an unequivocal manner that processing of *digitally encoded numbers* works. Digital storage and processing now has recognized advantages. What does digital storage and processing do for us? It allows us to remotely re-target the Minuteman missile. It allows us to correct problems on a missile that's halfway to Jupiter. Right now, *digital* is taking over in areas like music. You get a little greeting card which plays music and that is stored as digital numbers. One of my first jobs was working on analog equipment. My boss came and said, "We're going to develop a digital computer, but we don't understand *digital*." The ENIAC experience demonstrated the value of digital processing. I became the project engineer of the first airborne military digital computer. Over 2000 such computers were delivered. And as you trace the actual effects, you'll find that it goes all the way from the ENIAC to the big computers, and down to the little musical greeting card.

Tim Bergin:

Thank you, Joe. Let me close with a story too. Last August, I got an aircraft to fly to Frankfurt, Germany, to attend a meeting devoted to the history of software engineering. It was a big aircraft out of Dulles Airport. After we were in the air, the man sitting next to me asked, "What do you do?" I replied that "I'm a Professor of Computer Science at American University." Then he asked, "So what kind of research do you do?" I answered that I did research in the *history of computing*. He said, "Computers aren't that old; there is no history!" That remark ended that conversation! [laughter]

What we've seen today is that we've merely scratched the surface. I believe this panel could go on, profitably, for many, many more hours. This morning's panel of the ENIAC women and this afternoon's panel on the many pioneering hardware and software efforts at BRL could also have gone on for many, many more hours. This evening, at the Museum reception, we have another chance to talk with, and learn from, our BRL pioneers. Tomorrow, we have another full day with two panels that will take us closer to the present. We look forward to seeing all of you, tomorrow morning. Thank you. [applause]

Day 2
November 14, 1996

6. Recent History: Supercomputers and Networking

Harold Breaux:
Yesterday's presentations were quite interesting, inspiring, and in fact, a very hard act to follow. We'll be talking about an era in computing at BRL and ARL that followed the period of time when computers were being developed, either by or for the Laboratory, and when we went to the era of acquiring commercial systems.

I'll introduce the three panel members briefly and then we'll hear from each of them in sequence. To my immediate left is Dr. **Bob Eichelberger**, who was Director of BRL from 1969 to 1986. His period was a time of excellence, a time when great science was done for the warfighter, as it continues to this day. Bob set quite an example for all of us. We were especially fortunate that he was such an advocate for computing and was the kind of advocate who made a lot of things possible.

To his left is **Mike Muuss**, who's a Senior Computer Scientist in the Survivability/Lethality Analysis Directorate. Mike came to BRL even before he finished his undergraduate days at Hopkins. Early on, especially when he came on permanently, he was an evangelist for the Unix operating system, for a computer on every desktop, for networking, and eventually got involved in computer-aided design and did great things, especially for the technology of lethality and vulnerability.

To Mike's left is **Bob Reschly**, who is a most interesting story. Bob came to BRL as a GI, involved in calibration, I think. He eventually wangled his way into Bill Barkuloo's project on the HEP. Later, as you heard yesterday, Mike Muuss began putting a Unix operating system on the HEP. Bob began working with Mike, and through a lot of self-study and being a very bright individual, he became an expert in networking. Over a period of years, Bob eventually became the architect of the Army supercomputing network, the Interim Defense Research and Engineering Network, and in his most recent *tour de force,* he has been the Program Manager that put together and just let a major defense-wide contract for what's called the Defense Research and Engineering Network (D-REN). He'll tell you about some of those things today.

Before I bring Bob Eichelberger on, I'd like to tell you an anecdote. As I mentioned, he was an advocate for supercomputing. The first big commercial system that BRL got was a Control Data System. We'd had it a number of years, and it was time to replace it. So, Bob began a series of "lobbying" efforts—in the good sense—to convince the Army hierarchy that we needed the funds to replace the CDC system. He began a process of working his way up to give a briefing eventually to the Under Secretary of the Army, Mr. James Ambrose. In a parallel track, Cray Research was doing the same thing. Brett Berlin, who I came to meet later on, was a Vice President at Cray, and he had been trying to get on Mr. Ambrose's calendar—but with no success.

Bob had a series of slides and I'll digress slightly here. One of his aides showed me his repertoire of slides once, and there was a picture of an outhouse. I asked his aide, I said, "What's that?" He said, "Well, it's one of many slides we've prepared for him. The thought would be, at this point, that he would tell whoever it is he's trying to convince that we need the money for new systems, that the state of computing at BRL is like an outhouse, it's grossly outmoded and we really need the money!" I don't know whether he ever used it, but it was in his repertoire!

But as Bob worked his way up, he eventually got on Mr. Ambrose's calendar. But right before he got there, apparently Mr. Ambrose had read about the great things that supercomputing could do for science in one of the trade journals. So he told one of his aides to "Get somebody in here to tell me more about this." Well it turned out that Bob was already on his calendar—and it was very close, like within a day or two. Meanwhile, that aide called Brett Berlin and said, "Can you come in and give that briefing you've been wanting to give?" Well Brett, on the side of Cray Research, arranged a special plane for John Rollwagon[1] to fly in to see Mr. Ambrose. So within a day or so of his seeing that trade journal article, Bob came in and as he made his pitch, Mr. Ambrose said, "You don't need to convince me, just tell me how are you going to do it." Then within a day, Rollwagon was there, and Mr. Ambrose said, "Is this serendipity or what?" Things don't really happen that fast. But it just turned out that it was a "scissors" move, and things just happened to happen.

[1] Chief Executive Officer of Cray Research during this period.

Things went on from there, and that effort led to the approval for funding for the first two Army supercomputers. Anyway, enough of that. Bob?

Bob Eichelberger:

This is your sole exposure to the "villain" of this opera. You've heard a lot from the heroines and heroes so far, and you'll hear some more. I guess I have to bear the responsibility for terminating the era of in-house procurement of specially built computers and in-house construction of computers. I would beg some pardon for that. Due to circumstances, however, there were at least three major trends that were coming to focus in the period around 1962–1967, when I first became involved in laboratory-level management. First, industry had finally heard the wake-up call and had decided that computers had some kind of a future for them, had pulled up their socks, and were beginning to get serious about developing computers.

Second, the DOE Weapons Laboratories, which were at that time the Atomic Energy Weapons Laboratories, and their contractors, had begun to disclose work that they had done in deep secrecy in the previous years, on solution of differential equations that were nonlinear, time-dependent, and in two dimensions—things that couldn't be solved before. They are now called hydro-codes.

Third, the Department of Defense had been in place long enough that it had begun to develop techniques for micromanagement. The days when a person could go to Washington for a day, talk face-to-face with the Chief of Ordnance, and if he were persuasive enough, convince the Chief that he needed some personnel and some money and come away with the insurance that he had those things—were gone. We were in the era—the beginning of the five-year plan—when you had to get into the budget five years ahead of time in order to accomplish anything. And the days when personnel were managed by a different set of people from those who managed the funds. So if you wanted to do something like increase your capability to design and build computers, you had to deal with one group of people to get the personnel, and another group of people to get the money. The likelihood that you were going to be able to do both was becoming vanishingly small.

Let me go back a moment. In 1962, when my role in this whole thing started, BRL—the Ballistic Research Laboratory—had the fastest computer in the world, BRLESC II. BRLESC II, however, was not capable of handling the problems of the hydro-code because it had that 50,000-word memory that you heard about yesterday.

My first undertaking in the computer realm was to increase the memory of BRLESC II by a factor of 10. That's 500,000 words. In present-day terminology, that would be equivalent to about four megabytes—about half the amount that you need in a personal computer to run Windows®95. [laughter] Nonetheless, at that time it would have been marginally sufficient to run the hydro-codes that we were then able to get from the AEC people and their contractors. So it was very important. You heard from Bill Barkuloo about some of the problems that we had with that memory. It took Bill and his people a long time before they got that memory actually operative on BRLESC II.

By that time it was very clear that people like IBM, Sperry Rand, and CDC were going to advance the state of the art in mainframe computers much faster than we could manage at BRL with the resources we had available. So villainous or not, the decision was made that we were going to stop building our own computers and buy commercial computers. We started to buy a CDC 6600, but by the time we actually got permission to buy, it wasn't being made anymore. We lucked out; we got a CDC 7600, our first commercial supercomputer.

But I don't want to leave the impression that BRL got out of the computing business then or became exclusively users. There were a couple of management policies that prevented that. Number one, I personally was very convinced, as Harold has said, that computers were the major tool for future research in essentially all the fields that BRL was interested in.

Secondly, the policy was that you hire talented people. If you're lucky enough to get them, and they have interest in parallel with the Laboratory's need, then you damn well better see that they get all the support that you can manage for them. You encourage them to do the thing that they are interested in. We were lucky enough at that time, in addition to people like Harry Reed and Paul Deitz, to have Steve Wolff, Mike Muuss, Harold Breaux, and a plethora of young people who were both talented and enthusiastic about computer-related technology.

So they got very much involved in the networking business; you heard about that. They made BRL one of the primary nodes in the ARPANET.[2] They built an in-house BRL network that essentially tied every computer that BRL had together and gave our people direct access from their desks. The dumb terminals or the personal computers that they had on their desks were tied in with the mainframe. Mike Romanelli, I think, yesterday said something about our going from a "closed shop" to an "open shop" operation. That was a major cultural change, I think, in the way the people who had the problems dealt with the computation.

[2] See Salus (1995) and Hafner and Lyon (1996).

We had very quickly developed local networks within each laboratory. I say each laboratory—in the early days what later became divisions were each called laboratories. So we had Interior Ballistics, Exterior Ballistics, and Terminal Ballistics Laboratories, a Weapons Systems Laboratory, and so on. Each one of those groups ended up with up to a dozen minicomputers, such as VAXes or Goulds. I think we had every brand on the market, and almost every professional or maybe every professional had a PC by then. Those all got tied into local networks within the laboratory, which then got tied into the BRL network, which then got tied into the ARPANET. It may have been "squirrely," but people like Harold Breaux and Mike Muuss kept us all honest and kept it operating.

I think we were among the first to make "management information" available to the technicians, the professional scientists, and the engineers at the bench. That took a lot of persuasion of the Aberdeen Proving Ground people who were our bookkeepers. Electronic mail became a way of life too. Even some of the more reluctant people in management were forced to use it, because that was the only way they got a lot of the information they needed.

Aside from networking, I think you've heard allusions, at least, to the work that was done by Mike Muuss and some of the other people in assisting in the development of Unix.[3] I think they had a great deal of influence on what Unix finally became, and on its adoption as a standard in many of the major mainframe and minicomputers that are being made today.

Paul Deitz and a group of the young people that he had working with him developed the computer graphics business, and BRL-CAD is a result of that.[4] I think that's become the world standard for people who do vulnerability and lethality analysis. We were among the very first to support the development of Eulerian codes as opposed to LaGrangian codes in the hydro-code business.

The work on HEP has been alluded to. HEP is not a very successful machine but the principles that were built into it, I think, proved valuable to future efforts. We weren't entirely out of the hardware support business but were mostly in a very high-risk venture sort of thing.

So despite the fact that we stopped building our own computers, there was a lot of excitement and a lot of progress made, in hardware networking especially, and the software business by the people at the Lab. It was not a dull time; it was not a time when the Lab had stopped contributing. The procurement of mainframe computers, I guess, has gone through its peak of difficulty and has become easier in recent years. At least it's much better supported at the DoD level, much more consistently supported than it was before. Maybe some good things are happening. Thank you. [applause]

[3] Unix is an operating system that was first developed at Bell Laboratories. Since AT&T could not, as a monopoly, sell Unix, it gave it to universities, government agencies, and private organizations. Although there are numerous versions of Unix, the operating system has been standardized.

[4] CAD (computer-aided design) is software that can be used to assist engineers in drawing diagrams. More than a simple drawing tool, CAD packages usually have data and shapes that can be manipulated with a mouse and keyboard.

Mike Muuss:

Ladies and gentlemen, good morning. My talk today could be called "Lions and Tigers and Bears, Oh My!" But instead I'm going to tell you about minicomputers, Unix, networks, BRL-CAD, and supercomputers. I've been at BRL, now ARL, for a little more than 15 years. In my opinion, this has been as exciting a time in the development of the computer as the first 15 years must have been for Dr. Goldstine and von Neumann and others. There's been just a tremendous amount of exciting stuff that happened in this interval, and I want to share some personal reminiscences about the most interesting highlights with you today.

I'm going to set the stage for what comes by talking about Harry Reed, who's sitting down here in the front. He was a reformed ENIAC programmer at this point. He was the Chief of the Ballistic Modeling Division and working for him was Dr. Steven Wolff, who had been a professor at Johns Hopkins University and then left to go to work for BRL. Well, my degree comes from Johns Hopkins, and there's a tremendous connection here between Johns Hopkins and BRL that I'm going to highlight a couple of times through the talk.

Before I showed up on the scene, Steve Wolff and Bruce Henrikson built an RS-232 interface between a GSA time-sharing system and some pen plotter.[5] They were so frustrated at not being able to get graphical representations of their scientific data that they went and built hardware and made custom software and made this all go. Well, things were happening in the commercial world. Digital Equipment Corporation had created the PDP (Program Data Processor) computers and they really created a landmark machine when they made the PDP-11, which was so inexpensive that any little department could afford one. So Harry and Steve decided they wanted to get some interactive computers for the people in the Lab, in particular for the Ballistic Modeling Division. So they asked Dr. David Van de Linde at Johns Hopkins what he would recommend and he said, "Oh, buy the PDP-11/70 and put Unix on it, of course." So they went and did that. But government procurement being what it was, they bought the computer from Digital, and all the peripherals from other companies. Back in the early days—even today, compatibility is not what it could be—you buy a card for your PC and it may or not work. And you have to get the drivers and all of that stuff going.[6] Well, life was very much the same 15 years ago. If the drivers didn't work you were in a big pickle. GSA managed to pick incompatible hardware where there were no drivers for Unix, and so they had this very lovely time-sharing computer that didn't work.

So Harry and Steve went back to Dr. Van de Linde at Hopkins and said, "Help, help, we did everything you said, and it doesn't work!" I was running the Computer Center for the Engineering School at Hopkins, while I was an undergraduate. At the time, they felt that that was too menial a job for graduate students to do, so they got the undergraduates to do things like that—which was a very enlightened view at the time and was very good for me. I enjoyed that. So Professor Van de Linde volunteered me to go to this "faraway place" called Aberdeen and write some drivers.

Now, at the same time as this, BRL had—as you just heard—gotten out of the special-purpose computer business and replaced the government-built BRLESC II with the Cyber 173 and a CDC 7600 from the Control Data Corporation. And as part of that procurement they bought three PDP-11/34's and some Vector General 3D [three-dimensional] display terminals, which never worked with the Cyber—a problem of driver software, again. They also put in an infrastructure of 56-Kb wide-band modems—56 Kb was a big deal back then.[7] None of that worked either because of software problems. So there was all this great hardware sitting around, just crying for somebody to do something.

As it turns out, I hit it off pretty well with Bruce Henrikson as I was working to make the PDP-11 go. So, he did some paperwork sleight of hand and certified me as an "expert consultant" to the Army Research Office, even though I hadn't graduated yet. And for some reason they believed him! He was a very persuasive fellow. So in the summer of 1978, they had me up at the Lab for the summer, and I created a terminal-independent plotting package so that Steve

[5] The General Services Administration (GSA) operated a number of time-sharing service centers that other government agencies could use. The RS-232 is a type of standard cable interface commonly used in networking.

[6] Peripheral devices such as monitors, printers, and plotters are all different and thus require a software interface to the operating system. These (usually small) interface programs are referred to as "software drivers" or just "drivers."

[7] 56-Kb modems can transmit data at 56 thousand bits (kilobits) per second.

and Bruce could finally get all those scientific plots that they wanted to get. This was still in the days where if you had a CalComp plotter, you bought software for making CalComp plots, but then your plot files couldn't be displayed on anything else.[8] If you had a Tektronix terminal, you could make plots on the Tektronix, but then you couldn't put it on the CalComp, because the two weren't compatible.

So the terminal independent graphics package (called a TIG Pack) created a vendor-independent meta-file so that you could put your plots on your Tektronix and then on the CalComp. That was very, very successful. People started really visualizing their data very nicely with these plots. So they had me back the next summer to work on a project much more near and dear to my heart, which was designing a multi-CPU Unix system so that we could go back towards the days of the big computer center where we only had one computer to worry about—even if it was made up of a lot of little parts working together.

After I graduated, I went and interviewed at a lot of different places. In particular, when Harry and I talked, he said, "If you come to work for me, I'll give you a little office in the corner and a computer to work with, and you can work on whatever you want, because we have so many problems. You can fix things for us no matter what you do." [laughter]

Well, the Army made me the second lowest job offer. The only people that were worse were General Electric down in Daytona Beach. [laughter] But I remembered what Harry had said, "You can do anything you want to," and I said, "That's the research job for me. This is the kind of place that I want to come to." I figured it would last about five years. I'm still here because they keep throwing neat new stuff at me to work on. So those were my summer jobs.

The first three years that I was here are the bulk of what I'm going to talk about for the rest of my time, because those were really the crucial formative times for what comes afterwards. Those Vector General displays that were bought with the CDC Cyber machine were just sitting around doing nothing, and that kind of pained me because they were like $100,000 machines at the time—probably a quarter or a half million dollars in today's dollars. So I managed to hook one up to the PDP-11, wrote some driver software for it, and I put a cube on the screen and had it spinning around. That worked really nicely. But I'm not an artist and I'm not a modeler. I had in mind to put complicated shapes up there and spin them around and look at them. This really appealed to me. But I didn't know how to describe those things.

Well, I was hanging out with a guy named Earl Weaver—who's not the baseball fellow but a scientist here at the Laboratory.[9] At the time, he was working on the design of the XM1,[10] in particular on the team that was trying to reduce the vulnerability of the tank to make it as survivable as possible. Those guys did a really good job, but they had a lot of hard problems they were trying to work on, and they had a computer-aided geometric design file that they had been working on that they'd never seen in three dimensions. They had only been able to get 2D [two-dimensional] CalComp pen plots of this vehicle. And Earl made the important insight that, "Hey, this is 3D data. Mike just made a 3D display spin around on the screen. Maybe I can get him to display my data for me."

Well, I was very gullible and Earl was a prankster. So, he came up to me one day and said, "I'll bet you can't make my tank spin around on your Vector General display." So gullible me said, "I'll bet I can!" The very next morning, I had a static plot of his XM1 on the Tektronix using the TIG Pack.

[8] California Computer Products was a manufacturer of plotting equipment that was very popular at this time.

[9] During this period, the manager of the Baltimore Orioles was named Earl Weaver.

[10] The XM1 was the designation for the Abrams M1 main battle tank while it was still experimental.

The next night, I had the thing spinning. Well, the Army went crazy! The ARRADCOM Commanding General flew in on his plane the next day to see this XM1 tank design. This was very important to the Army; this was an important tank, *and nobody had ever seen it before*. People just kept coming, and for the next two weeks we did nothing but demos showing people this rotating tank. So I have here a picture of Earl and me standing in front of the display.

It's a little hard to see, but you can see a wire frame in blue on the screen of an XM1 tank. And behind it is the original PDP-11 computer.

Having one computer doing useful work for the laboratory is nice, but that doesn't get us to today. There was a "proliferation" stage, which was really pushed down from the top. Dr. Eichelberger gets all the credit for that. He saw what was happening in Harry's operation and said, "Maybe I can use this to make the Office of the Director a little more efficient." So he went and bought himself a PDP-11 and CRT[11] terminals and printers for every Division Chief.

Muuss and Weaver with PDP-11 displaying wire frame diagram of XM1 tank.

[11] Cathode ray tube: the tube used in televisions and computer terminals on which the information is displayed.

There's a funny story here. Dr. Eichelberger was kind enough to provide enough money to put these things into every Division Chief's office. Some of them accepted it right away and said, "Oh, this is great, I'm really going to be able to use this; I can prepare documents and make reports and stuff." Charlie Murphy, on the other hand, was a little bit more traditional, and he said, "What's this thing good for? Take it out of here; I don't want it." And Harry Reed said, "Oh, there's an extra available? I'll take it off your hands." And then Charlie Murphy said, "If Harry wants it, maybe there's something to it. Maybe I'll hang on to it and try and learn this thing." [laughter] That's a funny story, but it's very important for what comes next. Because what this means is now the Director of the Laboratory and every Division Chief is "on board" with electronic mail, interactive time-sharing computing, document preparation—all at their desktops!

Now, everybody else wants to be involved too. Rather than trying to force the workers to do something that management doesn't believe in, we're now having the workers trying to catch up with management who were actually out in front. This is a very rare occasion in history. [laughter]

This is not something I accomplished by myself; this has been a big team effort [on the part of the following people]:

Bob Eichelberger	Doug Kingston†	Harry L. Reed†
Harry L. Reed	Ron Natalie†	Gary Moss
Steve Wolff†	Chuck Kennedy†	Paul Stay
Bruce Henriksen	Bob Reschly	Keith Applin
Nikki Wytias	Phil Dykstra	
Lou Colano-Romano	Howard Walter	
Mike Muuss†	Joe Pistritto†	
Earl Weaver	Bill Mermagen, Jr.	
Paul Deitz		
Bob Miles		

†*The "Johns Hopkins University" connection*

The little daggers after the names indicate all the people who came from Hopkins, including Steve Wolff, Bob Miles, Doug Kingston, Ron Natalie, Chuck Kennedy, Joe Pistritto, and Harry's son Harry L. Reed.

So, in fact, there was this whole group of us in the space of just a couple years that sort of moved *en masse* from Hopkins up to BRL and really infused a lot of this new computing technology into the Lab.

One thing the Army likes to do is to write plans for things. So in the 1979–1980 time-frame, we had to write the "Vision for Computing in the Eighties." This was a very frustrating thing. This was at a time when not everybody had their own telephone and telephone number yet. We had party lines and shared phones, and things like that. So I was a bit of a revolutionary and said, "Everybody ought to have a desk, a chair, a telephone, their own personal computer terminal—that they don't have to share, a little bit of a computer— some slice of a time-sharing computer, and 10 MB of disk space." This was in the days when a big disk drive held 80 MB. Since we had 700 employees, more or less, we were talking about just unthinkable quantities of disk space to provide that much to everybody. Nowadays, a 10-MB hard drive—that I'd pop that in my PC—is not big enough to do anything useful. But in those days, that was a lot of storage. On the other hand, 10 years is a long time. This wasn't the plan for 1981, this was the plan for all the eighties. We actually achieved this vision in 1986. So we actually beat it before the decade closed out.

There's another thread that ties things together and I call this "ARPANET Envy." When I was at Hopkins, I was using the computers at MIT through the ARPANET, and sort of bouncing around the country. That was a very rare privilege at the time. There were only a few thousand "ARPAnauts," as we called ourselves, who were at the different universities working on stuff. Well, BRL was one of the very first sites on the ARPANET. It was, in fact, one of the few military R&D facilities on the ARPANET. Don Taylor, whom I met last night at the party, and I were reminiscing about some of the early days of making all of that go. We had an ARPANET terminal server (ANTS) system, but none of the actual host computers were connected to the network. Again, it was a problem with software. They had hoped to plug the CDC Cyber in, and do remote job entry to the Cyber and so on, but nobody had been able to make it go.

Furthermore, there was—at that point—a fairly entrenched big old Computer Center that didn't want to change things very much. It was a major battle for me to get a 9600-baud wire from the ARPANET system to Harry's PDP-11/70 computer. But the world is a changing place. In 1981, on January 1, 1981, New Year's Day, the ARPANET changed protocols to a long leader format. The software that had been running for many years stopped working. We had warning that this was going to happen, and we had prepared a version of Unix which we were prepared to plug in. Dr. Eichelberger had lent us his PDP-11/34 from the front office, because he had upgraded that to a bigger machine at that point. We replaced the ANTS system with a Unix computer, and all of a sudden a major quantum increase in our capability occurred. Suddenly, for the first time, we had a host on the Internet, or what was to become the Internet—it was still called the ARPANET then. The birth of the Internet is what happened after that.

Anyway, there was a whole bunch of hardware that came into being at the same time that we at BRL helped to create, such as the Ikonas Framebuffer, which is a 24-bit color-shaded display. We bought the first VAX and the first Megatek 3D color display. So again, we were getting vendors to build us custom hardware to our specifications rather than building the hardware ourselves. This was the theme of what we were doing.

With the birth of the Internet, the long leader protocol turned into the TCP/IP protocols.[12] And we at BRL actually had a major hand in helping develop these. These became MIL standards, MIL-STD-1777 and -1778, and became the *lingua franca* of the Internet. Now, everybody in the entire world—who uses the network—"speaks" the TCP/IP protocols, which were developed, in part, here at BRL.[13]

We needed to deploy this networking capability now, out from this one ARPANET node, to all the different buildings. Dr. Eichelberger alluded to this. We had a three-tier network scheme. We had come up with "building-area networks," the "campus area network," and the "wide-area networking," which started with the ARPANET.[14] I'll spare you the stories about that in the interest of time.

Another thread comes along now. Paul Deitz was trying to get the old GIFT (Geometric Information From Targets) code converted to "C" so we could start doing some more interesting ray tracing of geometric targets work.[15] His project was way behind schedule. They'd been struggling for half a year to get this new project on line. Finally he took me aside one day and said, "Mike, is this really that hard?" I hadn't thought about it at all, until then. I said, "Gee, Paul, I don't know. If I can't do it in a week, it's probably hard." So he said, "Ok, go take a week and try it for me."

So, I started on a Monday and by that Friday I was producing ray-traced images of an ellipsoidal-shaped man. This was a big breakthrough. This is what his year-long project—that hadn't worked—was trying to accomplish. So I said, "Well, that really wasn't that hard; I guess we can go forward from here."

Then Gary Moss popped in a couple days later and said, "This is really cool stuff, and I want to use your subroutines." So we created a library for doing ray tracing, and split it all apart, and this was the birth of BRL-CAD. I'll tell you a little more about BRL-CAD this afternoon.[16]

We also had parallel supercomputing in the form of the Denelcor Inc. HEP.[17] Parallel computing is a very important thread in everything that happened, but I'll cut short what I was going to say on that as well.

There were three kinds of computers that we were deploying in the Lab: work stations, departmental minicomputers, and supercomputers—and we had interesting stuff happening in all of those. We had a lot of influence with Silicon Graphics and Sun Microsystems in their early days. We caused the Gould 9000 computers to be custom built for us; the Alliant FX8 and FX80 computers were custom built for us. Those were all wild commercial successes when they got out into the marketplace.

I'm going to summarize now with the "Attack of the Supercomputers." We bought an interim Cray XMP on the way to getting a "real computer," and it lasted for nine years. (Time scale in the government is very different from in the outside world. "Interim" lasts nine years.) In the process, we got tagged to help build the Army supercomputer network and we also worked on the NASA Science Internet. It turns out that a lot of the technology we had built for

[12] Transmission Control Protocol/Internet Protocol (TCP/IP) developed by Vint Cerf and Robert Kahn; see Salus (1995) or Hafner and Lyon (1996).

[13] See Salus (1995, pp 129–130) for discussion of these activities at BRL. Salus states: "It was BRL's PDP-11 TCP/IP that was distributed nationally in 1983, after BRL became a host on the Internet."

[14] The "building-area network" would now be called a "local-area network" or LAN; wide-area networks are referred to as WANs.

[15] The "C" programming language was developed by Dennis Ritchie at Bell Laboratories; see Ritchie (1996).

[16] See Session 8, Future of Computing, pp 114–135.

[17] The Denelcor, Inc., Heterogeneous Element Processor (HEP) was the world's first massively parallel supercomputer.

the Army net transferred directly over to NASA. This is one of those delightful cases where the Army was able to help NASA instead of the other way around.

The figure shows Phil Dykstra on the right side, standing next to the Cray Research XMP as we're uncrating it from its boxes and putting it together. This was a very exciting time for us, getting our first Cray supercomputer, and it had Unix on it—before too long.

Uncrating the Cray Research XMP (Dykstra in background).

There's one last person that I want to talk about and that's Steve Wolff. He should have been an important scientist for BRL but was destined for obscurity, unless he changed jobs. What happened was he took a one-year assignment at the Army Research Office and then went to a position at National Science Foundation, where they asked him to build the NSF network. He said, "Oh, that's easy; that's just like what we did for the Army supercomputer network at BRL." So he proceeded to turn the crank and do for the nation what we had done for the Army here at BRL. That's how the global Internet got started.

There was one other key insight; he said, "We really need to push this to our research collaborators overseas." So he struck a deal with IBM, saying, "The NSF will bear half the cost of all the international lines if you'll run TCP/IP on it and hook it up to the NSF net"—because IBM was paying for all that at the time. They said yes. Suddenly the Internet burst from the United States out to all the European and Asian nations that we were collaborating with. And the Internet was born.

I'll share with you a final anecdote, and then sit down. The campus area network that we put in first was made out of BRLNET IMPs.[18] What we did was clone the ARPANET; we duplicated all the hardware and software exactly and plunked the hardware and software system down in each of the buildings, saying, "We're going to have a little teeny ARPANET of our own to support our early communication needs." Well, Ron Natalie and I were chasing the hardware installers, with cables ready to plug in, and as soon as they installed one of these racks of equipment and turned it on, Ron and I would plug the connectors in and the computers would start coming on-line. Literally, within 10 minutes of the machines having been turned over to us, they were on the net and starting to communicate.

When we got them all connected and running, we called up the Network Operations Center to celebrate and tell them, "We've got it working, everything's great!" Ron was on the phone, and they told him, "It can't be done; it won't work; you're lying, there's no way this could possibly be happening!" Ron said, "I'm glad you didn't tell me that before we made it all work." [laughter] But it all worked. We were sufficiently upset about this, so we went to commiserate with Steve Wolff for a while. He said, "All that matters is that it works. It doesn't matter what they said; it doesn't matter who did what. All that matters is it works."

That's a pretty good summary of BRL's tradition. It doesn't matter who did it; it doesn't matter how you did it; all that matters is that it works. We have a heritage now, of 50 years of Army computing, solving important problems and

[18] The IMPs (Interface Message Processors) were the packet switching computers for the ARPANET, linking network hosts with distant IMPs.

doing useful stuff. Thank you very much for your attention. [applause]

Harold Breaux:

I just wanted to mention that Bob Reschly is pinch hitting for Phil Dykstra, who is on the west coast and couldn't be here.

Bob Reschly:

Good morning. This has been a very interesting week, what with helping with the preparations and stuff and getting all of the pieces pulled together. Mike did such a fine job that I probably don't even really have to talk. A lot of what I've been doing the last 10 or 12 years has been working, first under Mike and then independently with a number of the folks here, on continuing to develop the networking, both within the Laboratory and to external sites. One of the things that I'd like to regale people with is that I'm convinced that computer networking is firmly grounded in physics, in that what we try to accomplish is to get *net* work out of all the *gross* work that we go through putting it all together. [laughter] That's solid physics! [laughter]

The networking was in place, and BRLNET[19] was up and running. There were these wonderful little blue boxes scattered around the campus when I first got involved. I learned a lot about Unix and how to make all that work with Mike. Then, when several of the people moved on, I inherited the system. The prime function that we had was to continue to expand the network out into the various laboratories and offices scattered around the campus. What we ended up doing was putting together a set of "leapfrog projects," so that we had a production network running at all times while working with the next generation of networking as an experiment. As that solidified and we got comfortable with it, we moved—or leaped—to our next generation.

The technology started out with things like the 9600-baud RJE lines, which were much faster than any of the long-haul stuff that we had available.[20] Going to the 56K stuff was the basis of the BRLNET. Then we made the jump to Ethernet, which was 10 megabits. This was fast. This was something that could fill your screen with graphics faster than you could hit the carriage return. That made a lot of difference. It had a major impact on how people started doing business. It was now convenient to use any of the resources within the Laboratories when we had that kind of connectivity.

From there, we had to push that out to all the other customers that we were working with. What we ended up doing was getting to the Program Manager for Army Supercomputing, and working to build a wide-area version of the types of things that we were doing within the Laboratories. In those days, 56K was all you had. This was also coincident with the early development of the Internet. We were pushing to go to the next-generation technology, which was the T1 or $1\frac{1}{2}$-megabit technology. That was very expensive then, relatively speaking, and actually rather difficult to get. But we persevered. We struck some deals with various folks and other organizations. There's a gentleman, Chuck McPherson, who had bought a bunch of equipment for use with a satellite network that ended up not being used, and he loaned that equipment to us so that we could use it for our network.

We ended up connecting about 15 sites across the nation with this T1 network, and providing a quantum leap in connectivity. Rather than just being able to share resources across the Laboratories conveniently, we were able to share resources across the nation conveniently. In the time frame of doing all of

[19] See *Ballisticians* (vol. III), pp 10–14.

[20] Remote Job Entry (RJE) allowed users to submit jobs to a mainframe, mini-, or super-computer through terminals connected by (usually coaxial) cables.

that, we were also looking at how to perform classified computing across the nation.

Historically, if you had a problem that was classified, you had to go to the physical computer and you had to sit in a cold computer room huddled with a lab coat over the terminals, because there was no way to get that information out of that secure location to the researcher's desktop. One of the big thrusts within the Laboratories that I've had a small piece in has been to provide networking and the technology that allows the researcher to sit at his/her desktop, where it's actually warm and tolerable, and do classified computing.

From there, we continued to march. The technology within the Laboratories was continuing to advance from the 10-megabit, Ethernet-based technology, up to 100-megabit-per-second, fiber-optic technology. The Laboratories was one of the first places on the east coast that got totally wired with fiber. Bill Barkuloo, who I worked for when I first came back here, was responsible for a contract that actually buried fiber all over the campus and out to the airport and places like that. So we moved to the fiber-optic technology on the campus and that provided us with something that would survive all the lightning strikes—which was a wonderful advance. Fiber optics was also where the phone companies were headed for national connectivity, in the industry in general.

As we were migrating through those technologies, the Army Supercomputing Program was eventually disbanded, and the DoD version of that, the High-Performance Computing Modernization Program, was born. I was asked, along with people from a number of laboratories, to help put together the networking portion of that program. That has been what I've been consumed with for the last three years now. And we've taken with the networking environment the same tack that Dr. Eichelberger had the Laboratories take in the computer environment, and that is, we've moved from something that we've built specifically for ourselves to off-the-shelf hardware and software. We string the wires together, design it, and that sort of thing, and then we contract with a commercial provider to actually get networking services. So, a lot of my time over the last couple of years has been spent designing a spec and writing a contract to provide those services. We've managed to take a real quantum leap with that contract, in the types of technology that are going to be provided.

The baseline that we're going to have for all research facilities is what they call T3 or 45-megabit technology, and we just go up from there. It's all going to be basically fiber connectivity. What we're finally getting in the national environment is the types of technologies we have here at the Laboratories, where it doesn't matter—for the most part—where the resource is. If you need to do something, the response is there.

If you look at the history of how computing has evolved, there are some neat models. I believe it was Mr. Gene Amdahl who talked about what a well-balanced computer looks like.[21] He basically said that for every million instructions per second of processor power you had, you needed a megabyte of memory and a megabit per second of I/O into and out of the system. If you follow the development of personal computers and mainframes, what you see is that Amdahl's rule has been pretty much a given. Every six or so years there is an increase of an order of magnitude in terms of processing power, in the amount of memory, and the amount of I/O bandwidth—except when you talk about wide-area connectivity.

What you see is that for a long time, from the early seventies until just

[21] Gene M. Amdahl was born in Flandreau, South Dakota, on November 16, 1922. He worked for IBM during 1952 to 1955 and 1960 to 1970. During the latter period, he designed the IBM System/360. He founded Amdahl Corporation in 1970 to manufacture IBM-compatible computers. See Lee (1995a), pp 22–23, and Slater (1989), pp 185–194.

the last five years or so, wide-area connectivity has been basically flat at the 56K-type bandwidth. And then, finally in the nineties, the T1's and the T3's at 1½ megabits and 45 megabits, respectively, have become economically viable. What that's done is it's forced a mind-set on people, that communication over a long distance is expensive, very difficult to do, very time consuming, and you don't want to do it, unless you absolutely have to or don't have any better choices!

New technologies are coming on line, in particular things like asynchronous transfer mode, which you have probably heard about from the phone company. We are finally in a position where we will see, in the next few years, a rapid catch-up of wide-area communications to the point where it's going to be balanced again, and we'll be looking at an ability to communicate that is commensurate with the processing power and memory that we have on personal computers today. That's going to be really neat, because now once again you will be able to get into a mode where being able to do the work you need to do is location-insensitive. You can just sit at your desktop, and what needs to happen can happen with relatively little pain. You don't have to go off and get a cup of coffee while you're waiting for your file to transfer. So that's been the focus of what's been going on from my perspective. It's been a wonderful place to work in. There's been an incredible cast of characters to work with, and lots of interesting learning experiences. We've done some neat stuff. So that pretty well summarizes what I have to say. Thank you. [applause]

Harold Breaux:

Later today we're going to be dedicating the creation of the ARL Major Shared Resource Center (MSRC), so I thought I would take a few minutes to talk about the period of time in which we evolved to that Center. In doing that, I'll just briefly talk a little about myself.

I came here as an Ordnance Lieutenant, 1961, and had about a 23-year career in the application areas, first as a ballistician and later applying computers to laser propagation, heat transfer, and laser effects, i.e., being a user of computers. In that period, I think I acquired an appreciation and understanding of the power and utility of computers in modern science. I view modern science as being a combination of theory, experiment, and computation.

After that 23-year period, Harry Reed came to me one day and said, "Hal, I want you to think about becoming a manager, a Branch Chief." This floored me, because up to that point I had been pretty much an individual doing his own thing, and except for a brief stint filling in as a manager, I had never really gotten into that arena. I said, "I don't think so. And besides, you want me to manage computer people. I'm a user of computers." Out of politeness I didn't flat out say no, I said, "I'll think about it, but I don't think so." I turned him off about three times.

Finally, in a moment of weakness, I said, "Well, if you're really in a pinch—in a bind—I'll do it just out of loyalty to you." So I did. Little did I know that I would go on a 12-year ride, if you will, into some major areas of the acquisition of computers and running a Computing Center.

It started off as something called the Advanced Computer Projects Branch. We had gone through a period where networking and other aspects of computing had sort of evolved through almost a "skunk-works"-like environment. We had another group of people who took care of the computers and had been working the traditional computing operations that had emanated from the old Computing Laboratory. It was clear that at some point we needed to bring these two organizations together. That was one of the things Harry Reed wanted to do, i.e., to restructure and reorganize BRL computing. Of course, Dr. Eichelberger was still Director then, and that was the grand plan. It started off as a Branch. It eventually became the High-Performance Computing Division—which it is now. I retired in March of this year, and Charlie Nietubicz, who you'll hear from later today, replaced me.

That [era] was marked by a period of acquisition of large systems on the one hand—to feed part of the high-end computing—and the kinds of things that Mike Muuss talked about, where there was the other part of the effort to get networking going and to get a computer on everybody's desktop.

One of the features of acquisition in this era was that because of the price of computers, we no longer were getting systems merely for our Laboratory. These systems were expensive. Their funding had to literally be put into the Army's budget. For example, the Cray-2 Supercomputer cost $25M. When we got these systems, it was made clear to us that we had to operate these systems as an asset for the Army Materiel Command as a whole, i.e., for the Army as a whole. While we had in place policies for sustaining these systems internally, since we provided access to these systems to other agencies, we had to recoup part of the operating costs through fees. This was one of the first pitfalls I learned about running a Computing Center.

One of the trade journals came up with the analogy of the "skater's death spiral." They said when you run a Computing Center and you can't meet budget, you up your fees and you find that people are now less interested in computing because the costs have gone up. So you have people turned away, you have less computing, and you find that you have to up the fees again. And it's like a death spiral. Soon you've chased everybody away. So that was one of the major problems we had to work with. While we could fund things internally, we needed outside customers.

So we worked different initiatives. Dr. Frasier, who was then head of BRL, worked with us.[22] We created something called the AMC Tech Base Initiative, where we were able to get funding for parts of our operations from the Army Materiel Command. Later, through our own efforts, we were able to convince the Army hierarchy that the Army should create a budget line for sustaining systems, in general. But it was always, if you will, trying to stay out of bankruptcy. Very fortunately, the Congress, in its wisdom, decided that the Department of Defense should create something called the DoD High-Performance Computing Modernization Program. Basically, the Congress stated that they'd observed that the Defense laboratories were lagging behind the Department of Energy and the National Science Foundation, etc., in the process of upgrading their computers.

Now with the technologies we're talking about, you would buy a $25M system, but the reality was that in about two to four years the system would be obsolete. Computer systems have a useful engineering life of perhaps twice that, but as soon as you get a system in—even though you may have worked one or two years to get it—you have to, almost immediately, begin to start working the next cycle, if you're going to stay modernized. Fortunately, when Congress gave the signal to the Director of Defense Research and Engineering to create this program, we were in a position to respond to it. We created a High-Performance Computing Working Group. I represented the Army, and

[22] Dr. John T. Frasier served as Director of BRL from May 1986 until its closing in September 1992. At that time he became the Director of the newly formed Weapons Technology Directorate of ARL.

we structured a program that had several components.

One component was to get well quickly, namely to get big systems for the key laboratories. The other component was to put together a network to link these systems together and to provide the services to all the scientists nationwide. The third component was what we called "early access systems." The architecture in computing now is going to parallel systems. The big problem with solving physics problems—the numerical solution of partial differential equations—is that it takes a great deal of effort to restructure lots of the programs into parallel versions. And, in fact, computers are getting far less user friendly, in that realm. We recognized that if DoD scientists were to migrate their applications to these new scalable systems, they would need support at the project level, because not every project is prepared to let their key scientists stop doing what they're doing for a year to change their application codes to parallel versions. So we thought we needed to jump-start that initiative.

As the program evolved and the planning moved on, it evolved to creating four Major Shared Resource Centers. Early on, we realized that we were in a position to do just that, and wanted to be one of those centers. So we went though a process, we competed, and we actually tied for first place in the "sweepstakes." We put together a package, we hosted a blue-ribbon panel that came to the Laboratories to look at our bonafides, and in the process we were selected. Interestingly enough, politics being what it is, and the pressures to have such a nugget at different laboratories, for the last two years we've been more or less struggling to keep that anointment, if you will, as one of those four centers. In this time of cutbacks and retrenchment in budgets, we found that we just couldn't sit on our laurels, and moreover, the process took a while.

But we were successful, and as part of the whole process we worked an acquisition project. A lot of our people were very instrumental in that whole program. We volunteered Tony Pressley, for example, who was one of my Branch Chiefs, as one of the key members to start a new Program Office to succeed the *ad hoc* committee that created the program. Tony became the first Program Manager. I mentioned that Bob Reschly became the Program Manager for Networking. We have a young lady, Valerie Thomas, who's the Executive Officer of the Program. Finally, we have another gentleman, Roger Johnson, who helped work the Interim Defense Research and Engineering Network. So our staff as a whole was very vital and made major contributions to the successful jump starting of this program.

We went through a roughly 18-month period in the acquisition, where about eight of our staff members had to move, literally, to Washington, D.C., for one full year of TDY,[23] to execute the acquisition of the systems and manage the integrators that came in to help run these Centers. E-Systems of Dallas, Texas, for example, was the winner of the infrastructure contract for our Center. The dedication of the opening of our Center is what the ribbon-cutting ceremony will be later today.

In summary, though, I should say this. There were two reasons we were chosen to be a Major Shared Resource Center. One is because we're the Army's "corporate laboratory." The Army Research Laboratory is the Army's corporate laboratory for technology, and it makes sense to put the MSRC here, because we have the dominant need and are the ones who are best in a position to exploit the supercomputer capability. The other critical reason we were selected is the kinds of things you've heard over these two days: the history, the tradition, the excellence that has been BRL and ARL computing—BRL and

[23] Temporary duty.

ARL's contributions to the warfighter, based on the use of computers in that three-pronged arm of science: theory, experimentation, and computation. So I think all of you pioneers, and all of those who followed the pioneers, should be proud of that tradition. And as one who worked the issue of the Major Shared Resource Center, I really feel I was in your debt for the tradition you handed down to us—that *tradition of excellence.*

I will finish with one anecdote. Dr. John Lyons, who has just joined us, is the Director of ARL. When he came on board, I had occasion to brief him. We were in the process of working this issue of becoming a Major Shared Resource Center. I thought it was important to have him understand that we were at a crossroads in the decision, and I said to him, "We can choose to be a Major Shared Resource Center, but it brings its problems and its difficulties and it takes spaces on the TDA[24] that you could fill with scientists and so forth." I said, "The structure of the Major Shared Resource Centers is such that, if we choose not to play in this arena, we can get all the free computing we need over networking and we won't have to maintain the infrastructure. On the other hand, we're good at this, we have a lot to offer, and we can bring a lot to DoD and help them run the program." I think it took Dr. Lyons all of one second to say, "No, we need to be a Major Shared Resource Center. We need to help out, and we need to go this direction." So I was, of course, hoping that would indeed be his answer, and it was indeed his answer. It didn't take him more than a second to say this is what we should do! [applause]

[24] Table of Distribution and Allowances. The TDA is the official document that authorizes an agency to hire people. Without it, you can't actually bring people in to form an activity.

7. Military Ceremony

On Thursday morning, November 14, the U.S. Army Ordnance Center and School honored Dr. Herman Goldstine and Colonel Paul Gillon with a review ceremony at Fanshaw Field to recognize contributions they made while serving in the Ordnance Corps.

The official host was Major General Robert D. Shadley, the Chief of Ordnance, the Commanding General, U.S. Army Ordnance Centers and Schools, and the Deputy Commanding General for Ordnance at the U.S. Army Combined Arms Support Command.

Colonel Roger F. Brown, Chief of Staff of the U.S. Army Test and Evaluation Command, pinned the Distinguished Service Medal on Dr. Goldstine. The citation with the medal read as follows:

> To Major Herman H. Goldstine, United States Army, for exceptionally meritorious service in a duty of great responsibility, 22 July 1942 to 29 May 1946, given under my hand in the City of Washington this 12th day of November, 1996.
>
> Dennis J. Reimer
> Chief of Staff of the U.S. Army

Colonel Brown also presented a plaque and flowers to Colonel Gillon's widow, Kay. The plaque read as follows:

> As an officer in the Ordnance Department, Paul H. Gillon contributed greatly to the advancement of Army research and development, specifically by supporting the ENIAC program (1943–1946) and the EDVAC program (1944–1949) at the University of Pennsylvania and the electronic computer project at the Institute for Advanced Study (1946–1952). This plaque is presented to his family in grateful recognition of his outstanding contributions.

Soldiers, Marines, and airmen of the 61st Ordnance Brigade, commanded by Colonel Dennis M. Webb, paraded around Fanshaw Field and passed in review. The 389th Army Band, "AMC's Own," provided the music.

Military Ceremony 103

The Ordnance Corps honors two of its own: (*clockwise from top*) Herman Goldstine reviews the troops; Herman Goldstine and Paul Gillon at the time of their work on ENIAC; Goldstine and Kay Gillon; Herman and Ellen Goldstine, Brendan Gillon, Kay Gillon, Theresa Gillon Heine, Paul Gillon, Jr., and other guests; (*opposite, top*) Colonel Brown and Dr. Goldstine.

8. Civilian Recognition and MSRC Ribbon-Cutting Ceremonies

Paul Deitz:
Ladies and gentlemen, General Benchoff, Dr. Goldstine, Dr. Farrington, Dr. Lyons, Ms. Kay Howell, Ms. Joanne Parrott [President, Harford County Council], Ms. Veronica Chenowith [Councilwoman, Harford County Council], and other distinguished guests. Good afternoon and welcome to the "50 Years of Army Computing" ceremony. Fifty years ago, the Army invested its resources in developing a technology that has revolutionized the way we live. Today we're here to commemorate the anniversary of the technology of the computer, and to honor those individuals who contributed to its development. We're also here today to officially dedicate a Major Shared Resource Center acquired through the Department of Defense High-Performance Computing Modernization Program.

But first, let us go back to where it all began. Even before the outbreak of World War II, scientists working at the U.S. Army's Ballistic Research Laboratory here in Aberdeen, Maryland, were pursuing methods to speed the calculation of firing and bombing tables. As we have heard in the last few days, Colonel Paul Gillon, anticipating the need for increased production, developed a working relationship with the Moore School at the University of Pennsylvania.

Following the outbreak of World War II, the inadequacies of even the enhanced methods became clear. Based on a bold proposal advanced by John Mauchly, Presper Eckert, and Herman Goldstine, a contract was signed with the Moore School in June of 1943 for the design and construction of the world's first general-purpose electronic computing machine. The completed machine was unveiled to the public and dedicated in February of 1946. Ironically, the first pressing task to which the machine was applied was not the computation of firing tables, but a series of calculations to aid in the design of the hydrogen bomb[1] in support of the Manhattan Project. But even before it was completed, the ENIAC team had begun developing plans for improving its performance and then started on a new machine called EDVAC.

Over the years, many advances occurred, sponsored and directly supported by the scientists at the Ballistic Research Laboratory. These include the construction of the ORDVAC at the University of Illinois (with support from the Institute for Advanced Study at Princeton), the construction of the machines BRLESC and BRLESC II, contributions to better input/output devices and faster memory, the development of high-level computer languages to aid in the process of computer programming, and support to the Defense Advanced Research Projects Agency, establishment of the ARPANET, and subsequent developments. You've heard about many of those contributions over the last

---

[1] Nicholas Metropolis and Stanley Frankel, two physicists at Los Alamos, used the ENIAC to test a mathematical model of the "Super," a new thermonuclear weapon, later known as the hydrogen bomb.

two days.

Those traditions continue even today, and at a later point in our ceremony, we'll hear more about the future. Right now, it's my pleasure to introduce the Director of the Army Research Laboratory, Dr. John Lyons.

Dr. John Lyons:

Thank you, Paul. Good afternoon, everyone: Dr. Goldstine, General Benchoff, distinguished guests. I'm asked almost every day in my job, and as recently as yesterday, "Tell me, Dr. Lyons, what is it that the Army science and technology budget has done for the Army lately?" It occurs to me as I think about this occasion and the events we're celebrating, you'd think that this one contribution of the Army's S&T budget would have lasted a couple of centuries. [laughter] But, in fact, they still want to know, "What have you done for me today?"

It's a very proud day for the Army Research Laboratory and its predecessor institution, the Ballistic Research Laboratory. It's a proud day for the Army. I'm honored to be able to recognize some of the outstanding people who are here today, people whose contributions to the ENIAC project were monumental. And we have to wonder, if they knew—if they had any idea 50 years ago—where their work would take them, and where it would take the rest of the world.

The advent of the computer has transformed many areas of modern life, but none more than that of science and engineering itself. Before the computer, we had theory, and we had experiment; we had the notebook, and we had the bench. Now, we have computer modeling and the possibility of running experiments on the computer that are impossible to run on the bench for reasons of size, cost, or complexity. Computer modeling is now considered a third branch of scientific investigation. So we technical people owe a special debt to you pioneers.

First, we'd like to recognize the family of **Paul Nelson Gillon**, who joined the Ballistic Research Laboratory in 1939 and was named the Executive Officer the next year. In 1942, Gillon contracted with the Moore School and put a young officer named Herman Goldstine in charge of the project. It proved to be a brilliant choice. In 1944, Colonel Gillon received the Legion of Merit for his research and development accomplishments, and he was honored earlier today by the Ordnance Center and School at a parade, where he was posthumously recognized for his significant contributions. We're honored to have Paul's wife, Kay, and her three children, Paul, Jr., Brendan, and Theresa [Heine], here with us today. Mrs. Gillon, could you and your family please stand?

The next person we'd like to recognize is **John von Neumann**. Von Neumann was introduced to the ENIAC project in 1944, when the design was already well established. In spite of this, von Neumann participated in the ENIAC modification for partial stored-program operation, and in 1946, along with Dr. Goldstine and Arthur Burks, von Neumann initiated the electronic computer project at the Institute for Advanced Study at Princeton. This project represented another turning point in computer evolution, because it changed the computer into a tool for scientific research and not just a production tool. Von Neumann was instrumental in the design of the next two computers, the EDVAC and the ORDVAC, and is now known as one of the greatest scientists of his time.

John von Neumann died in 1955, at the age of 53. Today, we have with us his brother Nicholas Vonneumann and his daughter Marina von Neumann Whitman. Would you please come to the podium?

Paul Deitz:

The plaque that Dr. Lyons is presenting reads as follows:

> Dr. John von Neumann.
> As a member of the Scientific Advisory Committee of the Ballistic Research Laboratory (BRL), John von Neumann provided a valuable boost to Army research and development, especially the support of the ENIAC project at the University of Pennsylvania and by helping to re-program ENIAC once it moved to Aberdeen Proving Ground. In addition, Dr. von Neumann helped draft the initial design for the EDVAC in 1945, and started the project at the Institute for Advanced Study that eventually resulted in the installation of ORDVAC at BRL in 1952. This plaque was presented to his family in grateful appreciation of his outstanding contributions.

Dr. John Lyons:

And now Marina would like to say a few words.

Marina von Neumann Whitman:

Thank you very much. I asked Dr. Lyons if I could say a few words. I've never been to Aberdeen before, and with the happy exceptions of Herman Goldstine and Arthur Burks, both of whom became lifelong friends, I didn't know the pioneers with whom my father worked. There are two reasons why this is a very special event for me. One is that throughout his life, my father made it very clear that one should never apologize for the need of the United States to have a strong military. This is something I had to remember as I lived and taught on the college campuses of the 1960s and 1970s, because having experienced both totalitarianism on the right (Nazism) and, at the beginning of the cold war, recognizing the same dangers from totalitarianism on the left, he was convinced that if freedom was going to survive in this world, it was going to because America maintained a strong military.

The other reason this is a special event for me is that I am, by profession, an economist. One of the articles of faith in my profession is that most things are better done by the private sector. But my involvement in the preparation for these ceremonies today made me realize that, were it not for the involvement of the Army, and not just the financial support but also the intellectual leadership and what you might call simply the guts and foresight of some of the people who are being mentioned here today, the IBMs and UNISYSs and the Microsofts would never have had a chance for all the major commercial developments that they have made. And, if weren't for the generosity of the Army in putting much of the advances in the public domain, the technological developments would not have moved as well or as fast, and the country wouldn't be in the kind of technological leadership position that it is today. So for that reason, I'm particularly delighted and honored to be here—along with my uncle Nicholas—to receive this award in honor of my father, John von Neumann. Thank you. [applause]

Dr. John Lyons:

Thank you, Marina. There are a few policy makers I'd like to introduce you

to. [laughter]

If you're attending this ceremony, you probably know a little bit about the ENIAC, and if you know anything about the ENIAC, you probably know about Dr. Herman Goldstine, and if you were out in the snow this morning, you know a lot more about him. Dr. Goldstine played a major role in the development of ENIAC. Initially, he was put in charge of the Ballistic Research Lab Section at the Moore School of Electrical Engineering at the University of Pennsylvania. He served as the Project Officer for the ENIAC and also helped develop the original plans for the Army's second computer, the EDVAC. He helped develop a line of computers that included the ORDVAC, BRL's third machine. Dr. Goldstine has received many honors. In 1985, President Reagan presented him with the National Medal of Science, recognizing these contributions. This is the highest award for scientific achievement that this country offers.

Today, however, we, his colleagues and intellectual descendants at the Army Research Laboratory, would like to make special recognition of you, Dr. Goldstine. Would you please join me at the lectern?

Paul Deitz:

Dr. Herman H. Goldstine is awarded the Decoration for Distinguished Civilian Service. The citation reads—

> Dr. Herman H. Goldstine, Assistant Project Director, Electronic Computer Project, has distinguished himself from June 1946 to June 1958. During this period, Dr. Goldstine continued his involvement in the development of the stored-program computer, which became the defining structure of today's modern electronic computer. He headed the Institute for Advanced Study Electronic Computer Project, which resulted in the development of a family of machines that included the Ordnance Variable Automatic Computer (ORDVAC), the ILLIAC, and the MANIAC.[2] During these developments, he continued to donate his time and knowledge by serving on several advisory boards, including the Mathematic Steering Committee, the Ballistic Research Laboratory Scientific Advisory Board, and as a consultant to the *ad hoc* group to the Joint Chiefs of Staff Joint Meteorological Committee on determining the computer system for the joint numerical weather prediction unit. Dr. Goldstine's achievements reflect great credit upon him and the Department of the Army.
>
> [Signed] Togo West, Secretary of the Army

[2] For information on the ILLIAC and ORDVAC machines, see Goldstine (1993), pp 306–307. See also Bigelow (1980), Robertson (1980), and Metropolis (1980).

Herman Goldstine:

As a graduate student, professor, program director, scientist, mathematician, military man, and corporate administrator, I have spent most of my adult life in designing and carrying out research backed by the United States Army. Over the years, this research has helped to make possible the design of modern computer architecture and programming, as well as advancing the use by the Army of modern computer technology. Much of this work was done in collaboration with John von Neumann, one of the world's greatest scientists. While he is not here today, he is very much in my thoughts, because he shaped my thinking forever. It was the Army's realization of the fundamental importance of computers and computing that made it possible for people like von Neumann and me to work in an open, supportive, and unfettered way to provide some of the early ideas and instruments on which modern computing is based. For myself, and on behalf of all those who shared in the intensity, commitment, and accomplishment of those years, I am proud to accept this honor, and I thank you very much. [applause]

Paul Deitz:

Thank you, Dr. Goldstine. There's one more group of individuals that I'd like to recognize today—possibly the most important group. Over the last two days, we've heard a wonderful accounting of the great progress made by the uniformed and civilian workers of the Army, together with their counterparts in the private sector. We are honored to have with us today, as we did yesterday, a group of returning pioneers who variously contributed to the great progress over those early years. Each of them, we hope, has already received a plaque inscribed with the following words:

> In recognition of your outstanding contributions to the development of the Electronic Numerical Integrator and Computer (ENIAC) and in the area of computational science, the Army and the world salute you. Your foresight and dedication planted a seed that has led to remarkable discoveries impacting the entire world, and have provided the technical community with a gift of unlimited possibilities. Well done.

So if each of you would stand at this moment, I'd like all of us to recognize you with a round of applause. Would you all stand, please? [applause] Thank you very much.

It is now my honor to introduce the Deputy Commanding General of the Army Materiel Command, Lieutenant General Dennis L. Benchoff.

Lieutenant General Dennis L. Benchoff:

Thank you, Dr. Deitz. I'm very pleased to be a part of this ceremony today celebrating the Army's computing accomplishments of the past and heralding a new era of the Department of Defense High-Performance Computing. General Wilson, the Commander of the Army Materiel Command, has asked me to pass along his compliments, as well.

I'd like to digress a moment from my prepared remarks, just to mention that I've seen this thing before; I've seen it in operation—maybe even gazed on that exact board. [See photo opposite] When I was a junior or a senior in high school in the suburbs of Philadelphia and in the college prep program, one of our field trips was to the University of Pennsylvania, and one of the things we were privileged to see was this wonderful machine. Of course, being a skeptical high school smart aleck at the time, I didn't know whether it worked or not. It just looked kind of good. We asked the programmers to do something on it to show us that it worked. So we asked them to compute the square root of 64. We knew the answer to that, and sure enough, it was 8! [laughter] Then we got a little more adventuresome and were quite impressed. They explained to us the fundamentals of binary computation, and the rest, of course, is history. In my master's degree days, I was able to go back and put away my slide rule and my log tables and actually do my own programming. Of course, now everybody carries around a watch that can do everything but tell time. [laughter] Such are the wonders of science.

The Army of today is very different from the Army of World War II. The

Major General Barnes and John Grist Brainerd in front of ENIAC Function Table "A" (the table was on display at the ceremony).

Army of tomorrow will no doubt be very different from what we know it to be today. Our speakers have talked about what the development of the computer has meant to our nation and to our world. Dr. Lyons talked about computer technology's enormous contribution to the scientific world. I'd like to talk about what the computer has meant to the soldier—which is the reason for our existence.

Fifty years ago, the only way to communicate with soldiers in the field was with a limited-range radio or an electronic teletype, which gave us essentially very slow but worldwide communications. Today, computer technology allows us to communicate, via satellite, with soldiers anywhere in the world. We use helmet-mounted video cameras and hand-carried Global Positioning Systems (GPS). No longer can soldiers be lost.

The dawn of the information age has given the soldier amazing new capabilities. We have, through the power of computers, changed and expanded the definition as well as the range of Army communications. When we talk about Force XXI, when we think about the Army After Next, when we think about digitizing the battlefield, I find myself thinking about 50 years ago. None of these capabilities that we take for granted now even existed. They hadn't even been dreamt of by such visionaries as Jules Verne.[3]

So as a soldier I'd like to say "thank you" to the pioneers, Dr. Goldstine and his fellows, that we're honoring here today. You may never know how many battles were won or how many lives were saved because of the advances made from your humble beginnings. I'd like to challenge the scientists and the engineers of today to continue this path of excellence and to continue to stretch the limits of this science. Now it's my pleasure to introduce Dr. Gregory Farrington, Dean of the School of Engineering for the University of Pennsylvania. [applause]

[3] Jules Verne (1828–1905), French author of such science fiction classics as *Twenty Thousand Leagues Under the Sea* (1870), *Around the World in Eighty Days* (1873), and *Voyage to the Center of the Earth* (1864).

Dr. Gregory Farrington:

Thank you, General Benchoff. It's a pleasure to bring greetings from Judith Roden, the President of the University of Pennsylvania; from all the faculty of the Moore School, which I actually have the pleasure of being head of today; and most importantly the students of the Moore School of Engineering of the University of Pennsylvania. I, perhaps alone among everyone in this room, every morning walk by ENIAC. Sometimes I wave. [laughter] And if no freshmen are around, sometimes I say "Hi!" [laughter] because a piece of ENIAC still sits in the entrance way to the old Moore School building.

To say "the old Moore School building" is to not give it proper credit. We're blessed at Penn with old buildings. The greatest thing about old buildings, for new people, is the spirit, the ghosts, and the memories they hold. Our building is full of memories, particularly the Moore building. Two names resound, Eckert and Mauchly, that great team of geniuses who—with Dr. Goldstine—made ENIAC a reality, from a dream in 1946. Personally, 1946 is important to me too, because I was born in 1946. [laughter] So as far as I'm concerned, there are really two great events, one is ENIAC, and one is me! [laughter] Like many people in this room, I've grown up during the growing force of the computer age.

It's hard to choose any one particular impact of the computer age which has been the greatest, because it's pervasive. It's everywhere. ENIAC lives in everything; it affects us in so many ways we don't even think about. But if I have to choose one, it has to do with communication. Our ability today to talk with each other, fly to see each other, communicate with each other, take pictures and broadcast them around the world from cameras that are almost as small as a portable radio was yesterday, has truly transformed the world. I believe that the more we know about each other, the less likely we are to hate each other. The less likely we are to hate each other, the more likely we are to live a long time and have long and happy lives.

The greatest contribution of a strong military, as we all know, is securing the peace. Our military, our Army, this great partner with the University of Pennsylvania—and people like Eckert and Mauchly and Goldstine in 1946—created a partnership that has done so much in our contemporary time to secure the peace. It's only begun. The new computer that the Army unveils today is somewhere in this room. The thing about new computers is that they're so small you can't always find them. That new computer is one more step on an evolution of computers that goes on as far as we can see and beyond that. If it's really successful, it will do great things. And if it's really successful, it will be out of date very soon. That's the fate of computers. All of which is to say, 1946 was a glorious beginning, 1996 is a very interesting punctuation point, and in terms of the impact of computing on our society and our lives, we haven't seen anything yet. Thank you, and "Hello" from Penn, and "Happy Birthday," ENIAC, and "Happy Birthday," great Penn-Army collaboration! [applause]

Paul Deitz:

Thank you very much, Dr. Farrington and General Benchoff. Ms. Chenowith, from the Harford County Council, is going to present us with an award.

[She is accompanied by Ms. Parrott.]

Veronica Chenowith:

If I could have Lieutenant General Benchoff and Dr. Lyons come up to center stage, please. A half a century ago, I was just a child of eight and had no idea what a computer was. But they certainly knew at Aberdeen Proving Ground. It is indeed an honor and a privilege to present this proclamation:

Whereas ENIAC, completed in the fall of 1945 and publicly unveiled in February 1946 at the University of Pennsylvania, was the first operational general purpose electronic digital computer;

Whereas ENIAC was first used to solve an important problem for the Manhattan project and subsequently provided a platform for testing major component concepts;

Whereas the success of ENIAC stimulated the development of other machines leading to the buildup of the modern computer industry and the presence of computers in everyday life;

And whereas the engineers and scientists at the Army's Ballistic Research Laboratory helped develop a series of machines and continued to experiment with computer hardware, software, and operations which eventually led to expansion of the ARPANET, now known as the Internet;

And whereas the dedication of the Major Shared Resource Center (MSRC) will enhance the already extensive research capabilities in such areas as simulation, virtual reality, and scientific visualization;

Now, therefore, we, the County Council and County Executive of Harford County, Maryland, do hereby congratulate the U.S. Army on the celebration of "50 Years of Army Computing" and wish them continued success and dynamic new high-performance capabilities.

[Signed:] Eileen M. Rehrmann, County Executive, and all seven members of the Harford County Council.

[applause]

Paul Deitz:

I guess that "just-in-time delivery" business really works, doesn't it? As I mentioned at the beginning of the ceremony, we're here today not only to commemorate the past achievements in computing, but also to herald in a new era of high-performance computing. The Major Shared Resource Center will act as a cornerstone for modernized defense R&D computational capability and challenge the established limits. Right now, I'd like to call upon Mr. Charles Nietubicz, Chief of the Army Research Laboratory High-Performance Computing Division, to come forward to talk about those capabilities, and to initiate the ribbon-cutting ceremony. [applause]

Charles Nietubicz:

Thank you, Dr. Deitz. Good afternoon, ladies and gentlemen. It is with great pleasure and pride that I welcome you to the ribbon-cutting ceremony for the ARL DoD Major Shared Resource Center. During the past two days, you've shared many details of the rich computing tradition that BRL and ARL have established. The accomplishments have had a major impact, not just within our Laboratory, but on the Army, the DoD, and the world in general.

Today's dedication and ribbon cutting, then, mark an additional important milestone in that rich tradition. The creation of the ARL Major Shared Resource Center has come about by a competitive process initiated by the DoD High-Performance Computing Modernization Program. The DoD program has as its primary goal the infusion of leading-edge high-performance computing technology and infrastructure into the DoD research, development, test, and evaluation community—all this, in order to be able to provide the DoD warfighter with the ultimate superiority in weapons systems.

In short, the program has three major initiatives: the establishment of four Major Shared Resource Centers and a number of distributed centers; the establishment of a robust network called D-REN, which you heard about this morning; and the establishment of common, high-performance, scalable software.

You'll hear more about this High-Performance Computing Modernization Program from Ms. Kay Howell in the "Future Computing" session, directly following the ceremony.

We at ARL are both pleased and proud to be able to carry on the established tradition of providing high-performance computing in support of our country's defense mission. On August 9th of this year, Raytheon E-Systems was awarded the integration contract for the ARL Major Shared Resource Center. As you heard yesterday from Dr. Goldstine, ENIAC had a capability to compute 300 multiplications per second. The initial capability of the ARL Center that we're inaugurating today is over 200 million times that of ENIAC. Through planned upgrades, the ARL Major Shared Resource Center will soon provide an aggregate of nearly one teraFLOP, or one trillion floating point operations per second, of computer power to our defense scientists and engineers. The first phase of the high-performance computing hardware upgrade consists of (in the unclassified arena) Silicon Graphics scalable parallel systems consisting of 32 central processing units with a distributed shared memory of 12 gigabytes[4] and two Cray Vector systems with 16 processors, each with a half-million-word memory.

On the classified side, we will have two Cray T90s with four processors and 512 million words of memory, and two Silicon Graphics scalable parallel systems consisting of 32 processors and a distributed shared memory of 12 gigabytes. Additionally, with that computing hardware come mass storage systems capable of storing 50 terabytes[5] of data, computational file servers, and major scientific visualization and production capability. And that's just phase one. There's phase two and phase three. So we have a long way to go.

I believe you can see that with this hardware, together with the developing software and an integrated government and contractor staff, we are in an excellent position to carry out the tradition so well established by the early pioneers. And we're so very proud to do that.

So at this time I would like to ask Colonel Roger Brown, Chief of Staff of the Test and Evaluation Command, together with Mr. William Mermagan, Director of Corporate Information and Computing Center, and Ms. Kay Howell, Program Manager of the DoD High-Performance Computing Modernization Program, to come to the stage and join General Benchoff, Dr. Goldstine, Dr. Lyons, and Dr. Farrington, to help us officially dedicate the new DoD ARL Major Shared Resource Center by cutting the ribbon.

The ribbon before you bridges the supercomputing of the past, represented by the ENIAC to my right, and the supercomputing of the future, represented by the Cray T90 to my left. I would ask that you now take your scissors, and in true computing tradition, recognizing that there are really only two numbers in this world that are important, "zero" and "one," we will do the countdown in binary form, where three is represented by "1 1." So, when I say "1 1," we will cut the ribbon:

0 1,
1 0,
1 1.
[cut]

Thank you very much.

Dr. John Lyons:
Ladies and gentlemen, thank you for attending this historic ceremony. I'd like

---

[4] A gigabyte consists of one billion (giga = 10^9) characters (or bytes) of memory.

[5] Tera = 10^{12}.

to thank the 389th Army Band, AMC's Own, and the Color Guard from the 61st Ordnance Brigade. I think they did a great job. [applause]

Before we leave, there's one more person I'd like to recognize. Paul Deitz, would you please come "front and center." This two-day event took a lot of hard work by a team of very dedicated people. Paul actually started this a year ago last summer. He filled up my e-mail many times with the details of the proposals. But it was his personal initiative that made it all come together. So on behalf of the team and the Army Research Laboratory, I'd like to present you with this plaque, which I will now read:

> Dr. Paul H. Deitz, this plaque is presented in recognition of your effort to bring to the forefront the Army's crucial role in the birth of the age of electronic computing 50 years ago. Your work on the February 1996 national celebration in Philadelphia and conception and bringing to fruition the celebration at Aberdeen Proving Ground in November 1996 have been exemplary. Your dedication to the Army, your peers, and your predecessors is a model to all who work for the Army Research Laboratory. Thank you for a job well done.

[applause]

Dr. Paul H. Deitz:

This is very nice. Thank you very much.

This was really a significant effort. I didn't think it was going to be at first, but it turned out that it was a significant effort by a lot of folks. We've got a lot of support from people like Walt Hollis and the folks at Anita Jones's office up at OSD. We've got a tremendous amount of support from General Shadley's folks at the Ordnance Center and School, and of course a group of folks within the Army Research Laboratory, along with Dr. Tim Bergin, and others. We tried to list all those names somewhere in the program; I think you have them. And just for the record's sake, those folks did a wonderful job. It's those folks who should get our thanks. Thank you very much.

[applause]

Ribbon-cutting for ARL MSRC.

9. Future of Computing

Carol Ellis:
Ladies and gentleman, good afternoon. My name is Carol Ellis. I work in that successor organization that was at one time the Computing Lab. Our organization is now the caretaker of the ARL Major Shared Resource Center that you heard a lot about during the ribbon cutting ceremony. With us today to discuss what to look forward to in the future of computing are four speakers.

Our first speaker is Ms. **Kay Howell**. Kay has been involved in the DoD High-Performance Computing Modernization Program from the beginning. She is from the Naval Research Laboratory, but right now she is serving as the Program Manager of the program in Arlington, Virginia.

Next, I have Mr. **Paul Weinacht**. Paul has 14 years of experience as an aerospace engineer. He is an expert in computational fluid dynamics. And specifically he is interested in the behavior of kinetic energy ammunition.

Next, we have with us **Kent Kimsey**. Kent has been with us for nearly 25 years, and is the Computational Technology Leader for structural mechanics for the High-Performance Computing Modernization Program. Kent is particularly interested in the modeling of the behaviors of materials and structures that are subjected to intense impulse loading.

Last I have **Mike Muuss**, who was introduced to you earlier today. Mike will have a discussion about future interests that he sees evolving: the megamodeling of a virtual world.

Without further ado, I'd like to introduce Kay and she'll lead it off.

Kay Howell:
Thanks, Carol. I'm very happy to be here today. I very much appreciate the opportunity to participate in the ceremony taking place today. This really is a great day, in spite of what you might see if you look outside the window.[1] It truly is a beautiful day, because we're celebrating ENIAC and the ribbon-cutting for the Major Shared Resource Center that's being hosted here at the Army Research Laboratory. The ribbon-cutting was a symbolic gesture of what I consider to be the next phase of the DoD High-Performance Computing Modernization Program. Fifty years ago, DoD initiated the modern computing age with the ENIAC, and today we continue that 50-year legacy, with the investment in high-performance computing represented by the Modernization Program.

The Office of the Secretary of Defense is investing over a billion dollars to

---

[1] There was about 2 inches of snow on the ground.

modernize its computing capabilities to support the science and technology and the development test and evaluation communities. The systems and the services that are being provided through the High-Performance Computing Modernization Program are strategic resources that are a key ingredient in DoD's process to provide materials to the warfighter. With these systems and services, DoD's scientists and engineers will routinely conduct world-class research to support the warfighter.

The Major Shared Resource Center that's being hosted at the Army Research Laboratory is one of four centers that the Modernization Program is funding. You heard briefly from Charlie Nietubicz about the three initiatives of the program. The first is High-Performance Computing Centers. We've selected four Major Shared Resource Centers, and to date we've funded 12 smaller centers that we call Distributed Centers. The Major Shared Resource Centers are designed to carry the bulk of the high-performance computing load for the science and technology and the developmental test and engineering communities. These are full-service computing centers. They support a variety of hardware architectures; they have full customer service support. We have technical experts available to support the scientists and engineers, as well as visualization capabilities and mass storage devices.

The Distributed Centers are smaller centers that are nominally funded with $5M size systems. Their role is to complement what's going on at the Major Shared Resource Centers. They do this to support needs that we can't support at the Major Shared Resource Centers, such as real-time analysis work. Some embedded systems work is also being supported at our Distributed Centers. We also use Distributed Centers to take advantage of specific pockets of high-performance computing (HPC) expertise that we want to be able to tap into.

The second initiative of the program is the Defense Research Engineering Network (D-REN). The purpose of the D-REN is to provide connectivity, not only from the users to the centers, but between the centers to each other and between the users. We're doing that with a vision of being able to support interactive collaborations in the very near future, so that any scientist and engineer within DoD and the community that we support can interactively collaborate with scientists and engineers in any other laboratory.

The third component of the program is a software initiative to develop a core set of DoD applications that run well on these new scalable architectures. So far, we've funded over 40 projects, which are representative of the 10 computational technology areas of our scientific support. This is a three-year effort. These projects range anywhere from $1M to $3M per year, and take applications that already exist and, if necessary, redesign the applications to run well on the new scalable architectures.

With this program, our goal is to be able to apply HPC capability to provide advantage to the warfighter. That is our ultimate customer, the ultimate bill-payer, for the program. You heard briefly today about some of the exploits that ARL has undertaken with high-performance computing, even in the days of ENIAC. We're very much looking forward to what ARL will be doing in its role as a Major Shared Resource Center for the High-Performance Computing Modernization Program.

ARL is a great site for the DoD Modernization Program's Major Shared Resource Center for many reasons. One is because of the great research that's done here. The quality, the breadth of the research, and its direct relevance to the warfighter give this Major Shared Resource Center a tremendous local base of users. A second reason is the proven track record that ARL has in its computing capabilities. You have a record for providing excellent service to your scientific community. ARL has also been a leader in many areas of computing, including networking, secure computing, and scientific visualization.

A third reason is the strong commitment that the Army Research Laboratory has shown in support of high-performance computing. The modernization effort started back in 1992, with an appropriation from Congress to start the effort and a direction to develop a modernization plan for how we would go about improving the HPC capabilities in DoD. ARL stepped up to the line very strongly, with support to help make that effort take place. There are a few names that I'd like to recognize for the support that they provided over the years.

Harold Breaux is called one of the "founding fathers" of the program. Harold helped develop the first modernization plan for the program and was active in the program throughout his career at ARL and continues to work with the program.

Tony Pressley, of the Army Research Laboratory, was the first Program Manager for the Modernization Program. It was during Tony's tenure that the Modernization Program developed the procurement for these Major Shared Resource Centers and for the Defense Research and Engineering Network. It was during Tony's tenure that we received the necessary approval from our oversight committees in order to deploy the resources to make this all happen.

Valerie Thomas, from the Army Research Laboratory, is Executive Officer today for the Modernization Program. She has worked tirelessly with these oversight committees to get us the approval that we need to continue, and as Executive Officer she does just about anything that needs to be done to make this program work.

Bob Reschly served as a Program Manager for the Defense Research and Engineering Network effort. Bob's tenure ended when we made our D-REN award. He's now back at ARL, but his tireless efforts have served us well. We have a very strong network contract in place, thanks to his efforts.

Roger Johnson manages the Interim Defense Research and Engineering Network. That network has served us for four years now, and will continue to serve us as we get the new contract in place.

I'd also like to thank *Phil Dykstra* for the work that he's done with the Technical Advisory Panel for our networking piece. Phil helps us with the vision that we need to get these things in place and has been a very faithful member of that committee and provided us with excellent advice.

Kent Kimsey, as a Computational Technology Area Leader, has been instrumental in helping us get the CHSSI[2] projects, the scalable software projects, in place. And as a Computational Technology Area Leader, he's responsible for several of those projects.

I'm trying to think if I've left anybody out here. All the people who participated on our Source Selection Evaluation Board were the folks who allowed us to get the five contracts in place: four for the Major Shared Resource Centers, and

[2] Common HPC (High-Performance Computing) Software Support Initiative. This is the software activity of the DoD MSRC at Aberdeen and the other MSRCs.

one for the Defense Research and Engineering Network. These folks dedicated a year of their lives to making those awards happen. What we're seeing today are the results of their efforts with this first ribbon-cutting for a Major Shared Resource Center.

What I wanted to do today is to present you with some challenges as a Major Shared Resource Center for the program. We think about all the hard work that it's taken to get us to the point where we are today, but I like to tell everyone that the hard part has just started. Phase One is behind us; we've made the acquisitions and we're now in the process of deploying the systems. Now we have to actually do great and wonderful things with the billion dollars that the Defense Department is investing in high-performance computing.

For those of you at the Computing Center, I challenge you to establish yourself as a world-class center. This year alone we've invested over $50M in hardware and several million dollars in support and sustainment of the Center. And with Level Two capabilities, we'll be looking at similar-level investments. With these resources you have what is necessary to come to great prominence in the national HPC arena, and also worldwide! In order for you to do that, I challenge you to become closely linked with the national HPC infrastructure, to take advantage of what's going on at other government agencies such as NASA and the National Science Foundation, and to tap into the academic community and all the great work that's being done there. I challenge you to become early adopters of innovation. The program environment and training component of our program is your vehicle for doing that. You're going to develop tremendous programming environments to support the scientists and engineers and to make sure they are as productive as possible in doing their research.

I challenge you never to lose focus on your customer, the warfighter, and to make sure that you provide the scientists and researchers who are supporting the warfighter with the best environments possible to get the research done.

I'm very excited about the Shared Resource Center that we've put here at the Army Research Laboratory. I eagerly anticipate the great progress that's going to be accomplished here. I look forward to visiting you next year, on your birthday, to see all the great things that you've done. So I say, "Happy birthday!" to ENIAC and "Happy birthday!" to ARL as a Major Shared Resource Center. Congratulations. [applause]

Carol Ellis:

There happens to be one person I neglected to introduce. I'd like ***Phil Dykstra*** to join me on the stage at this moment. Phil has been involved for close to 17 years with what is now known as the Army Research Laboratory. And as Kay has mentioned, Phil has been involved in the networking aspects of the program, and he's going to share with us something we can look forward to in the future in networking.

Phil Dykstra:
You heard this morning from Bob Reschly about networking history, so I'm going to talk a bit about where it's going and try to use a crystal ball. I will say a little bit about the technology, where that's headed, and what limits there might be, what kinds of things we're doing with it, and how that's changed and is changing. Finally, I'll say a bit about the political scene and agenda, such as what's happening now at the national/international levels. I always have more to say than I think I do, so I'll try to talk fast and see how much of it I can get through.

I have only two slides. They give you something to look at besides me. The first [right] just shows graphically the progress we've had since ENIAC, by plotting computer speeds over the years on a logarithmic scale. You can see that there's been roughly a factor of 10 increase in computing power every six years, or about a 47-percent increase per year. So in these 50 years, we've gone through eight or nine orders of magnitude of computational increase, and we don't see any slowdown in that rate of progress at least for the next 20 years.

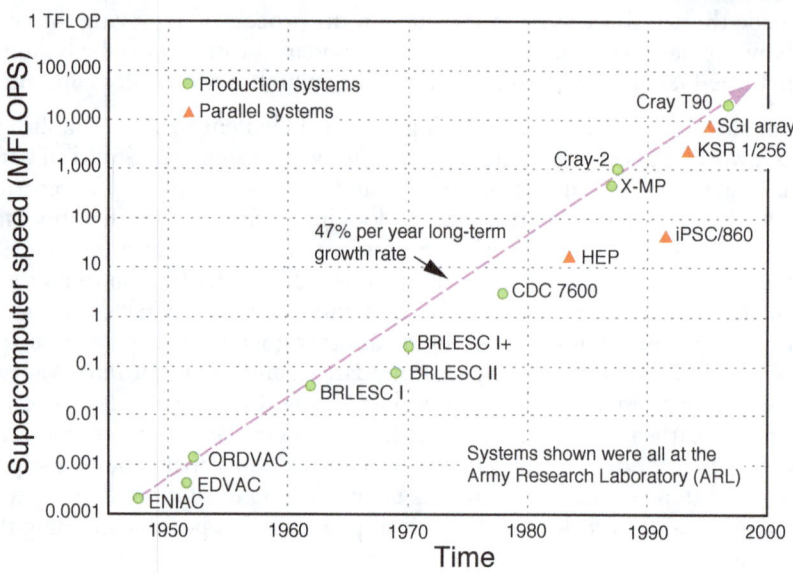

Speed of supercomputers versus time.

So where does networking fit into all of this? There's a rule of thumb that computer designers use, called the "Amdahl/Case rule," that says for every million instructions per second (MIPS) of processing power, you should have about a megabit per second of I/O capability.[3] What this means is that the machine has to be able to read and write data—in and out of itself—at roughly the same speed that it can process it. So this, in turn, means that our networks should keep pace with this rapid increase in computer power—and they have pretty much. Networking, at least in the sense that we know it, is about 30 years old—rather than 50 years old. Certainly, some of our first machines were tied together in local-area networks; we had remote access to them very early on. But really, just as the ENIAC was the birthplace of modern computing, the ARPANET was the birthplace of wide-area networking as we know it today. The ARPANET began in 1969.[4] So we've had about 30 years of wide-area networking, as well as steady progress in local-area nets that tie all these machines together. We've seen, in fact, in recent years, a growth rate that is faster than an order of magnitude every six years [see figure opposite].

So where are we today? We have commercially deployed gigabit-per-second-type links, depending on whether you're looking at the wide-area carriers, or research LANs, so we're at about 10^9 bits per second today.

How far can it go? It's predicted that a single fiber-optic cable, a single piece of glass, can carry up to 10^{15} bits per second. So we've got about six more orders of magnitude to go before we hit the limit of our fiber, which should probably happen in about 40 years. So within many of our lifetimes, we will see something on the order of 15 bps over fiber. To put that in perspective, that's about three orders of magnitude higher than the amount

[3] See Reschly's remarks (pp 96–98, this volume) for a discussion of Gene Amdahl and his thoughts on computer architecture.

[4] Salus (1995) contains an excellent timeline, from George Stibitz's demonstration of long-distance calculation in 1940, to 1994, when America Online connects to the Internet.

of traffic carried by the worldwide telephony system today, and that would be in *one* fiber!

If we get this fiber to every household, that would mean every house in America could carry 1000 times more traffic than is in the entire communications spectrum today. What would we conceivably do with that? It means that the possibilities are limitless, as far as everyone running their own TV stations or having collaborative virtual reality between our households. There are no technological limits, at least from a scientific level, to achieving the kind of communications support we need for those applications. Instead it will require a shift in our economic or social structure, to determine how we pay for this kind of infrastructure.

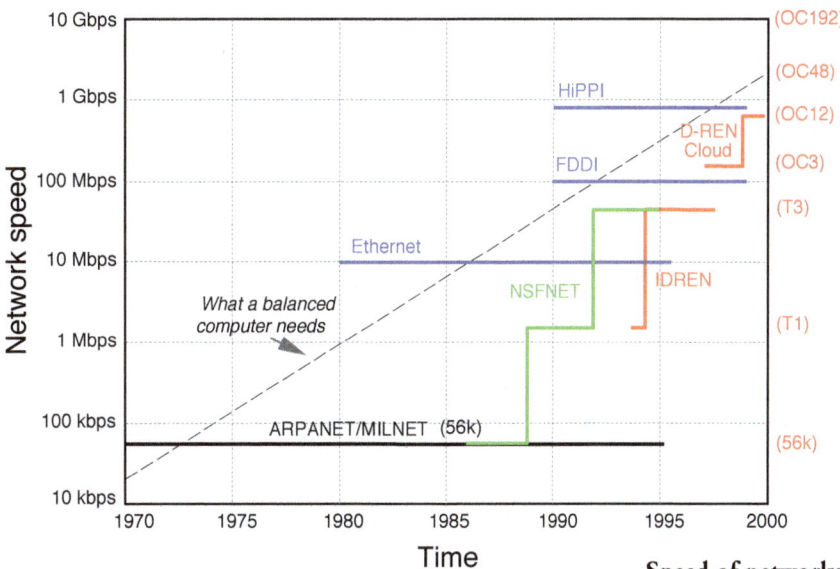

Speed of networks versus time.

You obviously all know that during these 50 years you haven't seen your telephone bill drop by nine orders of magnitude, yet it's become increasingly cheaper to carry your voice traffic. Why is that? It is because there is a somewhat constant price of maintaining our communications infrastructure, leading to what some people believe will be a cost per bit of zero; that is, the cost of actually making a voice telephone call will not be measurable—as far as the amount of bits that it consumes. Instead, we'll just be paying to maintain this shared communications infrastructure. So that means it doesn't matter what you do with it, whether it's a voice call, a fax, or a virtual reality session consuming "zillions" of bits. The amount of data you're consuming should be essentially irrelevant, and that's the environment we're headed into.

There are other interesting details, but I don't have time to delve into the technologies that will give this to us. But there are many exciting things, such as solutions over fibers, which means that we might be able to cross the Atlantic, for example, with no repeaters whatsoever. There's deployment now, in the Internet, of a technique called "tag switching" or "IP flows," which is bringing ATM[5]-like high-speed technology to the Internet as we know it today. That's fairly exciting, and a new generation of networks is emerging based on wave division multiplexing (WDM), which switches light in fiber independent of what may be carried over it.

But what are we using all this for? For many people, the Internet is the World Wide Web. The Web is an *application* that has taken off that has caused millions of people to want access to the Internet.[6] For many people, it's very new. It actually began about seven years ago, and is an example of how things take a long time over in the research environment before they explode into the public domain. There are at least 20 million domestic Internet web users today, and this number is growing extremely rapidly. I think the next wave of this kind of thing will be voice telephony. There are many people playing with this, who can make free telephone calls worldwide over their Internet connection. We're doing that with video as well. In fact, in the HPC program, we're trying to deploy that to all 4000 of our users, so that we can routinely see and talk

[5] Asynchronous transfer mode, a technique for high-speed transmission of data.

[6] The Internet is the physical network of computers and communications media; electronic mail, the World Wide Web, and Gopher are all applications. The World Wide Web is an amalgamation of "objects" (documents, photographs, sounds, etc.) that are linked through sets of pointers associated with the objects. The software used to "surf" the WWW is called a "web browser." Popular web browsers include Netscape Communications' *Navigator* and *Communicator* and Microsoft's *Internet Explorer*.

to each other from our desktops. It's a way of sharing an office—potentially worldwide. As for this type of telephony, it will—once we get high enough data rates into the home—become a thing of the masses, just as the Web has. Stu Personicks, who's the head of one of the technology divisions in Bell Communications Research, said, "The future of the voice telephone system is the Internet." Who's going to control voice telephony over the Internet, and how will they do it? These are big questions. But it's inevitable that eventually this communications infrastructure will be used for everything, as opposed to there being a separate voice system, for example.

Because of this high-speed interconnection, there's an old rule of thumb in computing that doesn't hold true anymore: the "80-20 rule" meant that about 80 percent of your access to information was local, and 20 percent was remote. In the area of networking, people looked at these numbers, and it's practically the other way around. We're now spending far more time talking to resources that are far away from us than we are to our own local machines. That's a very big change, brought about by the increased usage of the Internet.

I guess finally, I should mention the politics of all this. As I said earlier, with all of these uses, the control of all this is a very big question. The U.S. government, which gave rise to all this technology, is trying to get out of this business. The "kid" has grown up and left home, and it's anybody's guess, really, as to how the market forces will battle this stuff out. Steve Wolff, who had been at BRL some time ago, went to the National Science Foundation and oversaw their networking program. He essentially oversaw the demise of the NSFNET.[7] That is, it was his role to commercialize the Internet and get the government out of this business. So he did that. About two and a half years ago, the backbone of the Internet, the whole Internet communications infrastructure that we knew, went away. It was handed over to a collection of private providers, who set up a system of network access points where we would all come together, and that's now been operational for a bit over two years.

And somewhat to our surprise, we're finding that the commercial forces don't like it, that they have their own ideas, and are instead setting up private interconnection relationships. Things are going very much in a different direction, I guess, than the government thought it might, a couple of years ago. And right now, we only loosely control that, because of cooperative agreements that will only last for about two more years. Now that commercial forces have gotten on to the Internet, and have started doing *commerce* with it, issues such as host names, address-spaces for your machines, etc., have become international issues. The questions are still "Who's in charge?" "Who has the authority to control the Internet?" The government and DARPA roughly hold control of things, such as Internet address space, but there are *ad hoc* international committees that are stepping up and saying, "We're going to pass rules about this stuff. We're going to control this stuff." It's not clear to anybody yet, really, who has this authority and how it's going to shake out.

On the political scene, I'll quote from Vint Cerf, who was an Internet pioneer. He had a three-part saying about the maturity of the Internet. The first part is that, "When lawyers get involved, you know you have a real product."[8] Lawyers got involved quite a few years ago, actually, in Internet issues when these first Internet companies were formed. Cerf also said, "When the masses get involved, there goes the neighborhood." That happened clearly a few years

[7] The NSFNET provided the "backbone" of the Internet after the demise of the ARPANET. The Advanced Research Projects Agency (ARPA) funded the ARPA Computer Network in 1968; the National Science Foundation funded the first five national supercomputer centers, which would be connected by the NSFNET backbone in 1985; the ARPANET was shut down in 1989.

[8] Dykstra heard Cerf say this at a conference years ago, but unfortunately has no reference for it.

ago, as services like AOL, Compuserve, etc., started providing Internet access and the Web took off—now there are millions of people using the Internet and the Web. The Internet is now very different from what it was when it was all scientists and engineers.

Finally, he said, "When Congress gets involved, it's time to retire." That's happening right now. Last term, Congress passed its first law with the word "Internet" in it, and the Federal Networking Council had to come up with a definition of what the Internet was. As we start to do things such as *commerce* over the net, all kinds of issues come up, such as "what does a *digital signature* mean?" and "what about *electronic cash*?" Some people talk about the demise of the penny. What about the demise of cash entirely? Cash becomes some sort of crypto-numbers on a card you carry around.

Another area of concern is censorship. The "Communications Decency Act" is working its way up to the Supreme Court today. There are concerns about cryptography export controls, and the trade-offs between privacy and national security.

It's in some ways a very exciting time, because it's causing us to re-examine all kinds of social infrastructure. We're looking at why do we do many of the things we've been doing for many years, such as what does it actually mean to sign a document? I have no doubt that there will be plenty of work for lawyers for years to come!

Finally, as for the federal role in this, just a few weeks ago the White House made a public announcement about the next-generation Internet (NGI). The research universities that started the Internet now find that the Internet is kind of swamped. They're being told to sign up with a commercial provider. The bandwidth isn't there yet, the Internet is congested, and they're asking, "How can we do our research?" So there's essentially a push to create the next-generation network, the next level of performance by the hundred or so top research universities in the nation, along with the government R&D labs. What happens to that program is now being defined by a Large-Scale Networking group under the Committee for Computing Information and Communications (CCIC), which reports to the White House. They're defining what that next-generation Internet will be. We hope that, through that kind of effort and through programs such as the HPC Modernization Program, the government can continue to shepherd the Internet to show what can be done 10 years from now. This is the kind of frontier we at ARL and DoD work on, to show what makes the most sense for deployment into the commercial sector. So I think many of the applications that we're doing today, such as *virtual reality*, will be things that you'll be seeing commercially 10 years from now. So I think it's a very exciting time for this program and a very exciting time for the nation. Thank you for your time. [applause]

Paul Weinacht:

As Carol mentioned, I'm Paul Weinacht and I've been working in the area of computational fluid dynamics for about 14 years here at ARL and in the past at BRL. This is a technology area that I was exposed to as an undergraduate nearly 20 years ago. The moment I saw it, I was very intrigued by it and knew exactly what I wanted to do. I'm glad to have had an opportunity to work in that field for the past 14 years, here at ARL.

Computational fluid dynamics (CFD) is one of the strong areas of focus here at ARL in terms of computational analysis. I'd like to first give a few examples of what CFD is all about.

One of the first steps in performing a CFD analysis is to discretize the flow field about a flight body of some sort, and this is done by gridding it up [see figure, right]. At each of the intersections of these grid lines, equations are solved that govern the balance of mass, momentum, and energy. There's an interrelation between these conservation laws at each of the points in the computational domain. Therefore, there are many calculations that have to be made, and these calculations are made continuously until there's a balance of the mass, momentum, and energy throughout the entire flow field.

Computational grid.

The result, when we finally get done with our calculations, is that we can completely define the flow field about a flight vehicle. The figure [below] shows a modern kinetic energy projectile that is an antitank type of weapon. From this we can determine what the aerodynamic forces are on the flight vehicle, and from that, we can determine how it would fly and see if there are changes that need to be made to the design or whether the design meets the design goals.

Research in the area of computational fluid dynamics dates back to the 1950s, when the Laboratory was known as BRL. Studies in refereed journals show that investigations included such areas as ablation of melting solids and prediction of forebody pressure drag on projectile configurations. And in some cases, some of these techniques can be traced to work that's ongoing today. However, much of the development in computational fluid dynamics really occurred over the last 15 years. This is most likely because sufficiently large computational resources became available at that time, and these were capable of solving the nonlinear partial differential equations that characterize fluid motion. These machines included the CDC Cyber 7600, as well as the

Flow field visualization.

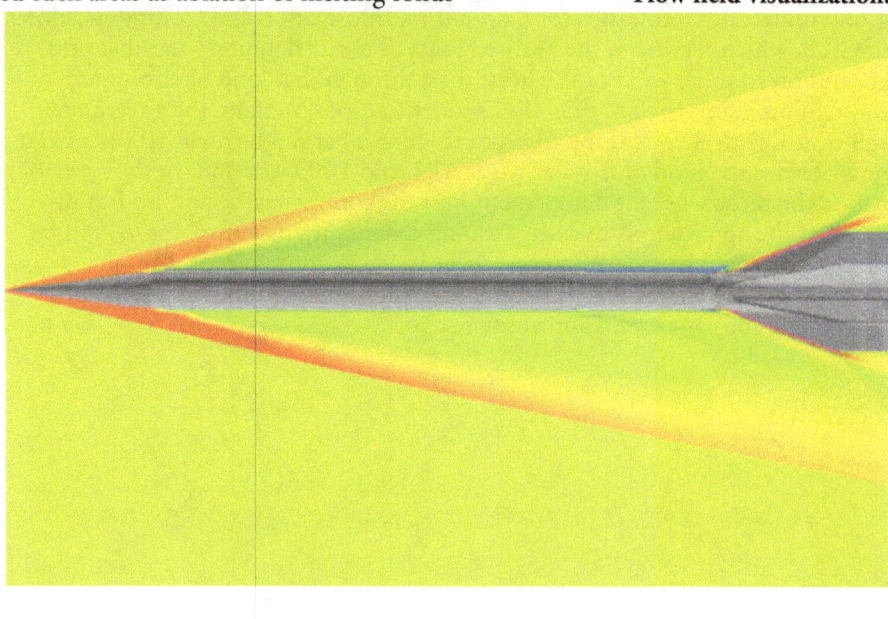

Cray machines that followed later on, such as the Cray XMP and the Cray-2.

Probably the landmark computation within the Army over this 15-year era was the prediction of the Magnus effect, or spinning axisymmetric projectiles, that was performed by Walt Sturek of BRL. The Magnus effect is well known to golfers or baseball players. This is the mechanism that causes the curvature in the trajectory of the golf ball or a baseball. This problem had defied solution through older techniques such as a coupled Euler and boundary layer code. In earlier studies of boattailed projectile configurations, Dr. Sturek collaborated with Dr. Schiff of the NASA Ames Research Center. They applied a recently developed Navier-Stokes code to this particular problem. Their successful solution of this Magnus problem paved the way for other significant advances in Navier-Stokes methods within the Army aerodynamics community. These include prediction of Magnus effects at transonic velocity and prediction of the critical behavior in the pitching moment coefficient at transonic velocity, which were performed by Dr. Sahu and Mr. Nietubicz.

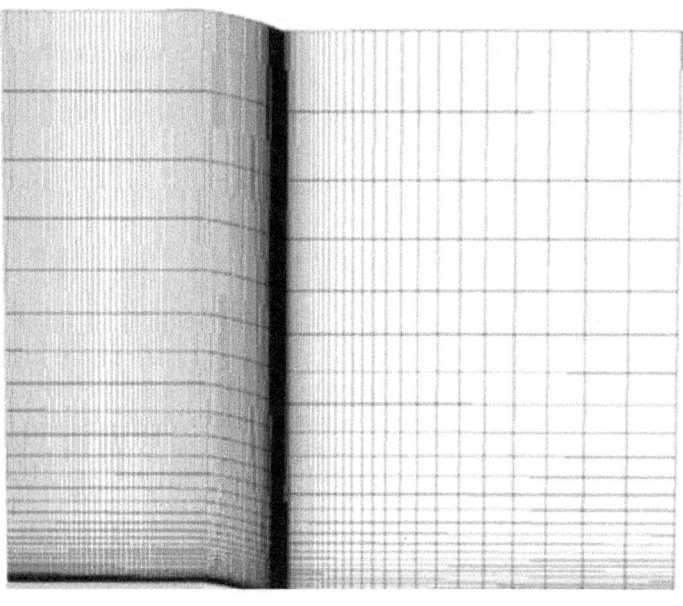

Computational grid for transonic computations.

Both of the accomplishments that I've just listed here were really paced by the available computational resources at that time. First attempts at solving these problems were not totally successful, although they did yield promising results. It wasn't until later generations of supercomputers that a predictive capability was fully established.

I think if we look at a grid for a transonic flow field calculation [right], you can see the large number of grid points that are required to fully define the flow field about the body, and this basically means that the calculation is going to take a very long period of time before the solution fully converges and you've got a successful result.

Now, another problem that was investigated during this time period was the problem of a wrap-around fin projectile [see figure, next page]. You will notice that on this particular projectile, the fins are curved, and when it's in a launch tube, the fins actually conform to the body so that the body is completely actually axisymmetric. When it is fired out of the launch tube, the fins deploy, and they maintain their curved shape. The problem with these types of fins is that as the projectile slows down, the projectile will begin to roll in one direction, and it will change direction at a particular Mach number.[9] For the particular projectile shown here, at about Mach 1.7 you'll get this change in direction of the roll. This has some poor effects on the flight performance, and in particular on accuracy. So therefore the projectile designers would like to try to avoid this type of problem.

The wrap-around fin problem was addressed by one of the engineers in our group, Mr. Harris Edge. He established a capability for predicting the magnitude of this type of behavior. This particular type of calculation was very challenging, in that it involves both a viscous boundary layer, which requires many grid points to resolve, as well as geometric complexity, which again requires

[9] Mach is a unit of velocity equal to the velocity of sound in a medium (usually air). Mach 1 is about 730 miles per hour at sea level. The unit is named in honor of the Austrian physicist Ernst Mach (1838–1916).

additional calculations. I believe this simulation required over 50 million words of memory on a Cray-2 computer.

One feature of all these computational accomplishments is that they taxed the state of the art in computer resources at the time. Typically this was due to the fact that they required so much computer time—although computer memory was certainly an issue. This is one of the real big benefits of the MSRC, as we see it, in that it will allow us to continue to advance the state of the art. There really are no easy problems left to be done.

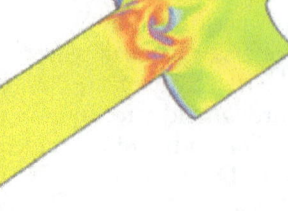

Pressure contours on a wrap-around finned projectile.

A second benefit of having these kinds of resources here at ARL is that it's going to be possible for engineers to do routine calculations, and many of them! In the past year or so, I've been involved in the development of an advanced kinetic energy concept, and for this particular project I was able to perform analysis computations for 340 different designs—over a period of a couple of months. This allowed the design space to be fully defined, so that it was possible to select several optimal designs based on different constraints. Such a study would have been prohibitively expensive using traditional experimental methods. To fire these rounds alone would have cost over a million dollars, and that doesn't account for the cost of actually manufacturing and building the rounds.

Thus, we can see that the new resources that will be part of the Major Shared Resource Center really will be used in two ways: one is to advance the state of the art to allow us to do problems that we couldn't do before, and the second is to perform important design studies for the Army customers that we have.

I would like to mention several research areas that we intend to investigate in the future. One area is related to control aerodynamics for maneuvering projectiles. Smart weapons are one of the things that's being pushed quite heavily in the Army. These are going to require additional resources, because these geometries are typically fairly complex.

Another area of investigation will be multibody systems. This might include things like submunition dispersal, as well as sabot discard problems. Again, these are very complex problems. Typically, they're time dependent, which again will tax the computational resources quite heavily. So we're very excited to be part of this MSRC and have these resources available to us.

As a final comment, on behalf of the people that work in this computational fluid dynamics area, I'd really like to thank all the people who worked so hard to bring these resources to ARL, particularly Hal Breaux, Charlie Nietubicz, and their staffs. I know it was quite a challenge for them to fight the battles that needed to be fought in order to get the site here, but we, the application specialists, really appreciate their efforts. It's really going to make a big difference for all of us. Thank you. [applause]

Kent Kimsey:

I'm Kent Kimsey from the Terminal Effects Division of the Weapons and Materials Research Directorate of ARL. I'm going to talk about the role of large-scale computations in weapons research. The following are some of the engineering and design functions made possible by large-scale simulations:

- Conduct two- and three-dimensional parametric studies
- Explore novel concepts
- Exploit and evaluate foreign technologies
- Supplement terminal ballistics test databases
- Exploit scientific visualization:
  - Capture the dynamics of complex projectile/target interactions
  - Identify and optimize critical defeat mechanisms

I want to talk specifically about using large-scale computations for conducting research in penetration mechanics. To set the stage, there are several approaches to addressing problems in penetration mechanics. The most obvious one is to go out and shoot a weapon at a target. The figure [below] is an example of the type of data you might obtain from a terminal ballistic test, using flash radiography, in which you have multiple flashes. You can see a picture of a steel rod penetrating an oblique steel plate. Now, perhaps on the surface, that may appear to be a fairly simple problem—just penetrating a steel plate by a steel rod. But this is a very complex problem, because there are many competing physical phenomena that occur during the penetration process. There is erosion of the rod, fracture of the rod, bending of the rod, and you can see the formation of a debris cloud behind the armor. Also, there is plate bending and bulging, there could be radial cracking, and there could be thermal mechanical instabilities that develop, which lead to shear bands that lead to failure.

So it's a complex phenomenon that we are trying to model numerically. Over the years we have enhanced the design utility of large-scale simulations for modeling terminal ballistic phenomena with each increment in high-performance computing resources. The design utility allows us to conduct parametric studies so that we can start to understand the basic penetration phenomena associated with different targets.

That kind of sets the stage. I was asked to speak about what we see in the future. Well, as I mentioned, this is a fairly complex problem, even for a simple

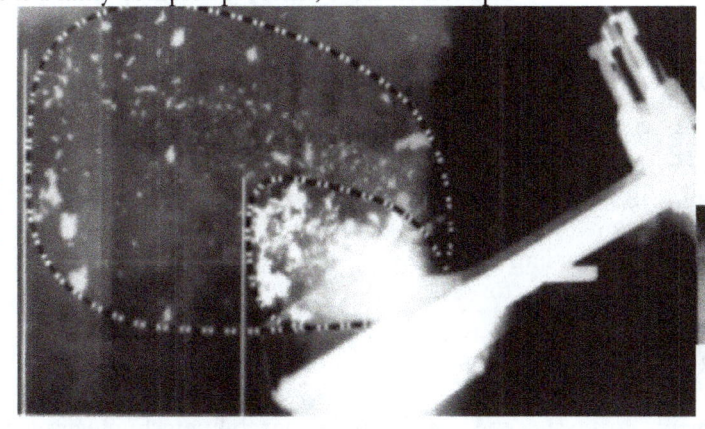

Image of steel rod penetrating steel plate, obtained by flash radiography.

490   140
Time after impact (ms)

target. For example, the figure [right] shows a three-dimensional simulation of long-rod penetration with combined yaw and obliquity. Today's modern armor and armaments technology—as well as those that are emerging—simply compound the complexity of the problem that we are trying to model. By coupling large-scale simulations with scientific visualization, we can capture the dynamics of complex projectile-target interactions, which cannot be gleaned solely from terminal ballistic tests.

Modeling long-rod penetration with combined yaw and obliquity.

Today large-scale calculations are an integral component of our basic research programs to develop and enhance the lethality and survivability technologies for armored vehicles. The problem sets for these emerging armor technologies are really what drive our high-performance computing needs.

Today, compared to the simple oblique impact problem I showed—where the penetration process mainly occurs over several hundred microseconds—in order to capture the complete projectile/target interaction process, our simulations must be carried out into the millisecond regime. Also due to the complex geometry and materials involved in some of these advanced technologies, we're having to use a finer mesh resolution in order to get accurate solutions and to capture some of those complex phenomena, such as bending and material failure during a penetration event.

Also, our physical domains are getting larger. That was a fairly small problem to model. Today, to do weapons simulations for applications for heavy armor vehicles, our physical domain is much larger than in the past. In addition, we're always faced with oblique impacts, and these are three-dimensional events. Through ballistics experiments, we can gain insight into the dominant physical characteristics of the problems. However, we really can't glean the critical defeat mechanisms or target interactions that occur in some of the more complex technologies solely from the ballistics experiments. We rely heavily on large-scale simulations to help us gain insight into these complex phenomena. In fact, in some scenarios today, the calculations are guiding the experiments that are conducted.

Penetration problems drive our computing requirements because of the size of the problems we have to model and the mesh constraints. Typically, for finite-volume calculations, if you double the mesh resolution, that corresponds to a factor of eight increase in memory requirements. Now, for a three-dimensional problem, if you maintain the same coordinate domain in each of the coordinate directions and you double the mesh, this results in having your mesh width or characteristic length reduced by a factor of two. And since we are using explicit time-integration techniques to follow shock-wave propagation in materials, the time step is governed by the minimum characteristic length in the problem. When you double the mesh resolution, you also cut your time step in half, so now you have to compute twice as many cycles to get to the same point in the simulation time. So for doubling the zoning in a particular problem, you can see CPU times increased by a factor of 16.

Today, we dedicated the high-performance computing resources available under the MSRC. We look forward to using them to model these complex phenomena, so that we can leverage the calculations, in concert with terminal ballistic experiments, to advance the lethality and survivability technologies for future land combat systems. [applause]

Mike Muuss:
Thank you very much for remaining for the very last session of this commemoration. It's my unfortunate honor to be the last speaker, and I'll try to provide you with a little bit of entertainment and keep you awake for the remaining minutes. Before I launch into the subject of the slides, I'd just like to point out that while the conference room you see here today is not very large, this commemoration is being carried live on Channel 3 here in Aberdeen. It's being transmitted by ISDN network links to Adelphi[10] and other Army facilities and is being transmitted live over the Internet's MBONE to many American and foreign facilities. This afternoon, we have 70 international people joining us (via the MBONE), and that's probably more people than are in the room at this time. We are currently live in Sweden, Germany, the United Kingdom, Finland, Japan, France, and Canada. So this is truly a testimony to how far we have come in 50 years—to be able to have researchers from across the world joining us here celebrating the birthday of the ENIAC.

[10] The Army Research Laboratory at Adelphi, MD.

What I'm going to tell you about is my vision for what we're going to do with some of this impressive new computing power. My personal interest is in creating virtual worlds and then coming up with useful things for us to do in those virtual worlds.

Everything I am going to talk about today is based on BRL-CAD and solid modeling, which is another technology invented by the Army. This was invented in 1958, the year I was born, and is one of those things that we don't get much credit for either, so hopefully we can keep pushing the message out to the public that the Army is in fact creating these useful technologies. The BRL-CAD product is in use now in over 1600 institutions worldwide. This is a tremendous technology transfer from the Army out to the world.

So what we plan to do in this project is to build a very, very large virtual world and then create a camera to look at it with. We want

1. A physics-based synthetic wide-band imaging spectrophotometer. That is, a camera-like sensor to look at any frequency of energy.

2. A set of virtual worlds for it to look at:

    - With atmosphere, clouds, smoke, targets, trees, vegetation, high-resolution terrain.
    - A dynamic world—everything can change.

So we don't want just any camera; we want an imaging spectrophotometer. It's going to have the ability to look at any frequency—not just light, but ultraviolet or infrared, or millimeter wave—and see what a camera would see. To put it more simply, we are trying to build "Superman's x-ray vision." We want to be able to tune our eyes—in simulation—to see what a soldier would see through a night sight or an infrared system, or what the nose cone of a missile might see as it's looking around the battlefield trying to find a target.[11]

[11] Gibson (1998) discusses this topic.

Our expertise for 30 years has been in solid geometry and describing material properties, and that's the center of this onion diagram. I saw Jim O'Bryon[12] in the audience earlier. I'd like to point out that going in the upper right direction—sort of at one o'clock—is our support of Army live fire and DoD live fire. That's a very important part of what BRL-CAD is used for. What I am going to talk about today really occupies the left side of this onion diagram, where on top of BRL-CAD, we have the ability to generate optical images, infrared images, radar images, and so on. And we are going to apply those to problems of interest to a soldier. But they also happen to be kind of fun, too! And what I hope to show you today is some of the fun that comes in solving these problems.

If I had to summarize the entire effort we've been working on, this list would be the way to do it.

- Ray-tracing, exact combinatorial solid geometry
- Enormous scene complexity, real targets
- Physics-based multispectral image generation
- Micro-atmospherics, smoke, and obscurants
- Near real-time (6 frames per second) operation
- Fully scalable algorithms
- Network distributed MIMD[13] parallel HPC
- Image delivery via ATM and HPPI[14] networks

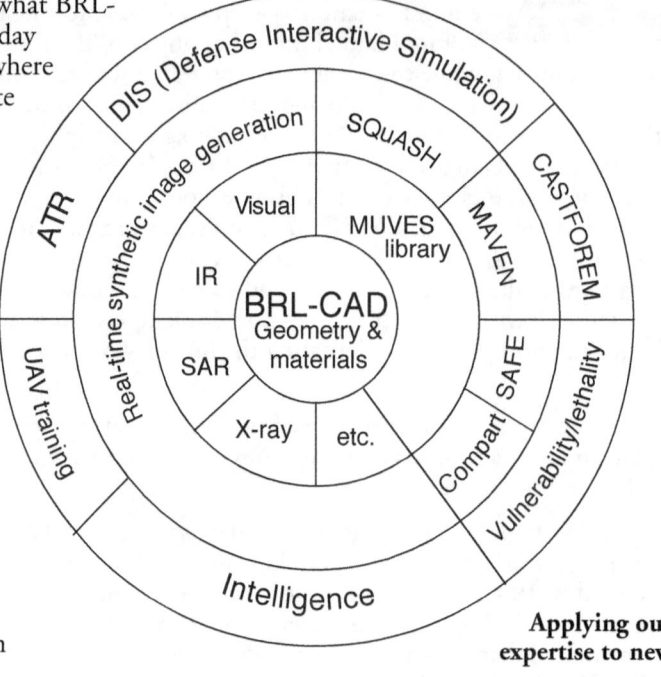

Applying our expertise to new

[12] Director, Joint Live Fire Office, Pentagon.

[13] Multiple instruction, multiple data stream, a form of parallel processing hardware. The other main form is SIMD—single instruction, multiple data stream.

[14] Asynchronous transfer mode; high-performance parallel interconnect.

[15] Combinatorial solid geometry combines volumes using Boolean expressions.

We're doing ray tracing of exact combinatorial solid geometry (CSG).[15] Ray tracing was invented hundreds of years ago for lens design, but it's proven to be very useful for studying arbitrary geometric shapes. I don't have time today to teach you much about it, but I think most of the folks in the audience have a little appreciation of this already.

We're working with scenes of enormous complexity. My current low-resolution test is a 12 ∞ 16 km chunk of land measured at 1 m spacing—that's about a yard. We have a measurement every yard for more than 10 miles in each direction. That's a tremendous amount of data, and that's the *low-resolution* test. Every tree was surveyed by satellite, and we know where they go and how big they are; each of those trees has individually modeled leaves. So we are modeling the leaves on the trees for 100 square miles worth of land. Just think of how many leaves there are in 100 square miles of land.

Everything we are doing is physics based. We are not making cartoons, and we do not work at Disneyland. We are not trying to make motion pictures for entertainment. We are trying to solve problems for scientific analysis, for evaluating new concepts, and for checking out weapons that have been built to see whether they are going to do the jobs the soldiers expect the weapons to do for them. And as a result, there is no hand painting of colors on things; there is no artist to go in and make Donald Duck look just right. The physics of the situation is what we depend on. We put the equations and all the input data in, and the computer tells us what is going to happen. That means we have to do a lot of work to make sure that the encoding of those equations, algorithms, and data structures, in the machine, is very carefully done, so that we get the right answers out, and that is a very challenging problem.

In addition to that, for the first time we are sticking in nano-atmospheric modeling. We are looking at being able to capture the plumes of smoke off the back of a tank. We are interested in being able to look at the hot rotor wash coming off a helicopter, and a more conventional example, the exhaust plume coming off the top of a tractor trailer—you see an 18-wheeler going down the road, and you know it's blowing a big cloud of smoke. We want to be able to model the effect of that smoke going into the environment, so we know what it is going to do. If that was a smoke generator truck instead of just an 18-wheeler, it would be making a whole lot more.

What's worse is that weapons systems run fairly fast. We want to do this in real time, so we're not making people wait overnight or until next week to get the results—so we have to generate these images at a rate of approximately six frames a second. In particular, for the first couple of weapons that want to be tested with this technology, the processing rate is six frames a second. So this isn't something we can do overnight and come back and get one picture from. We have to be making pictures constantly at a tremendous rate.

As a result of that we need fully scalable algorithms. These are things that will use 100 or 200 CPUs from a high-performance research center, combine them together in solving this one problem, and deliver the answers to the customer.

Now we're generating images. This is like producing television pictures except it's not just red, green and blue colors like you'd see on your TV. This is going to be multispectral data, many more bits of information than a regular color television signal. And we don't want this in the Computer Center, we want this in the laboratories and in people's offices so they can study the results. So this has forced us into looking at supporting technologies in ATM networks and HPPI networks—it causes us to become somewhat expert in the intricacies of those networking technologies. And also we must delve into the details of parallel processing—how to make these codes use those huge numbers of processors efficiently and coordinate together, over the network.

This picture of a tank is an example of a medium-resolution vehicle that we will be incorporating in one of the simulations. In fact, we will probably be using much higher resolution vehicles than this, but I want you to take note that every pad, every rubber pad on the track is modeled, every pin that holds the track together is modeled, every hydraulic line, every electrical line inside that vehicle is there. You can see some of that in the figure. We've stripped the armor away here so that it is more interesting to look at, and you get a sense of the detail inside. This is not the highest level of resolution modeling that we do; this is almost 12 years old now, but I had to use old stuff that is unclassified, so I could show it to you today.

Tank simulation: medium resolution.

Of course, the whole problem is that military systems aren't just one vehicle. We don't have just one tank fighting itself. There's lots of vehicles involved, lots of men involved trying to work together as a team. This figure shows an example of a Corps Command Post study that was done several years ago. We have a whole gaggle of trucks pulled together to form a temporary Command Post. And the purpose of this study was to see what would happen if an artillery round exploded nearby—whether that would damage one of the vehicles—and the impact it would have on the functioning of the Command Post.

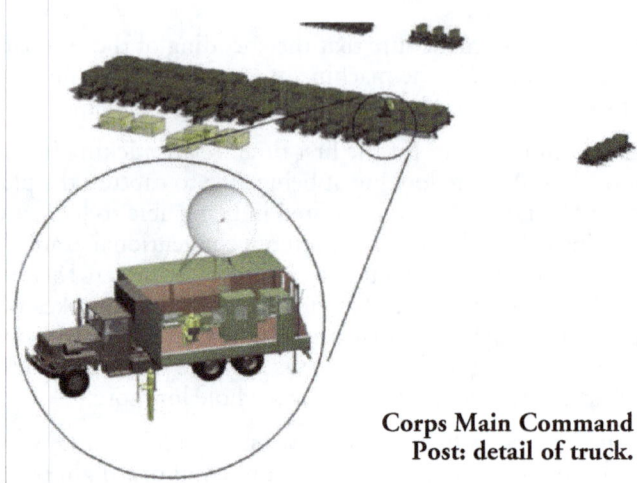

Corps Main Command Post: detail of truck.

But again, the quantity of detail that we are wrestling with is just staggering. This figure includes a blowup here of just one of those trucks, and you can see inside. The men are there, and the equipment racks are there. Inside each rack of equipment there are circuit cards, and on the circuit cards there are circuits, and there are wires connecting the circuit cards together! And all those things are modeled.

The figure [below] shows one frame out of a video that shows part of the prototype work we've done to justify going forward with this project. You can see a ground view of a piece of Fort Hunter-Liggett in California, and you can see on the ground the 1-m^2 patches. If you look very carefully, you can see a kind of a rectangular pattern on the ground. That's actually the 1-m measurements that we got off the satellite. So you can see the artifacts introduced by that measurement. We need better measurement of the terrain. You can also see my trees, the *virtual trees* there, which have the *virtual leaves* on them, and they cast shadows that are very realistic. This does not look much like a cartoon. And this is just the prototype.

Model of terrain at Fort Hunter-Liggett.

In the next figure [opposite], you can see what we call the "steps of Hunter-Liggett." Of course, it's not really like that—it's smooth, but there's a quantitization error in the measurement by the satellite, and so you can see the ground going along smoothly and then jumping up and then going along smoothly and then jumping up again. Since that's the way the data comes to us, we displayed it that way here. The interesting part of this is in the lower right hand corner. It's a little hard to see, but there's a shadow of a Tomahawk missile there. This

simulation was actually done for a Tomahawk missile flying in Fort Hunter-Liggett. Hopefully, there will never be any missiles flying there, but we just let it loose in the simulation to see what it would look like. And in particular, it's afternoon and the sun is setting in the west, and so the missile is casting a shadow down on the ground, and our simulation predicted that correctly. We didn't go paint the shadow in; we didn't have anybody plan that in advance; it just turned out that the missile was flying east, the sun was in the west, and the shadow turned up in the field of view.

Terrain model showing quantization error ("steps").

Now, if you're designing the sensor system that goes on the nose-cone of the missile, looking for military targets is your job. So you build a machine that looks for military targets. Well, if you're a missile, and you see your own shadow, you say, "Ah ha, I see a military target. There's a missile right there. I think I'll blow it up." And the missile does a good dive and blows your shadow up! [laughter] This is not the correct functioning of that weapon.

So we need to be able to provide those guys with the accurate shadows of their missiles and their other weapon platforms. And that is just one of the many little details that our simulations get correctly because we do the physics correctly.

One of the things I want to point out: most of you are familiar with the very high-quality television pictures you get in your homes now, especially if you have cable TV. The picture looks really good. Well, the television cameras we're giving our soldiers these days, in particular their night sights or FLIRs, the forward-looking infrared systems, have better picture quality than your television set, by quite a bit. And if we're going to simulate how those things work, that means we have to produce pictures of better quality than you would put on a television set. And that's really, really hard. If you look at "Toy Story" made just recently in the theaters, they had to labor very hard to make a clearly cartoon-looking movie. "Toy Story" is a very entertaining movie, but it was a lot of work for them to come up with those pictures.

We need to be able to come up with something that soldiers can pretty much believe is real. They'll know it's not real—we're not going to be quite that good for a while—but they need to be able to *believe* they are real, and we need to start studying how things are going to respond in that environment.

There's a whole bunch of input data that goes into this:

- Highly detailed terrain (≤1 m spacing)
- Highly detailed target geometry (1-cm features)
- Highly detailed trees and vegetation
- Highly detailed target signature modeling (spectral BRDF[16]/absorption/emission data)
- Highly detailed nano-meteorology model
- 1-nm atmosphere reflection/absorption/emission model
- Sensor response, modulation transfer function (MTF)

[16] Bidirectional reflectance distribution function: a mathematical formula describing how a surface reflects light as a function of incident and view angles.

In addition to all the equations that we have to describe for the computer, we have to find a huge amount of data. So this is research in the traditional library sense. I've been running around talking to people who measure bidirectional reflection functions, who measure terrain, and who measure numerous shapes, collecting all this input.

After taking all those words and putting them into a picture, the situation looks more like this [below]. We need to have *virtual terrain* for things to sit on—I've been talking about the satellite measurements for that. We need a collection of targets, and we have an excellent library already. You've seen a few examples of the simulated vegetation, trees, grass, shrubbery, and so on. Energy is being provided primarily by the sun, but could also be provided by flares, fires, and things burning in the battlefield, and it has to transport from the source down through to the target that's being illuminated. And there might be clouds in the way! Those might be water clouds like you see in the sky, or those might be military obscurant clouds trying to conceal something. Once the energy gets to the target, it has to bounce off, go back maybe through some more smoke, maybe exhaust smoke or maybe some more military smoke. And finally, it gets to a sensor array, which I've drawn as a little eye in the sky there.

And that sensor array has a two-dimensional grid of pixels on it looking into the scene. And for each one of those pixels, we have to make a measurement of the energy coming in. But that's not the end of it. Once we know how much energy is impinging on the sensor, the sensors themselves have a characteristic transfer function, which describes how they take the energy and make a picture. If you are familiar with a camcorder, you know you usually have a contrast knob or a gain knob or some color knobs that you can twiddle. Well, the soldiers operating the military sensors have that same set of knobs inside the

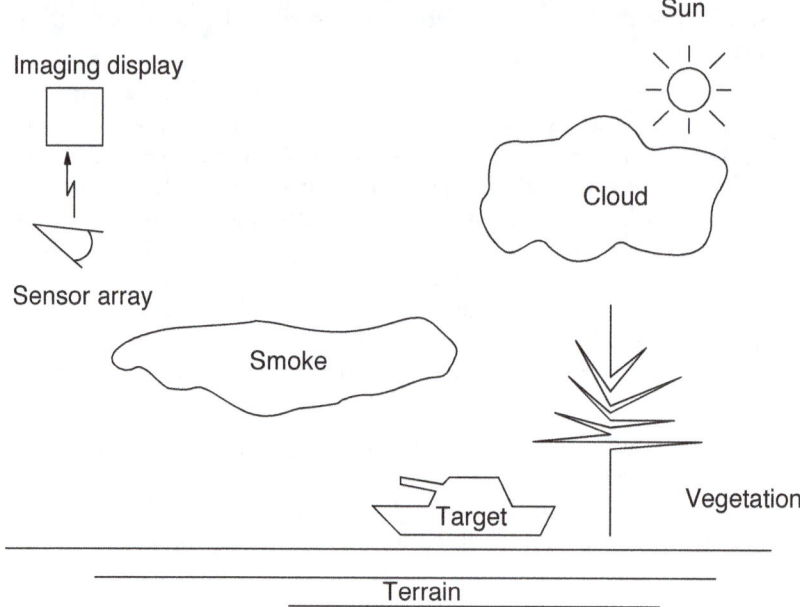

transfer function controlling the display they get to look at. So we have to model all of that as well.

At the start of my talk, I used the word "multi-spectral." And I haven't really defined that yet, other than to allude to the fact that we look at ultraviolet and other frequencies. On the sensor array, which is this two-dimensional array of pixels or picture elements, each one of those pixels has a waveform coming in on it, which is a plot of energy versus frequency. And what you see here is the plot of that energy versus frequency function for one pixel in a sensor. The units on the y axis are in milliwatts per centimeter squared—so they are physically based units; the x axis is wavelengths in microns. And the range goes from ultraviolet, on the left—in a fraction of microns—all the way through optical infrared up to 12 μm, which is about the border of the high IR. So for every pixel on the screen, we have to make a highly accurate plot like that.

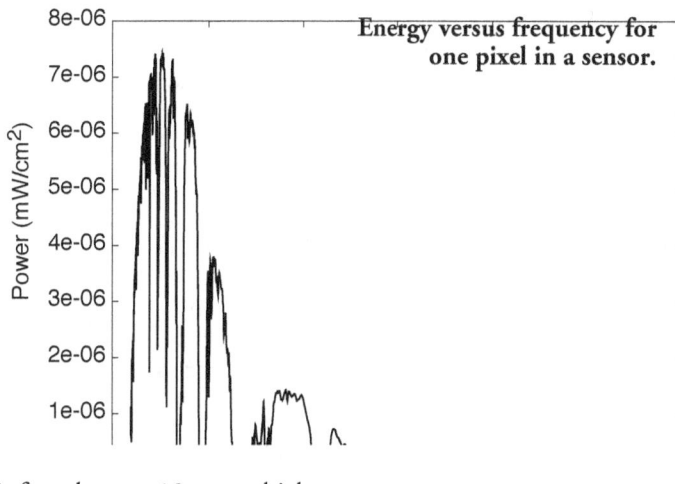

This figure is a model of a tank being observed through a very realistic-looking cloud of smoke, and Lee Butler, who is in the back running the sound for me right now, is in fact the leader of our "smoke and mirrors" working group, which has been working very hard to take all the knowledge acquired over the years in modeling smoke and atmospheric effects, and put it into the computer. So for the first time, we can take these very good atmospheric simulations and merge them with our sensor simulations and weapons simulations, and produce these accurate images for the soldiers.

Model of tank in smoke.

Energy transport through the atmosphere is a difficult problem [right]. In addition to the transmission and absorption in a straight line, you have in-scattering and out-scattering when the energy from the target hits a dust particle or something, and doesn't make it to your camera. And finally, there is emission itself—the air itself puts a little bit of energy in and distorts the image as a result. All those effects have to be modeled.

In the next figure [opposite page] you can notice that the distant mountains are blue, whereas the foreground is not. And that has not been hand-painted in by some artist. This is because we are beginning to get the correct atmospheric processing built into the simulation, so that the mountains just turn blue because that's what happens to distant mountains. That's the physics of light moving through earth's atmosphere, not because we're cartoonists painting on things.

Energy transport: basic sensor scenario.

We're actually building this in a very careful manner, just like electronics are built with back planes and circuit cards that plug into those back planes. I visualize what we're doing here, in software, the same way. We're coming up with a software simulation back plane. It's going to have standardized connectors on it—software connectors if you will—where you can plug in special cards, where these cards are going to be the synthetic image generators, the atmosphere models, the countermeasures models, which are very important to the soldiers and so forth.

The whole business of creating virtual realities and wandering around in them is really fun. And I enjoy it just for that, but we need to never lose sight of the fact that we are doing this to help our soldiers get better equipment, and to train them better to do their jobs.

And there are lots of different ways that a tool like this, a virtual reality tool like this, can be applied:

- Better materiel.
- Better data for "weaponeering."
- Intelligence: the image analyst's workbench.
- Training: give soldiers physics-based simulators—especially smoke, chem/bio, countermeasures. Within five years, hardware will be cheap enough.

Because we are part of AMC, which builds equipment for the soldiers, our primary job is, in fact, to help make better equipment, to help assess the vulnerability and the quality of the equipment, to see how it's going to work, and so forth. But this is a general-purpose tool. It could be applied to just about anything. And in particular, right now soldiers don't have much of an opportunity to train with smoke. We give them smoke grenades and smoke launchers and

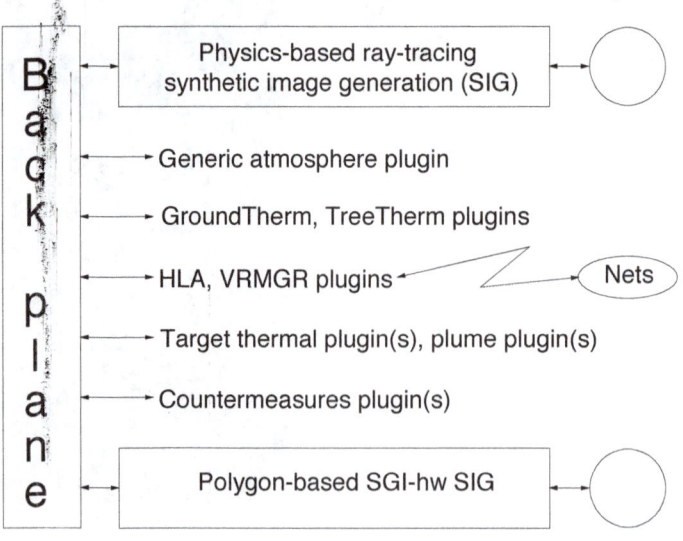

Software simulation back plane.

Simulation showing effect of distance on color (compare background and foreground).

smoke generators and things like that, and they can take them out in the valley at Fort Knox or someplace, and make smoke and see how it works. But they really don't get a chance to see what it's like on a dewy morning versus a sunny afternoon. There is just not enough money, or enough time in the day, to train soldiers in all these different circumstances. When we can make this kind of simulator cheap enough to give to soldiers while they are training, they can start playing "what if" games and say, "What would happen if I used this particular kind of smoke in this way in this circumstance?" And within five years, I think the hardware will be cheap enough that we can start training soldiers with the technology we are building today. But today, it's still a high-performance computing issue. It's a "grand challenge" problem, merging atmospherics with targets and terrain modeling and so on. This is one of the hardest computational problems in the world, and we are trying to do it here.

I'd like to acknowledge the help of my collaborators at the Army CECOM (Communications and Electronics Command) Night Vision Lab, for their support and assistance in this. They have been full and equal partners with ARL in pursuit with this project. I would also like to acknowledge a little corporate activity here in Aberdeen, by Geometric Solutions, Inc., which has been participating in this effort as well.

So with that, hopefully I've shared with you an idea of virtual reality, not as seen in the television show VR5 and some of the other cheesy things you see on television, but real physics-based virtual reality, to make better equipment for the soldier and to train our soldiers better. Thank you very much for your attention. [applause]

Presenter Biographies

Adams, Armand

Armand Adams worked at the Frankford Arsenal from 1942 to 1952, when he left to found his own company. He later worked for Sperry Rand Corp. from 1957 until he retired.

Antonelli, Kathleen McNulty Mauchly

Kay McNulty was one of the early Moore School "computers" and one of the initial six selected as the first ENIAC programmers. She moved to Aberdeen Proving Ground with ENIAC in 1947 but returned to Philadelphia in 1948 to marry John Mauchly.

Barkuloo, William

Bill Barkuloo held a variety of positions at BRL from 1951 until his retirement in 1985, working on every major computing system at the lab from ENIAC through the HEP. From 1985 until 1991, Barkuloo worked at Systems Support Agency, Inc., for whom he installed BRL's XMP/48 and consulted on the Cray-2 installation. Since 1991, he has been under contract with the Lab, preparing for the DoD/ARL Major Shared Resource Center.

Bartik, Betty Jean Jennings

Betty Jean Bartik was one of the first five programmers of the ENIAC. She started at the Aberdeen Proving Ground in 1945, working on many of the firing table calculations and on the UNIVAC. After a year at APG, she joined the Eckert-Mauchly Computer Company.

Bergin, Thomas J.

Tim Bergin is a professor in the Department of Computer Science and Information Systems at the American University. He serves as an Assistant Editor-in-Chief of *The IEEE Annals of the History of Computing*. He co-edited *The History of Programming Languages* (ACM Press and Addison-Wesley, 1996), and he chaired both the "Pioneer Day Retrospective Program" and the History Track at the 1996 ACM Computer Science Conference in February 1996. In his spare time, he serves as the Curator for the History of Computing Museum at American University.

Breaux, Harold

Harold Breaux joined BRL in the early 1960s and is noted for applying mathematical techniques to ballistic problems. He has made many contributions to the acquisition of computers and networking capabilities for ARL, the Army, and DoD, serving as chief of the High-Performance Computing (HPC) Division and Army Lead on the DoD HPC Working Group that created the HPC Modernization Program. In that role, he helped develop DoD's "shared access" policies that enable science and technology researchers in the Army, Navy, and Air Force to share supercomputers and networking.

Butler, Lila Todd

Lila Todd joined BRL in 1942 to work in the Firing Tables Section. Major Gillon sent her to Philadelphia to supervise a section of mathematicians at the Moore School, and she returned to Aberdeen Proving Ground in 1945. In 1951, she was assigned to work on ENIAC, and she went on to serve as a programmer for EDVAC, ORDVAC, and BRLESC I, playing a significant role in the development and use of FORAST software for BRLESC I.

Deitz, Paul Hamilton

Paul Deitz joined BRL in 1964, working in the area of air turbulence and its effects on optical propagation. He became chief of the Vulnerability Lethality Division in 1990 and is now chief of the Ballistic Vulnerability/Lethality Division of the Survivability/Lethality Assessment Directorate of ARL. Recently, he served on the Senior Scientific Advisory Committee during the DoD High-Performance Computing Major Shared Resource Center procurement action.

Dykstra, Phillip C.

Phil Dykstra joined BRL in 1985, working in such areas as Unix system development, networking, image processing, computer-aided design, scalable computing, and scientific visualization. He serves as the Army representative for networking on the High-Performance Computing Modernization Program (HPCMP) and chairs the Engineering and Operations Working Group of the Federal Networking Council (FNC). Currently, Dykstra is head of the Advanced Development Team in the High-Performance Computing Division.

Eichelberger, Robert J.

Robert Eichelberger retired as director of BRL in 1986, having served in that position since 1969. His technical achievements include work in detonation physics, combustion, high-speed and high-pressure fluid dynamics, and development of computer models and systems engineering. Eichelberger strongly supported BRL's acquisition of the Army's first supercomputers.

Ellis, Carol

Carol Ellis began her federal career at BRL in 1978. Her background in computer science drew her, in 1991, to join the descendant organization evolved from the Computing Lab of the ENIAC days. A participant in the DoD High-Performance Computing Modernization program from its inception in 1992, she has been involved in building program goals and strategies, and in source selection for the four major computing centers created under the modernization effort.

Fritz, W. Barkley

Barkley Fritz worked at BRL from 1948 until 1955 as an ENIAC programmer, a numerical analyst, and as ENIAC branch chief. He held a number of jobs in industry before joining the Computer and Information Sciences Department at the University of Delaware. During his retirement, Fritz has written and lectured extensively on early developments in computing.

Giese, John H.

John Giese joined BRL in 1946 as a mathematician. He later served as chief of BRL's Computing Lab from 1959 to 1968 and as chief of the Applied Mathematics Division from 1968 to 1974. He retired in 1974.

Goldstine, Herman Heine

See biography, Special Honors (p 5, this volume).

Gregory, John G.

John Gregory started his career at BRL by monitoring vacuum tubes on ENIAC. Then he supervised putting EDVAC into operation and, later, supervised the design, development, and operation of BRLESC I. After he left BRL in the early 1960s, Gregory worked on SOLOMON, an early parallel computer design. Earlier this year, he retired from Westinghouse. He is active in the Institute of Electrical and Electronics Engineers (IEEE) and the Aerospace Electronics Systems Society (AESS).

Holberton, Frances Elizabeth (Betty) Snyder

One of the original six programmers, Betty Snyder joined the computing unit at Moore School in 1942. She moved with ENIAC to Aberdeen Proving Ground early in 1947, only to return to Philadelphia later that year to work for the Eckert-Mauchly Electronic Control Company. She devised the first "sort-merge generator," and she has been credited with developing much of the software for UNIVAC. In 1950, she married John Holberton, himself a major computer pioneer. Betty Holberton worked at Remington-Rand before joining the David Taylor Model Basin and, later, the National Bureau of Standards (NBS). She played a major role in the evolution of COBOL, helping to monitor and control its standardization.

Howell, Kay

Kay Howell has been involved in the DoD High-Performance Computing Modernization Program from its start. Originally from the Naval Research Laboratory, Kay now serves as the Modernization Program Manager.

Huskey, Harry D.

Harry Huskey joined the ENIAC team in 1944, working first on the punched card input/output equipment, and then on preparation of manuals and drawings to explain operations and procedures. In 1947, he went to England and worked with Alan M. Turing at the National Physical Laboratory. In 1948, he returned to this country, joining the National Bureau of Standards and moving to California to the Institute for Numerical Analysis. At NBS, he was involved in designing both the SEAC (Standards Electronic Automatic Computer) and the SWAC (Standards Western Automatic Computer). For many years, he was a professor at the University of California (Electrical Engineering, then Computer and Information Science), first at Berkeley and then at Santa Cruz.

Kimsey, Kent

Kent Kimsey has had over 20 years of experience in modeling the behavior of materials and structures subjected to intense impulsive loading. He is currently serving in the Modernization Program as the Computational Technology Area Leader for Structural Mechanics.

Lyons, John W.

Director of the Army Research Laboratory from 1993 to 1998, John Lyons is a chemist by training. He joined the National Bureau of Standards (now the National Institute of Standards and Technology, NIST) in 1973; he became the Director of NIST in 1990. He is a Fellow of the American Association for the Advancement of Science and of the Washington Academy of Science.

Merritt, Donald F.

Don Merritt has worked at BRL/ARL since 1961, first as a co-op student and then as an electronics engineer and computer engineer. He contributed to the design and construction of both BRLESC I and BRLESC II and later worked on BRL's first Unix machines and the BRL Gateway machines. He currently is involved with high-speed networking.

Moye, William T.

Bill Moye was the Historian for ARL and its predecessor organizations from October 1985 to February 1999, joining the U.S. Army Laboratory Command (LABCOM) on the day it was activated. Before that, Moye was at the U.S. Department of Labor, with special focus on the Bureau of Labor Statistics.

Muuss, Michael John

Mike Muuss has worked at BRL since his college years at Johns Hopkins, and since 1981 he has been leading ARL's Advanced Computer Systems Team. He made substantial contributions to the early development of the Unix operating system and to the TCP/IP network protocols; he was the architect of BRL-CAD, the Army's third-generation constructive solid geometry CAD system; and he was the architect for both processing and communications within the Army Supercomputer Network, which has now grown into the DoD-wide D-REN network.

Nietubicz, Charles J.

Charles J. Nietubicz has 25 years of experience in basic and applied research, focusing on experimental and computational aerodynamics. He is currently Chief of the High-Performance Computing Division of ARL and also serves as Center Director of ARL's Major Shared Resource Center, created under the DoD High-Performance Computing Modernization Program.

Reed, Harry L., Jr.

Harry Reed started out at BRL in 1950 as a mathematician working on ENIAC. Reed continued at BRL until his retirement in 1987 (except for about two years at the Department of the Army), completing his career as chief of the Systems Engineering and Concepts Analysis Division. In the 1980s, he oversaw acquisition of two Cray supercomputers for the lab.

Reitwiesner, Homé McAllister

Homé McAllister reported to work at BRL in 1946, to do hand computing for firing tables. The next year, she transferred to the ENIAC, where she worked with Richard F. Clippinger and others. Later, she worked on both the EDVAC and the ORDVAC before leaving in 1955. In 1951, she married George Reitwiesner, another of the pioneers.

Reschly, Robert J., Jr.

With more than 10 years of networking experience, Bob Reschly is a primary architect of the Army Supercomputer Network, designer and technical lead for the Interim Defense Research and Engineering Network, and most recently served as Project Manager for Networking for the Modernization Program.

Romanelli, Michael J.

Mike Romanelli retired from BRL in 1979 after serving as chief of the Computer Support Division. Romanelli started at BRL in 1950 as a mathematician working on ENIAC and later worked as a programmer for EDVAC, ORDVAC, and both BRLESC I and II. In addition, he helped prepare specifications for the acquisition and installation of BRL's IBM 1401, EAI 690 Hybrid, and CDC Cyber 7600.

Smith, Jill H.

Jill Smith has worked for the Army (BRL/ARL) for 20 years and is currently Deputy Director, Survivability/Lethality Analysis Directorate. Smith was project manager of the LABNET Program to network all the laboratories within the Laboratory Command (LABCOM), was both member and chair of the AMC Functional Coordinating Group for Supercomputing, and was the initiator and project leader of the Army Supercomputer Network (ASNET) until it transitioned to PM Supercomputer.

Weik, Martin H.

At BRL, Marty Weik worked on the ENIAC, EDVAC, and ORDVAC. In addition, Weik conducted three surveys of U.S. electronic digital computing systems, assembling the characteristics of the early computers. His "computer tree" appeared in Karl Kempf's historical monograph in 1961. After BRL, he worked at the Department of the Army on the major information programs.

Weinacht, Paul

Paul Weinacht has 14 years experience as an aerospace engineer. He is an expert computational technologist in the area of fluid dynamics, specifically, the behavior of kinetic energy ammunition.

Woodward, Viola

Vi Woodward worked at BRL for many years. In 1974, she was identified as one of only four members of the ENIAC team still employed at BRL, the other three being Lila Butler, Mike Romanelli, and Clyde ("Skeet") Hauff.

Appendix.
February 18, 1996:
ACM History Track Panel

Appendix. ACM History Track Panel: The Army, the National Need, and the ENIAC

This panel took place on Sunday, February 18, 1996, as part of the History Track for the 1996 Association for Computing Machinery's Computer Science Conference. Since the ACM Conference did not publish proceedings, we decided to include it in this volume, since this panel was really the genesis for "50 Years of Army Computing, from ENIAC to MSRC," the anniversary celebration at Aberdeen on November 13 and 14, 1996.

Paul Deitz:

I'd like to welcome you to this next history track session. The title is "The Army, the National Need, and the ENIAC." In the off-chance that you were meant to be somewhere else, I'm glad you made a mistake. I think you will be happy you stayed here.

My name is Paul Deitz. I'm with the U.S. Army Research Laboratory at the Aberdeen Proving Ground. The particular element that I am with changed its name from the Ballistic Research Laboratory, or BRL, to the Army Research Laboratory about three years ago. The history of the ENIAC is a chapter in the history of computing for the U.S. Army and in particular for the U.S. Army Ballistic Research Laboratory at Aberdeen Proving Ground, Maryland.

But before going further, I want to express my personal thanks, and also the thanks of the U.S. Army, to the ACM for creating this session for us. For those of you who had looked at the early advertisements for these meetings and the History Track, this session wasn't there, and then magically, it appeared in the final publication. I am very much indebted to various members of the ACM: Bert Herzog,[1] Diane Martin,[2] Frank Friedman,[3] and particularly Tim Bergin who is sitting here in front.[4] Tim is going to be giving us a few words at the end of this session, but it was through his energy, foresight, and openness that we have a chance to tell our story here.

BRL actually came into existence in 1938, and before we start the session, I want to mention the business of firing tables. The problem of putting ordnance on targets was the reason that the Aberdeen Proving Ground was actually established. Mathematicians as well as experimentalists were working at the Proving Ground during the early '20s and early '30s, and in 1938, BRL was established.

The first Executive Officer for the Ballistic Research Laboratory was Colonel Paul Gillon. Colonel Gillon was very much involved with the problem of supporting mathematics and the preparation of firing tables. He became very instrumental in the story that you are going to hear unfolding later on today. Colonel Gillon was the Executive Officer for the Ballistic Research Laboratories, and did much of the work in establishing the liaison between the Ballistic Research Laboratory and the Moore School of Engineering.

Colonel Gillon was, in fact, invited to this conference, but just a few weeks ago, Colonel Gillon died at the age of 88. We mourn his loss, and we are very privileged today to have two of his children in the audience: Brendan and Theresa Gillon Heine. We are very grateful to have them here. [applause] I ought to mention that Mr. Nicholas Vonneumann, brother of John von Neumann, has also joined us today. [applause]

[1] Dr. Bertram Herzog is a Professor of Computer Science at the University of Michigan and served as the Chair of the ACM 50th Anniversary Committee.

[2] Dr. Diane Martin is a Professor of Computer Science at George Washington University and served as Special Events Chair of the ACM 50th Celebration.

[3] Dr. Frank Friedman is Professor of Computer Science at Temple University and served as Chair of the ACM Computing Week Steering Committee.

[4] Dr. Thomas J. Bergin (see Presenter Biographies, p 136, this volume) served as Chair of the History Track for the ACM Computer Science Conference and as Chair of the Retrospective Program for ACM Computing Week.

Colonel Gillon's work was very significant in the story that our first presenter is going to bring, and I am happy that you will see pictures [in front of the room] of all these people, including Colonel Gillon.

Our first speaker is Dr. Herman Goldstine. Dr. Goldstine earned three degrees in mathematics from the University of Chicago in the 1930s. He, at that time, had already interacted with some professors who were interested in ballistics; I think he had a love for ballistics, and of course things employment-wise were a little lean in the late '30s. He was doing some teaching at the University and like many individuals was in the Army Reserves. And in 1942, events were in motion, and he was called to active duty. So I suppose you could say in today's lingo that he was given an opportunity to "be all he could be!" And Dr. Goldstine, by pulling some strings, managed to get assigned to the Ballistic Research Laboratory at Aberdeen in 1942. After six months, Colonel Gillon assigned Lieutenant Goldstine to Philadelphia to establish a firing tables group at the University of Pennsylvania. It was out of that environment that the ENIAC ideas and programs sprang.

Dr. Goldstine has gone on to great things. He has had tremendous interactions with lots of folks, including John von Neumann, and I think we will hear more about him later. Later, Dr. Goldstine went to the Institute for Advanced Study, in Princeton. After the session, you might ask him about his great story about getting a traffic ticket while speeding to Albert Einstein's house to deliver a birthday present of a hi-fi system that he and some friends built.

Then Herman went to work for IBM, where he had various influential positions, including Chief Scientist. And now as he is approaching the prime of his career, he is back in Philadelphia, where he is Executive Officer of the American Philosophical Society. We are very much honored to have Dr. Goldstine with us today.

Herman Goldstine:

It is very kind of you to have me come. I hope my talk is not going to be too boring. I am perfectly willing to have you interrupt me with questions or challenges.

A description of my own experience might perhaps serve to introduce the ENIAC project. I obtained my Ph.D. at the University of Chicago in 1936, and then for a number of years was a research assistant at the Mathematics Department, teaching (among other things) a course in exterior ballistics. Thus, when I was called into the Service, I was assigned to the Aberdeen Proving Ground Ballistic Research Laboratory. I reported for duty on 7 August 1942. I was a First Lieutenant and assigned at once to Colonel Gillon, a regular Army officer who had charge of all ballistic computations. In fact, it was he who coined the acronym ENIAC: *Electronic Numerical Integrator and Computer*. Since he died just a few days ago, I'd like to take this moment to recognize his great contribution to science. Not only did he have an influential role in the development of ENIAC, he was also influential in funding the IAS computer of von Neumann and me, and founded the Mathematics Department of the University of Wisconsin.

He was a great friend of applied mathematics. Someone at Aberdeen called him the "Grandfather of the Modern Computer," and I think that is a very apt title. On September 1, 1942, Gillon and I went to inspect the small activity that the Laboratory had at the University of Pennsylvania's Moore School of Electrical Engineering. We found things there in a not very good state. I was placed in charge of the entire operation in Philadelphia and proceeded to make it operational.

Dean Pender of the Moore School had assigned the task of liaison with ordnance to John Grist Brainerd, who was then a professor in the Moore School and was later to be Director. Brainerd was perhaps the best qualified member of the faculty for this purpose. He combined a considerable interest in computation with substantial ability as a leader of men and a manager of affairs. He did an excellent job of handling this assignment, which was soon to occupy him full-time. At all times, it was a distinct pleasure for me to deal with this honest, kindly, and well-meaning gentleman. He undoubtedly deserves the credit for being the University's key man in the manifold relationships that were to be developed between it and Aberdeen.

Sometime in the fall of 1942, I first became acquainted with John W. Mauchly, who displayed considerable interest in Aberdeen's computing problems. He was both concerned about the technology of computing machines and the usage of them to do statistical weather predictions. His concern with these applications did not materialize in the usual way, and result in the production of papers on the subject. However, it did suffice to keep him thinking about machines to handle the underlying mathematical problems.

In 1941, Mauchly was so stimulated by his conversations with J. V. Atanasoff, a professor at Iowa State, that he was sketching in his laboratory notebook various emendations to the man's ideas. By August 1942, he had advanced his thinking enough to write a brief memorandum summarizing his ideas. This was circulated among his colleagues, and perhaps most importantly, to a young graduate student, J. Presper Eckert, Jr., who was undoubtedly the best electronics engineer in the Moore School. He immediately, as was his wont, immersed himself in the meager literature on counting circuits and rapidly became an expert in the field. This was to have inestimable import just a year later.

Barkley Fritz, Herman Goldstine, and Harry Reed at Philadelphia ACM Meeting.

Mauchly and I had frequent and mutually interesting conversations about computational matters during the fall of 1942. These talks served to emphasize Mauchly's point about the great gain in the speed of calculation if the devices used employed electronic data for the performance of the calculations, because the speed of such devices can be made very much higher than that of any mechanical device.

In March 1943, I indicated my considerable interest in all this to Brainerd, who made available Mauchly's ideas and his own judgement that they were not unreasonable. I then conferred on the problem at some length with Gillon, and we agreed on the desirability of the Ordnance Department underwriting a development program at the Moore School, looking for the ultimate production of an electronic digital computer for the Ballistic Research Laboratory.

Gillon, in his positive and enthusiastic way, pushed the matter forward with great celerity. There was some concern voiced over the large number of tubes the machine would contain—over 17,000. Some electronics experts expressed apprehension on this point. However, in spite of that, the work began on 31 May 1943, and a definitive contract was entered into on 5 June 1943.

To gain some rough measure of the magnitude of the risks, we should realize that the proposed machine turned out to contain over 17,000 vacuum tubes, of 16 different types, operating in a fundamental clock-ring of 100,000 pulses per second. This latter point means that the machine was a synchronous one, receiving its "heartbeat" from the clock, which would issue the signal every 10 μs. Thus, once every 10 μs an error would occur if a single one of the 17,000 tubes operated incorrectly. This means that in a single second, there were 1.7 billion chances of a failure occurring. In a day, which is equal to roughly 100,000 seconds, this is about $1.7 \infty 10^{14}$ chances.

In other words, the contemplated machine had to operate with a probability of malfunction of about one part in 10^{14}, in order for it to run for 12 hours without error. Man had never made an instrument capable of operating at this degree of fidelity or reliability. And this is why the undertaking was so risky, and the accomplishment so great.

Indeed, to this day, the computer represents man's most complex device. Man has never before or since produced a device where the probability of failure has to be so low, unless it be the space capsules with all their attendant computers. It has been said that, in addition to its 17,000 vacuum tubes, the ENIAC contained about 70,000 resistors, 10,000 capacitors, and 6,000 switches. It was 100 feet long, 10 feet high, and 3 feet deep. Its operation consumed 140 kW of power.

Above all others, the man who made it possible to achieve the almost incredible reliability needed for success was Eckert. He was the Chief Engineer and had Mauchly as his consultant. Eckert fully understood at the start, as perhaps none of his colleagues did, that the overall success of the project was to depend entirely on a totally new concept of component reliability and of utmost care in setting up criteria for everything from the quality of insulation to the types of tubes.

Eckert's standards were the highest, his energy almost limitless, his ingenuity remarkable, and his intelligence extraordinary. From start to finish, it was he who gave the project its integrity and assured its success. This is, of course, not to say that the ENIAC development was a one-man show. It was most certainly not, but it was Eckert's omnipresence that drove everything forward at whatever cost to humans, including himself.

It was stated in the ENIAC contract that the University, in cooperation with and under the direction of representatives of the Ballistic Research Laboratory, "shall engage in research and experimental work in connection with the development of an electronic numerical integrator and computer." The University agreed "to furnish copies of reports, and in the event that the contract results in the fabrication or completion of any part or unit, it shall be delivered to the government."

At the beginning, at least, Mauchly was to play a key role in the ENIAC project. He alone of the staff at the Moore School knew a lot about the design of standard electromechanical IBM machines of the period, and was able to suggest to the engineers how to handle various design problems by analogy to the methods used by IBM. Then, as time went on, his involvement decreased until it became merely one of writing up patent applications. Mauchly was at his absolute best during the early days, because his was a quick and restless mind best suited to probing problems of the moment.

There has been considerable controversy over exactly who invented the ENIAC and the follow-on EDVAC. In the first place, Eckert's contribution taken over the duration of the project exceeded all others. As Chief Engineer he was the mainstream of the entire mechanism. Mauchly's great contributions were the initial ideas, together with his large knowledge of how in principle to implement many aspects of the project.

Instead of my trying to summarize each person's contribution to what was, at least to me, a joint effort, let me just say that the senior engineers were Arthur Burks and Kite Sharpless, who somehow divided the overall systems responsibilities with each other, and with Eckert and Mauchly, who designed large pieces of the machine. The others were also important to the project, and not one of them could have been easily dispensed with. Their contributions were entirely noteworthy.[5]

Let me now introduce the person, who above all others had the greatest influence on the EDVAC, the Moore School's successor to the ENIAC and to all other computers, John von Neumann.

Let me just play you a small amount of tape:

> Mr. President and Mr. Chairman, President [...], Mr. Watson, Mrs. Watson, ladies and gentlemen. Thank you first of all for that very kind introduction. I don't know how to comment on it ...
>
> It seems that, when there is a new problem, you must resign yourself to solving it first a few dozen times the long way, before you gradually find out, by trial and error and by coming to grief, a reasonably good way. Consequently, one will simply not do it, unless one can make the individual test plan ...
>
> The last thing, which is very important, is said in fewer words, but I think it is nonetheless important, and this is this. In planning new computing machines, in fact in planning anything new, we are trying to enlarge the domain of time in which we can work. It is, of course, customary and very proper that one should consider what the demand is, what the price is, whether it would be more profitable to do it in a bold way than a cautious way, and so on. This type of consideration is necessary. The world would very

[5] According to Goldstine (1993, p 155), the engineering team, in addition to J. P. Eckert, consisted of Arthur Burks, Joseph Chedaker, Chuan Chu, James Cummings, John Davis, Harry Gail, Adele Goldstine, Harry Huskey, Hyman James, Edward Knobeloch, Robert Michael, Frank Mural, Kite Sharpless, and Robert Shaw.

quickly go to pieces if these rules were not observed …

It's very important that there should, however, be one decision in a hundred with some differences. And we will use the definition which Dr. Hazen pointed out 20 minutes ago, namely to occasionally do what the U.S. Navy did in this case, and what IBM accepted in this case, to draft a specification essentially to build the most powerful machine which is possible in this case with the present state of the art. I hope that this will be repeated very soon and will never be forgotten.

That was von Neumann giving a speech of introduction at a dedication for a machine called the NORC, which IBM built in the 1950s for the Navy.

Let me repeat it was his training in formal logic that made him very much interested in a result that foreshadowed the modern computer: this was the so-called *Turing machine*. Indeed, Alan Turing worked at Princeton under von Neumann's eye, on his fundamental paper.[6]

Von Neumann possessed, along with his other accomplishments, a truly remarkable ability to do very elaborate calculations in his head at lightning speeds. This was especially notable when he was making rough order of magnitude estimates, mentally, and would call upon an unbelievable wealth of physical constants he had available. His great interest in the application of mathematics was to become increasingly important, as time went on.

By 1941, it had become his dominant interest. This was to have the most profound implications for the computer field, in particular, and for the United States in general. The story used to be told about him in Princeton that, while he was indeed a demigod, he had made a detailed study of humans and could imitate them perfectly. Actually, he had great social presence, a very warm human personality, and a wonderful sense of humor. These qualities, together with his incredible mental capacity, made him a superb teacher.

Eugene Wigner,[7] a lifelong colleague of von Neumann and I, wrote this obituary of von Neumann: "No appraisal of von Neumann's contributions would be complete without a mention of the guidance and help which he so freely gave to his friends and acquaintances, both contemporary and younger than himself. There are well-known theoretical physicists who believe they have learned more from von Neumann in personal conversations than from any of their colleagues. They value what they learned from him, in the way of mathematical theories, but they value even more highly what they learned from him in methods of thinking and in ways of mathematical argument. With real justice, it can be said of him in the words of Landor,[8] 'He's warmed both hands before the fire of life.'"[9]

The contract between the University of Pennsylvania and the government was typical of research and development contracts of that period. As far as patents were concerned, the contractor had two options available to him. Either he could take out the patents and grant the government various royalty-free licenses, or the government would take over the task of patent preparation for him. In either case, Title 3 inventions will remain in the inventors' hands, and an appropriate license to the government would be executed.

Most universities in this era were quite naive about business matters, and the University of Pennsylvania was no exception. Its officials never bothered to consider how they were going to get their engineers to execute the appropriate

[6] Turing (1947).

[7] Eugene Paul Wigner was an naturalized American physicist, born in Budapest, Hungary, in 1902. He became a professor of mathematical physics at Princeton in 1938. Wigner worked with Enrico Fermi on producing the first nuclear chain reaction in 1942. Wigner developed many practical uses of atomic energy. He shared the 1963 Nobel prize in physics.

[8] Walter Savage Landor (1775–1864), English author.

[9] Goldstine and Wigner (1957), as reprinted in Goldstine (1993), p 177.

licenses that were required under the contract. The University of Pennsylvania had in those days a vague policy of permitting each employee who requested it all rights to his inventions. This was not an automatic procedure and required a petition by the employee to the Board of Trustees. There was much confusion in the Moore School as to who was entitled to be considered the inventor.

Now the problem of patents on the ENIAC, and then a little later on the EDVAC, was to have an explosive impact on the University of Pennsylvania. As far back as November 1944, Dean [Harold] Pender[10] was writing to George McClelland, then President of the University, asking for a clarification of the University's patent policy. Dr. McClelland responded that the Executive Committee had done nothing in this matter.

However, after much discussion, Eckert and Mauchly wrote to President McClelland asking for rights to the inventions made by them in the course of work. McClelland wrote them in March of 1945, granting them this right, waiving the University's right to a patent assignment with one stipulation: he provided that they grant the United States government a nonexclusive royalty-free license, and the university had the further right to sublicense any established eleemosynary institution to build and to use such devices for essentially noncommercial and nonprofit purposes.[11]

However, a month earlier, Eckert and Mauchly had assurances from President McClelland that he would act favorably. Most universities in this era were quite naive about business matters, and that's what caused the problem. Eckert and Mauchly hired an attorney to assist the Ordnance lawyers in preparing the necessary applications. As might be imagined, there was great heat generated over this entire question of patents. It served to place Eckert and Mauchly apart from the University and Moore School officials. And it created tensions between Pender and Brainerd, and finally between Eckert and Mauchly on the one hand, and Gillon, von Neumann, and me on the other.

The reasons for this last rift had to do with publicity and correctness. Gillon and I were very anxious to declassify ENIAC and EDVAC and to give wide publicity through the scientific community. We did not, however, want to hurt Eckert and Mauchly in the process.

Thus, in November of 1945, Gillon and I were corresponding on this subject. Gillon wrote, "On the protection of Eckert and Mauchly, how much time do they require to file? And how will that change our present publicity plans?" Eckert was loath to have any publicity until he and Mauchly had filed their patent applications. Indeed, Eckert "thinks we should say nothing ... but simply attend as auditors."[12]

A further exacerbation of this problem had to do with authorships. Both Eckert and Mauchly were much offended that Brainerd had been asked to write an NDRC [National Defense Research Council] report, and Mauchly was upset about the fact that Brainerd and Eckert had been originally invited to an MIT conference and he had not. While each of these crises was eventually smoothed over, each served to deepen the rift that was rapidly developing between Eckert and Mauchly on one side and Brainerd and Dean Pender on the other.

It should be said in connection with the above-mentioned grievances that Eckert and Mauchly felt, with some justice, that no one in the Moore School

[10] Harold Pender was the first Dean of the Moore School of Electrical Engineering, University of Pennsylvania.

[11] Letter, McClelland to Mauchly, 15 March 1945. This letter is the university's response to a request to Dean Pender from Eckert and Mauchly, dated 9 March 1945. See Goldstine (1993), p 222.

[12] Goldstine (1993), p 222.

administration had any deep technical understanding of the ENIAC or the EDVAC. There was truth in this. The way the Dean organized things, Brainerd was so deeply immersed in all the administrative details of the research commitments of the Moore School that he didn't have time or strength to follow in detail the ENIAC or EDVAC projects.

Indeed, the work of Burks,[13] Goldstine, and von Neumann in planning and coding have been viewed as seminal in the design of modern machines using "von Neumann" architecture.[14] Much of this latter work was included in the patents.

I don't want to go through the full discussion of the patents, which were fought out in a United States District Court in Minneapolis involving a Minneapolis corporation[15] and Sperry Rand, but in any event, the Court held that the patents were invalid. And it held so for a variety of reasons, which included not only the Atanasoff prior invention, but also various other facts, including, first, that not all the inventors were named in the patents, and that made them invalid. Second, that Eckert and Mauchly had attempted to offer for public sale a computer before they finished their patent application work. And there were a variety of other reasons why the patents were set aside.[16] At that, I'll leave the story. Thank you. [applause]

Deitz:

Thank you very much, Dr. Goldstine. Our next speaker is Barkley Fritz. Barkley Fritz is a Baltimore native, for those of you from those parts of the woods. He earned his bachelor of science degree from Loyola College and later a master's from Johns Hopkins that he is very proud of. His idea of what to do during the war was apparently to "join the Navy and see the world." There were two spots that he saw, and they were Iwo Jima and Okinawa, and I'm not sure he would have chosen to see those spots.

After the war, he came to BRL and was there from 1948 to 1955. He started programming the ENIAC and worked his way up to being Chief of the ENIAC Branch. He went on to other lives at Westinghouse, Sun Ship, and the University of Delaware in the Computer Science Department. We are happy to have Barkley Fritz with us today.

Barkley Fritz:

It's always a pleasure to be on the program with people like Herman Goldstine. I remember a couple of years ago—20 years ago—my being on a program with Pres Eckert. Pres spoke before I did, and a lot of the things I wanted to say had already been said. In fact, my feeling here today is that I'm personally kind of saturated with this whole thing. In fact, my own papers have been quoted, and that always makes me feel good.

Today, I'd like to direct my remarks towards the fact that 1940 to early 1950 was a time much different from the world today. Today, I want you to enter that work world that existed in 1941. In fact, I guess I could entitle my remarks today "Three Summer Jobs."

In 1941, I got a job; I was a kid at college, and it was for the summer, and I had just finished my freshman year. And I worked with the New Amsterdam Insurance Company, a now defunct organization like many others swallowed up by General Insurance and so on—American Insurance, I guess it is.

At any event, at that time, I learned IBM equipment. I learned to punch cards.

[13] For a comprehensive discussion of the ENIAC, see Burks and Burks (1981).

[14] See Burks, Goldstine, and von Neumann (1946). A copy of the second edition was provided to attendees.

[15] Honeywell Corporation.

[16] For an excellent discussion of the patent dispute, see Rosen (1990).

I hauled boxes of cards out of the basement, and prepared some actuary data for the insurance people. Those were the cards with those little funny rectangular holes. This was the data media—the way we stored data to be processed. That philosophy of doing things affected the design of ENIAC. ENIAC had a punched card input. It punched cards with its answers.

You could see in the lights—the demonstration the other day was pretty bad, I thought, because it didn't really bring back the flavor of ENIAC.[17] Many of you here, those with gray hair anyway, have seen ENIAC, and have seen it in operation—the way the lights kept flashing in the accumulators and how one could see how the results were going. You could see a trajectory moving.

It's not in my written paper, but one of the fun things that I did during the period of ENIAC was to explain ENIAC to the President of the United States, who came to BRL on February 19, 1951. He was making a tour, and all the generals were with him. After being oriented at the BRL conference room, he came into the ENIAC room when I was there and prepared. Homer Spence had spent the night trying to get the thing working. We were having problems, as we sometimes did. And ENIAC was performing beautifully. I mean the President was coming, and what's going to happen? Things are going to go great, and everything did. It was a beautiful demonstration. And I had the pleasure of spending about 10 minutes, one on one, with the President of the United States. I was in my 20s, and I was glad to be there at that time and to have had the opportunity to be a part of history.

That first summer job exposed me to one aspect of it. And what I had to learn, and what I did learn from that summer job with the insurance company, was exactly what the women programmers had to learn. I'm referring to the first six women who were the key people in the development and use of ENIAC in its early applications, and who worked with Nicholas Metropolis and Stan Frankel, who ran the nuclear computations.[18] And they worked with them, along with Mauchly and Eckert. There were six people working around the clock, two from Los Alamos, two from the design team, and two of the women who were helping, Betty Holberton[19] and Kay Mauchly.[20]

The important aspect of ENIAC, the part that I like to emphasize because I didn't have anything to do with the design, is the programming. I did have something to do with the use of ENIAC to solve problems—to do things when it was the only game in town. For five years, from 1946 to 1951, the ENIAC was the only electronic computer. It was a thousand times faster than the electromechanical Bell machines.[21] The development, in England, of the EDSAC probably snuck in during that time, but it wasn't available to the individuals in the U.S.[22]

People came from all over the country to see ENIAC, especially from the universities. Herman describes in his book quite well the attitude of the government, which was to make ENIAC available to everybody.

This was at a time when the feeling was, "How many of these do we need?" I mean, it was so fast, you could hardly keep it busy with some of the applications. For example, trajectories could be calculated faster than the projectile itself. So the question, "What are you going to do with all this speed?" was an important one.

Well, most of us were finding out about lots of problems in wind tunnel design, the solution of systems of differential equations, and some of the work that Dick Clippinger was doing for other labs at BRL and so on.[23] And we were

[17] On the morning of February 14, 1996, the University of Pennsylvania had a commemorative program during which a few units of the ENIAC were ceremoniously turned on by Vice President Albert Gore.

[18] Nicholas Constantine Metropolis and Stanley Phillips Frankel were two young theoretical physicists from the Theoretical Physics Division at Los Alamos. According to Goldstine (1993), p 214, "They were to have the honor of running the first problem on the ENIAC."

[19] Betty Holberton, one of the original six programmers selected for the ENIAC, was at this time known as Frances Elizabeth (Betty) Snyder. She went on to have a distinguished career in the private and public sectors.

[20] Kay Mauchly, one of the original six ENIAC programmers, was known at the time as Kathleen McNulty.

[21] Under the leadership and inspiration of George Stibitz, the Bell Laboratory constructed a number of relay-based calculators. The first of these, the *Complex Number Calculator*, was fully operational on January 8, 1940.

[22] Inspired by a summertime series of lectures at the Moore School, Maurice V. Wilkes returned to Cambridge University and started to design and build a computer, later called the EDSAC, for Electronic Delay Storage Automatic Computer. This machine was fully operational in May 1949.

feeling, doggone, we are going to need other computers! And maybe someone said at one time, that five would take care of everyone's needs but, you know, I think that those of us who were working with it realized that we had the problem of getting things moving faster. In other words, getting programs prepared to run on the computer more rapidly than it took with the old connecting cables. I'll quote myself. Barkley Fritz has said:

"Programming a problem for ENIAC by the original method involved taking the component parts of the ENIAC and designing a special-purpose computer out of those circuits and boards and accumulators and multipliers and so on, and creating a special computer out of those component parts to solve the problem."[24]

And that is almost what had to be done. It's as good an analogy as I can think of to present to you today.

Since I have abandoned my speech, I need to emphasize the importance of what the "five-year head start," as I call it, meant to the computer field at the time. During that five years, we learned—and I mean all the people who were involved with ENIAC, including the users from around the country—to use numerical analysis techniques that were in various texts, and that some wouldn't do the job anymore, and that we needed new techniques. ENIAC was so much faster than anything that ever existed that it caused us to rethink our approach to numerical analysis.

One last thought. In this period, the word *computer* was used to refer to the people who operated the Marchant, the Monroe, and Frieden desk calculators. Only later was a machine known as a "computer."

In a second summer employment, in 1942, I learned about engineering. I was a tracer for Martin Company. And the Martin Company was a designer that built sea planes. The U.S. Navy used sea planes. I was responsible for copying drawings and making small changes in the drawings. And I used a pen which you dipped in a bottle of India ink. I was a tracer. And that work gave me an appreciation, while I worked at Sun Ship and Westinghouse Electric, for having this all done automatically by a computer and the drawing done by a CalComp plotter.

In these two summer jobs, I got a chance to learn fields that were radically changed by the impact of computing—as a result of ENIAC and subsequent developments.

I think it is important to mention that ENIAC was never copied. It was great. If you're interested in women in computing, I have another paper coming out in the *Annals of the History of Computing* in April.[25] It didn't quite make it to the ENIAC issue,[26] but they decided it was more about women than it was about ENIAC and it's called "The Women of ENIAC."

The advertising for this meeting today showed a picture of 12 people, seven women, five men, who were employed at BRL in 1949. And we went to an ACM meeting in Oak Ridge, Tennessee. That was my entry into a professional society. George Reitwiesner was the only one who went officially; the rest of us took vacation time to go, because we felt it was good to get exposed to what was going on in this fast-growing field. By that time there were hundreds of people going to ACM meetings. We knew everybody, and practically everybody knew everybody else, because it was a small bunch.

[23] Richard Clippinger was the head of the Computing Laboratory at BRL at this time. He is credited, along with Adele Goldstine, with making the ENIAC into a stored-program computer by clever use of the function tables. See Goldstine (1993), pp 233–234.

[24] No specific reference is available; however, see Fritz (1994).

[25] Fritz (1996). This was in a special issue of *Annals* devoted to "Women in Computing" (vol. 18, No. 3).

[26] Volume 18, Number 1, *IEEE Annals of the History of Computing*, was a special issue devoted to "Documenting ENIAC's 50th Birthday."

My third summer job was after the war. I had finished a master's degree at Hopkins. I taught for a year at Loyola, and I spent two and a half years in the Navy, starting off as an enlisted man but having been smart enough to apply for a commission before I got drafted. I ended up getting to be in amphibious operations, and I ended up at the Navy Proving Ground at Dahlgren, Virginia, where I was exactly 50 years ago at the time ENIAC was being shown to the public. I was down at Dahlgren operating theodolites.[27]

Then I talked myself into the first summer job that BRL ever gave anybody. So I went to Dr. Dederick, head of BRL, and chatted with him for a few minutes and said, "I want to be a programmer." It's a good thing he didn't ask me what a programmer was, because I didn't know until after I had done it for a while how to define programming, and I'm still not really clear what a programmer should be described as.

[27] Surveyor's instruments for measuring horizontal and vertical angles.

My earlier paper discusses some 100 applications. And this was my whole point for doing this lecture. Fifty years later, ENIAC hasn't been given enough credit for doing a lot of useful stuff. And there were people from all over … everybody who was anybody that was interested or had important problems came to BRL to use ENIAC during that period. Even the President came to see what was going on.

I have a great paper here that I was going to read until Herman talked and I decided I am going to have trouble wading through it. So for those of you who came to hear me give my paper, you'll have to read it. But you got the gist of it. My Aberdeen summer. My three summer jobs. I decided to stay. They liked me, I guess.

Thank you all for coming today. I hope I have given you a little bit of the flavor of the times and the enthusiasm that I still share for the whole field of computing.

Paul Deitz:

Thank you very much, Barkley. If Dr. Goldstine stole a little of your thunder, I'm sure you wouldn't be the first person to whom that's happened. So don't feel bad. The four papers will be showing up in our World Wide Web site. We have a Web site in our research lab, which has virtually exploded in the last month, with lots of wonderful pictures and copies of papers and whatnot. For those of you who are able to surf electronically, we invite you to put on your scuba gear and surf on down.

Our third speaker is Mr. Harry Reed. Harry earned a bachelor of science degree from MIT in 1950 and later did some graduate work at Johns Hopkins. He started work at BRL in 1950, in the ENIAC Section, and Barkley Fritz was the gentleman who welcomed him aboard (kind of a mixed metaphor there). Some of his work in ENIAC programming was actually noted in the excellent article that Barkley Fritz advertised a while ago, and I encourage you to read his article. At the very end, he has a long list of major computer tasks that were done by the ENIAC.

Harry has had a long, prosperous career with the Ballistic Research Laboratory and retired a number of years ago, but not before he was involved in a rebirth of computing at BRL in terms of being a key person in the acquisition of the

Cray XMP48 and the Cray-2 and supporting the Bellcore parallel machine. We're very happy to have Harry Reed with us today.

Harry Reed:

I sort of thought the title for my talk should be something like "My Life with the ENIAC: A Worm's Eye View." I came to BRL in August of 1950, and I guess the first thing I learned was about bureaucracy. I showed up at Personnel, and they informed me that, "By golly, we don't have any form so-and-so available." They said, "Not to worry. Come back after lunch. Go and visit the Ordnance Museum. Everything is all right. You're being paid, so you don't have to worry about it." By the end of the day, I finally met Barkley, and as he pointed out, he said, "Welcome aboard," and I was a little taken aback, because I thought this was an Army installation, but apparently it wasn't.

I wanted to say a few words about how computing was at that time and how, to a certain extent, that would shape the nature of the ENIAC. Indeed, some of the traditions that came about during this period we tended to live with quite a while.

To understand ENIAC, of course, for those of you who don't know too much about it, think about it as a processor chip with 20 register positions. That was it. That was the RAM that you had available to you, and about half of those register positions were involved intimately in the various arithmetic operations and not available for general storage. You had the function tables, which contained 3000 decade (10-position) switches, that could be set ahead of time (like a read-only memory). And of course, you had cards for input and output, which were used for intermediate storage.

The ENIAC itself, strangely, was a very personal computer. Now we think of a personal computer as one which you carry around with you. The ENIAC was actually one that you kind of lived inside. And as Barkley pointed out, you could wander around inside it and watch the program being executed on lights, and you could see where the bullet was going—you could see if it happened to go below ground or went off into space or the wrong direction. So instead of your holding a computer, this computer held you.

Given its somewhat fragile nature, there was a sort of intimate contact with it. Probably one of the biggest problems we had was the IBM cards. The only rooms at BRL that were air-conditioned were those that were used for the handling and storage of IBM cards. Nothing else got air-conditioning, but those rooms did, because the IBM cards had a nasty habit of soaking up moisture, and the readers and printers that we had in those days were extremely intolerant of changes in the size of the cards.

Interestingly enough, about 50 years later, I find that some of our computer rooms have more problems associated with air-conditioning than they do with things associated with electronics.

Given the limited storage—extremely limited storage—on the ENIAC, things like the use of subroutines were just out of the question. There was no way that you could have a prewritten subroutine—that you could plop in—because you had nothing in the way of free space that you could use for local variables and/or stacks and/or things like that. So you might have a routine that you would embed in your program, making sure that it didn't interfere with other storage. In fact, you would usually replicate the subroutine, because you didn't have enough storage to put a return address to get back to where you were coming from. So it was easier just to put in the subroutine and then not have to worry about transferring back.

To give some idea of how crowded this thing could become, Barkley at one point asked me to program a guided missile for the General Electric Company. I said, "There is not enough room; there are too many variables." And he said "Oh, go do it anyway." So, it ended up we had to split the registers and store two things in each one of those, which added to our agony. We had to use all 3000 switches on the function tables, which at that time were being used for both program storage and for data storage. And just to make everything fit, we still had to write a special piece of *microcode*, if you want to call it that; we had to rewire a new instruction because we had to preserve one register and some of the transfer operations. So this was the kind of thing that you had to do, to get a program on the ENIAC.

Setting the programs up was something like a several-week job, writing the codes and figuring out how you were going to do it. Then you spent a couple of hours turning switches—depending on how many people you could draft to help do that process. And then you spent a certain amount of time in trying to figure out whether what you had done worked or not.

One of the few cases in which you actually fooled around with the wiring of the ENIAC was when you would pull the plug off the cable that sent the command to trigger the next instruction and then would walk around the computer with a little box and a button, and push the button and watch as the various numbers bounced around from place to place as you had programmed it.

ENIAC operation itself was done with a mathematician and an engineer on each of the 8-hour shifts, and you ran 24 hours. So you had a mathematician who was responsible for getting the program together, and who would go out and recruit two other mathematicians to supervise on the other shifts, and then you would run for 24 hours a day. It was a darn nuisance to set the program up too many times.

I might also mention that, as far as reliability was concerned, the ENIAC was rather remarkable. You hear lots of numbers about failure rates and so forth, but once you got the computer settled down, the computer had a habit of running for about a couple of weeks with no errors whatsoever. This is quite a remarkable achievement.

The whole thing had a certain amount of *bailing wire* in it. People talk about the "bailing wire days of aviation." Barkley was lucky I guess, or maybe he just tells the story that way. When he was with the President, he was able to show him a trajectory. Every year at springtime, the West Point graduating class would come down to the Proving Ground. They would visit all the various functions and get a demonstration of big guns firing. Among the things they came to see was the ENIAC. So you had this troop of cadets wandering through the room.

And when you had large groups of people wandering through the ENIAC room, things always went wrong. People always bumped cables and so forth and so on. So we would usually take out a deck of punched cards that contained some special diagnostic tests, and we would load these cards into the ENIAC and run those, because we won't have to worry about whether or not our results are any good. It was a great display, because these tests were constructed so that you could watch the numbers sort of flow through the registers in their patterns. So it reminded you of Times Square in New York, and you could diagnose what was going on in the computer.

So we would put these diagnostic tests on, and as I said, it sort of looked like Times Square. Then this escort officer would come in with these cadets, and he'd been briefed ahead of time. He would say, "Over there, you can see in this register that this is the velocity of a bullet, and you can see how it is moving …" None of this was true. It was just these tests going on. But we got away with it, and it did look good.

I wanted to spend the rest of my time talking about the big program for the ENIAC, which was firing table calculation. The ENIAC's basic construction, the number of registers and so forth, was quite well tailored to the problems associated with firing table calculations and in particular the calculation of trajectories.

Now, the basic problem in a firing table calculation is to calculate where the bullet is going. I've got this very simple-minded trajectory here. [see figure below] These are the kinds of things the ENIAC would calculate, for all sorts of angles, elevations, velocities. Then it would generate data about where the bullet was in space and, in particular, where it would hit the ground—which, of course, was the principal concern to most of the artillery officers at that time.

Of course, what you are getting is the wrong variables. You are getting the data for where the shell lands, given where you aimed the gun. What you really want is how to aim the gun so it will hit a specific target. That seems like an extremely simple problem for a computer today. If I worked on my PC, I obviously would have it record the data and go back through the interpolations, resort the data, and come out with what I want. Unfortunately though, it wasn't quite that simple with the ENIAC. You had no intermediate storage, so you had to take what you got out on IBM cards, and then if you were going to do something with these, you would have to resort them with a mechanical sorter, and then reprogram something on the switches so you could go back and get these new answers.

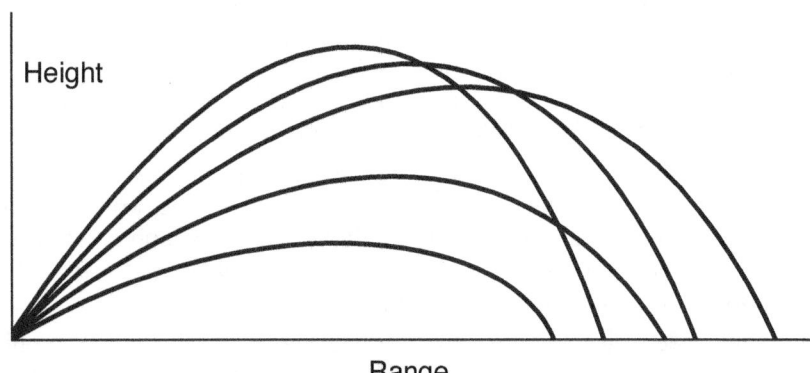

A simple set of trajectories.

Now, that actually was not all that hard to do. In fact, at one point Margery Fields from the Bombing Tables Branch was looking for some of this work, and Barkley shuffled me off on it. They wanted to do essentially the same thing for bombing tables. They wanted to generate the data for the people who designed the bomb sights rather than trajectory data. We went through quite an elaborate process of creating data and sorting it. (I thought I could qualify as a faro dealer in Las Vegas by the time I got done with the card shuffling that had to be done with this.) Essentially, we would take the punched cards, sort them, put them back, run them through rather elaborate fifth-order interpolations and smoothing processes, and generate the data.

The firing tables people were a bit more recalcitrant about that. This is a pair of pages from a firing table. This is a firing table for a 105-mm howitzer. It is just loaded with pages like that. And that's the kind of stuff we were generating.

Firing table for 105-mm howitzer.

Now people don't use these anymore. The data goes into computers that are embedded in the system, but they still print these things, because I think they ought to have them as a backup, or as a piece of history, I guess.

This contains a whole bunch of stuff starting with the *range*, the *elevation* you would shoot at, and a whole bunch of things that would tell you how you have to change things if the *wind* were blowing or if there were more *dense air* or whatever. The firing table people would take these data, and they would then perform an operation that they called "smoothing." Then they would start "differencing" all this, and create large sheets that they would write all this stuff on and then give it to a typist who would type all this stuff—and in fact, her grade was based on the fact that she went through this agony of typing these firing tables.

And I said, "Hey, I can do all that on the computer. I can even print it out for you." It wouldn't be great with an IBM tabulator, but it wouldn't be all that bad. And they said, "Oh no, no, you can't do that, because we have to smooth the data." I said, "I can smooth the data the way I did for the bombing tables people." "No," they said, "We have to do it our way." So I said, "Tell me what your way is." They said, "Well, it's hard to explain."

So I don't know whether it was sort of intellectual privacy or something they were dealing with, but they would look at me and say, "Gee, I think I better raise that number a bit or lower that number a bit." Now, nobody really cared, because anybody who thinks you can take too many of these numbers all that seriously is somewhat misled. [laughter]

But nevertheless, they did generate, among other things they called graphical firing tables, which were slide rules. And the people who made the slide rules had a terrible time if you gave them data that didn't have nice smooth higher differences. It just didn't work well when they tried to put in the graduations. But anyway, they went through this process, and it seemed terribly inefficient, although it did represent a certain trend in using the ENIAC.

Basically, the resource was extremely scarce. It was the only computer. It was busy; everybody wanted to use it—particularly after Herman and Adele[28] [Goldstine] and Clippinger[29] made it so you could set these switches and program it instead of doing all this wiring. So, what was usually done in the ENIAC was to take a high-intensity calculation problem and do that. And all the other stuff would then be relegated to other activities and to other people.

Well anyway, that all sort of persisted in the firing table business, until we came to the 280-mm atomic cannon. Once again, I think my friend Barkley said, "Hey, we need firing tables for the 280-mm atomic cannon, and there's a problem. The problem is that with atomic things, you have to burst them up in the air." And so all of a sudden, this one-dimensional table became a two-dimensional table, because I had to know where I would aim the bullet to hit each of these points up *here* [hands over his head]. And now I had a humongous human problem.

The firing people just sort of threw up their hands. What we essentially needed was something that would look like this [see below].

Every one of these pages represented a column on this sheet. So I was talking about a lot of calculations. So finally, the firing tables people had to give up. We did the calculations on the computer. We then took the data, played with various sorting games to do the double interpolations, did all the differential effects, took all the differences, and then I put a brand new ribbon in the IBM tabulator and put some nice bond paper in there instead of the usual stuff, and actually printed the firing tables. It was quite a dramatic experience for the folks. I don't think they ever felt that a computer could take over their business.

There was a tendency, particularly as I say with the ENIAC, to reduce the problem to something that would fit on the computer. Now when the human computers were calculating trajectories, they used very high-order numerical integration techniques, probably fourth- or fifth-order integration techniques at relatively large intervals. So, it was essentially a minimal computational problem, but unfortunately it was a fairly sizable memory problem. The ENIAC couldn't handle that. It didn't have the data storage necessary to do high-order integrations; it just couldn't "remember" the immediate results. What we had to do then was to revert back to a very simple trapezoidal integration, and, of course, then run the integration interval back so that we now had an adequate approximation to the problem. There was a good bit of that which went on.

[28] Adele Goldstine, Herman's wife, was one of the ENIAC team members; Adele wrote *Report on the ENIAC (Electronic Numerical Integrator and Computer) Technical Report 1* (of 2 vols), Philadelphia, 1 June 1946. Adele later played a major role in reconfiguring the ENIAC to use the function tables for programming.

[29] Clippinger (1948).

Quadrant elevation table.

QUADRANT ELEVATION - MILS

Height of Target - Meters

Range Meters	-400	-300	-200	-100	0	100	200	300	400	500	600	700	800	900	1000
10000	318.3	329.9	341.5	353.2	364.9	376.6	388.4	400.1	412.0	423.8	435.7	447.7	459.6	471.7	483.7
10100	323.1	334.6	346.1	357.7	369.4	381.0	392.7	404.5	416.2	428.0	439.9	451.8	463.7	475.7	487.7
10200	327.8	339.3	350.8	362.3	373.9	385.5	397.1	408.8	420.5	432.3	444.1	455.9	467.8	479.7	491.7
10300	332.6	344.0	355.5	366.9	378.4	390.0	401.6	413.2	424.9	436.6	448.4	460.2	472.0	483.9	495.8
10400	337.5	348.8	360.2	371.6	383.1	394.6	406.1	417.7	429.3	441.0	452.7	464.4	476.2	488.1	500.0
10500	342.3	353.6	364.9	376.3	387.7	399.2	410.6	422.2	433.8	445.4	457.1	468.8	480.5	492.4	504.2
10600	347.2	358.4	369.7	381.0	392.4	403.8	415.2	426.7	438.3	449.9	461.5	473.2	484.9	496.7	508.6
10700	352.1	363.3	374.5	385.8	397.1	408.5	419.9	431.4	442.9	454.4	466.0	477.7	489.4	501.2	513.0
10800	357.1	368.2	379.4	390.6	401.9	413.2	424.6	436.0	447.5	459.0	470.6	482.2	493.9	505.7	517.5
10900	362.1	373.2	384.3	395.5	406.7	418.0	429.4	440.8	452.2	463.7	475.3	486.9	498.5	510.3	522.1
11000	367.1	378.1	389.2	400.4	411.6	422.9	434.2	445.5	457.0	468.4	480.0	491.6	503.2	515.0	526.8
11100	372.2	383.2	394.2	405.4	416.5	427.8	439.0	450.4	461.8	473.3	484.8	496.4	508.0	519.8	531.6
11200	377.3	388.2	399.3	410.4	421.5	432.7	444.0	455.3	466.7	478.1	489.7	501.2	512.9	524.6	536.5

A previous way of doing firing tables was to use a differential analyzer, which was a predecessor to the ENIAC. On the differential analyzer, you didn't have a terribly bad job of generating trajectories. As I pointed out, the accuracy is not all that critical, when you come right down to it.

But where the problem came in was, if you wanted to calculate trajectories under standard conditions and under some nonstandard conditions, you didn't have enough accuracy in the computer so that you could take two sets of results and difference them and get a meaningful result. So to accommodate that, people went to things like adjoining systems of equations. So they first would solve the basic equation, and then they would mathematically have worked out the adjoining systems, feed the trajectories back, calculate the joint equations, and from those, be able to get the differential effects—very elegant way of doing business. If you like to read about it, Bliss's book on exterior ballistics,[30] I believe, probably goes into great discussion about the joint system and such.

[30] Bliss (1944).

A lot of these "pretty things" got lost. The ENIAC, again, did not accommodate that kind of calculation. It was much easier to just calculate 10,000 trajectories for all the conditions you wanted. So a lot of that kind of—what I might call "quality stuff"—got lost, at least for a while. I think it took a fair period of time before people got back out of the mentality that says the easiest thing to do is just put the simplest version of the problem on the computer and calculate the *hell* out of it.

I think that probably covers just about what I wanted to say. The whole idea of computing with the ENIAC was sort of a *hair-shirt* kind of thing. Programming for the computer, whatever it was supposed to be, was a redemptive experience—one was supposed to *suffer* to do it. And it wasn't until the 1970s that we finally were able to convince people that they were not going to have programmers continually writing little programs for them. I actually had to take my Division and sit everybody down who hadn't taken a course in FORTRAN, because, by God, they were going to write their own programs now. We weren't going to get computer specialists to write simple little programs that they should have been writing. Programming, indeed, had become a simple process, and I think to some extent, some of the earlier experience on the ENIAC convinced people that you should suffer to use a computer, whereas it had become something that was easy. [applause]

Paul Deitz:

Thank you very much, Harry. Bert Herzog has shown up, and I did thank ACM for this opportunity. Thank you very much. Frank Friedman was around the back, too, and may have slipped out. Again, our thanks to ACM. We will have these talks up on the Net as soon as possible for those who would like to do surfing. Bill Moye has copies of a wonderful brochure that he put together for those of you who want to read a little bit more about 50 years of computing in the U.S. Army.

Epilog.
High-Performance Computing at ARL

Epilog. High-Performance Computing at ARL

During the three years that have elapsed since the gathering described in these pages, the Army Research Laboratory has continued to serve the computational needs of Defense scientists and engineers in their quest to enhance the U.S. warfighter's capabilities. The ARL Major Shared Resource Center, modernized and dedicated in 1996, has grown to be one of the largest supercomputer facilities in the world, providing nearly two teraflops (peak) of large-scale, shared-memory, scalable processing power.

The ARL Center continues to provide the specialized high-performance computing (HPC) configurations needed to accommodate the large memory requirements characteristic of the most challenging defense scientific and engineering problems. The Center's HPC environment also focuses on the near-real-time, data-intensive computational requirements facing weapons systems developers in the test and evaluation community. Companion technologies—computational postprocessing, data storage and retrieval solutions, robust local and wide-area networking, and support for classified programs—are integrated into the Center's computational facilities. The entire set of resources is supported by a world-class on-site staff and linked to collaborative partners at universities and within industry.

Computational scientists develop mathematical algorithms from complex laws and theories describing the physical world. These algorithms are the basis for computer codes that are used to simulate physical phenomena. The results of these simulations can be interrogated, analyzed, and displayed through the technique known as scientific visualization, which has, within the last decade, revolutionized data analysis. Since 1991, ARL has dedicated a team to visualization support and development, providing specialized hardware and software that enable immersive and interactive display of scientific results. High-end graphics interfaces allow real-time review of data during calculations, large-format displays allow scientists to create simulations in a three-dimensional virtual environment, and other companion devices, which transmit a parameter's intensity to the human hand as a force, permit the researcher to "feel" a dataset.

When the Defense High Performance Computing Modernization Program was established in 1992, Defense computational science and engineering programs (under the auspices of the Director, Defense Research and Engineering) were served by an inadequate and outdated HPC infrastructure. Available resources were so stretched and overburdened that response to computational challenges was limited at best. The HPC Modernization Program was established first to modernize and then to sustain renewal of the Defense research and engineering HPC capability and capacity. The vision was to make resources available that would compare to those elsewhere in government, in academic research centers, and throughout industry.

The program's goals and strategies led to (1) establishing and developing the four comprehensive HPC environments under the auspices of separate defense laboratories; (2) linking remote scientists and engineers with very high-speed networking; and (3) providing systems and application software designed to enable effective use of the latest architectures and methodologies. ARL provided the program leadership and expertise to devise and implement both the interim high-speed point-to-point network solution for defense HPC users, and the longer-term networking alternative, the Defense Research and Engineering Network (DREN), a virtual private HPC network over the public grid.

Another basic precept of the Modernization Program is the rapid implementation of the best emerging HPC practices in government, industry, and academia, which, coupled with the drive to seek and foster beneficial collaborative partnerships, creates synergistic opportunities for in-house and partnered talent. This basic precept has been successfully applied, but there is a continuing need for collaborative arrangements with both scientific subject-area experts and computational researchers to ensure that science and HPC technology are coupled to achieve Defense research goals.

What fundamentally separates research computations from business applications is the exploratory nature of scientific and engineering endeavors. In the research arena, large resources are very quickly absorbed, and the sometimes unpredictable nature of cutting-edge technology is taken in stride. The output from R&D calculations frequently holds surprises that may reveal uncharted aspects of the physical world, or help refine scientific hypotheses. The scientific knowledge derived from increasing the fidelity of a model, or the precision of a parameter, is worth the stamina spent to harness the newest technology.

As a leader in the HPC community, ARL continues its commitment to providing the computational tools and scientific partnerships that enable leading-edge defense research and development programs. The computational infrastructure built on that commitment brings to the scientist's desk powerful tools, the newest techniques, and expert support to address previously intractable computational challenges. This combination of management, resources, and scientific talent is fundamental to ensuring the invincibility of our nation's defense and the safety of our men and women in uniform.

As Defense scientific and technical challenges require increasingly adaptable and sophisticated infrastructure, the ARL information technology program will continue to integrate both maturing HPC technologies and the newest computational science concepts. Emerging fields—knowledge management and data mining, distributed interactive scientific visualization, computational steering, solution of large interdisciplinary coupled problems, information assurance, and metacomputing—will hold the answers to many of the persistent computational and information management dilemmas that researchers encounter. At ARL and throughout the Department of Defense HPC community, the quest for discovery and the pursuit of excellence continues—for the defense of our nation.

Literature Citations

Ballisticians in War and Peace, A History of the United States Army Ballistic Research Laboratories. [various authors, n.d.] Volume I, 1914–1956; Volume II, 1957–1976; Volume III, 1977–1992 (by Harry L. Reed, Jr.).

Belzer, Jack, Albert G. Holzman, and Allen Kent, editors (1975). *Encyclopedia of Computer Science and Technology*, Marcel Dekker, Inc.

Bergin, Thomas J., and William Moye (1997). "Fifty years of Army computing, from ENIAC to MSRC," *IEEE Annals of the History of Computing* **19**, No. 3 (July–September), pp 76–77 (with photographs).

Bigelow, Julian (1980). "Computer development at the Institute for Advanced Study," in *A History of Computing in the Twentieth Century*, N. Metropolis *et al*, editors, Academic Press, pp 291–310.

Bliss, G. A. (1944). *Mathematics for Exterior Ballistics*, New York.

Burks, Arthur W. (1980). "From ENIAC to the stored-program computer: Two revolutions in computers," in *A History of Computing in the Twentieth Century*, N. Metropolis *et al*, editors, Academic Press, pp 311–344.

Burks, Arthur W., and Alice R. Burks (1981). "The ENIAC: First general-purpose electronic computer," *IEEE Annals of the History of Computing* **3**, No. 4 (October), pp 310–399.

Burks, Arthur W., Herman H. Goldstine, and John von Neumann (1946). *Preliminary Discussion of the Logical Design of an Electronic Computing Instrument*, The Institute for Advanced Study, prepared under Ordnance Department contract W-36-034-ORD-7481 (28 June).

Clippinger, R. F. (1949). *Description and Use of the ENIAC Converter Code*, Ballistic Research Laboratories, Technical Note No. 141 (November).

Clippinger, R. F. (1948). *A Logical Coding System Applied to the ENIAC*, Ballistic Research Laboratories Report No. 673 (29 September). (also posted at http://ftp.arl.mil/~mike/comphist/48eniac-coding/)

Eckert, J. Presper, Jr. (1988). Interview, "Development of the ENIAC, Session One," *Smithsonian Video History Program,* David Allison, interviewer (February 2), pp 15–16.

Eckert, J. Presper, Jr. (1980). "The ENIAC," in *A History of Computing in the Twentieth Century*, N. Metropolis *et al*, editors, Academic Press, pp 525–539.

Fritz, W. Barkley (1996). "The women of ENIAC," *IEEE Annals of the History of Computing* **18**, No. 3 (Fall), pp 13–28.

Fritz, W. Barkley (1994). "ENIAC—A problem solver," *IEEE Annals of the History of*

Computing **16**, No. 1 (Spring), pp 25–45.

Fritz, W. Barkley (1951). "The ENIAC—A five year operating survey," ACM Annual Meeting, Wayne University, Detroit (March); see Fritz (1994).

Garfinkle, Boris G. (1951). "Minimal problems in airplane performance," *Quarterly of Applied Mathematics* **9**, pp 149–162.

Gibson, Tom (1998). "Seeing in the dark," *Invention and Technology* **14**, No. 1 (Summer), pp 46–55.

Goldstine, Adele Katz (1946). *Report on the ENIAC (Electronic Numerical Integrator and Computer), Technical Report 1* (2 volumes), Philadelphia, PA (1 June). (also posted at http://ftp.arl.mil/~mike/comphist/46eniac-report/)

Goldstine, Herman H. (1992). "The Jayne Lecture: Computers at the University of Pennsylvania's Moore School, 1943–1946," *Proceedings of the American Philosophical Society* **136**, No. 1, pp 73–78.

Goldstine, Herman H. (1993). *The Computer, from Pascal to von Neumann*, Princeton University Press (second edition).

Goldstine, Herman H., and Adele Goldstine (1946). "The Electronic Numerical Integrator and Computer (ENIAC)," *Mathematical Tables and Other Aids to Computation* **2**, No. 15, pp 97–110; reprinted in *IEEE Annals of the History of Computing* **18**, No. 1 (Spring 1996).

Grosch, Herbert R. J. (1991). *Computer: Bit Slices From a Life*, Third Millennium Books, Novato, CA.

Hafner, Katie, and Matthew Lyon (1996). *Where Wizards Stay Up Late: The Origins of the Internet*, Simon and Schuster.

Huskey, Harry D. (1997). "SWAC—Standards Western Automatic Computer: The Pioneer Day Session at NCC, July 1978," *IEEE Annals of the History of Computing* **19**, No. 2 (April–June), pp 51 to 61.

Huskey, Harry D. (1980). "The SWAC: The National Bureau of Standards Western Automatic Computer," in *A History of Computing in the Twentieth Century*, N. Metropolis *et al*, editors, Academic Press, pp 419–431.

Huskey, Harry D. (1946). *Technical Description of the ENIAC, Technical Report 2*, University of Pennsylvania.

Huskey, Harry D., R. Thorensen, B. F. Ambrosio, and E. C. Yowell (1997). "The SWAC design features and operating experience," *IEEE Annals of the History of Computing* **19**, No. 2 (April–June), pp 46–50.

IEEE (1996a). "Documenting ENIAC's 50th anniversary," special issue, *IEEE Annals of the History of Computing* **18**, No. 1 (Spring).

IEEE (1996b). "Women in computing," special issue, *IEEE Annals of the History of Computing* **18**, No. 3 (Fall).

Kempf, Karl (1961). *Electronic Computers Within the Ordnance Corps*, Historical Monograph, Aberdeen Proving Ground (November). (also posted at http://ftp.arl.mil/~mike/comphist/61ordnance/)

Klopcic, J. Terrence, and Harry L. Reed, editors (1999). *Historical Perspectives on Vulnerability/Lethality Analysis*, U.S. Army Research Laboratory, ARL-SR-90 (April).

Lee, J.A.N. (1995a). *Computer Pioneers*, IEEE Computer Society, Los Alamitos, CA.

Lee, J.A.N. (1995b). "J. Presper Eckert, 1919–1995," *IEEE Annals of the History of Computing* 17, No. 3, pp 3, 5.

Lindgren, Michael (1990). *Glory and Failure: The Difference Engines of Johann Muller, Charles Babbage, and Georg and Edvard Scheutz*, MIT Press, Cambridge, MA.

MacKenzie, Donald (1991). "The influence of the Los Alamos and Livermore National Laboratories on the development of supercomputing," *Annals of the History of Computing* 13, No. 2, pp 179–202.

Mauchly, John W. (1980). "The ENIAC," in *A History of Computing in the Twentieth Century*, N. Metropolis et al, editors, Academic Press, pp 541–550.

Mauchly, John W. (1973a). "The use of high-speed vacuum tube devices for calculating," in *The Origins of Digital Computers, Selected Papers*, Brian Randell, editor, Springer-Verlag, Berlin, pp 355–358.

Mauchly, John W. (1973b). "Preparation of problems for EDVAC-type machines," in *The Origins of Digital Computers, Selected Papers*, Brian Randell, editor, Springer-Verlag, Berlin, pp 365–369.

Metropolis, N. (1980). "The MANIAC," in *A History of Computing in the Twentieth Century*, N. Metropolis *et al*, editors, Academic Press, pp 457–464.

Metropolis, N., J. Howlett, and Gian-Carlo Rota, editors (1980). *A History of Computing in the Twentieth Century*, Academic Press.

Moye, Bill (1996). "Postal service unveils computer technology stamps with help from Army's ARL," *Focus* 11, No. 9 (October), p 16.

Naur, Peter, and Brian Randall, editors (1969). *Report of the NATO Conference on Software Engineering*, NATO Scientific Affairs Division, January.

Randell, Brian, editor (1973). *The Origins of Digital Computers, Selected Papers*, Springer-Verlag, Berlin.

Redmond, Kent C., and Thomas M. Smith (1980). *Project Whirlwind: The History of a Pioneer Computer*, Digital Press.

Ritchie, Dennis (1996). "The development of the C programming language," in *History of Programming Languages*, Thomas J. Bergin, Jr., and Richard G. Gibson, Jr., editors, ACM Press and Addison-Wesley, pp 671–698.

Robertson, James E. (1980). "The ORDVAC and the ILLIAC," in *A History of Computing in the Twentieth Century*, N. Metropolis *et al*, editors, Academic Press, pp 347–364.

Rosen, Saul (1990). "The origins of modern computing," *ACM Computing Reviews* 31, No. 6, pp 449–481 (September).

Rutland, David (1995). *Why Computers Are Computers: The SWAC and the PC*, Wren Publishers.

Salus, Peter H. (1995). *Casting the Net: From ARPANET to Internet and Beyond ...*, Addison-Wesley Publishing Company.

Slater, Robert (1989). *Portraits in Silicon*, MIT Press.

Slotnick, D. L. (1982). "The conception and development of parallel processors, a personal memoir," *Annals of the History of Computing* 4, No. 1, pp 20–30 (January).

Slutz, Ralph J. (1980). "Memories of the Bureau of Standards' SEAC," in *A History of*

Computing in the Twentieth Century, N. Metropolis *et al*, editors, Academic Press, pp 471–478.

Stern, Nancy (1980). "John William Mauchly: 1907–1980," *IEEE Annals of the History of Computing* **2**, No. 2, pp 100–103 (April).

Stern, Nancy (1981). *From ENIAC to UNIVAC, An Appraisal of the Eckert-Mauchly Computers*, Digital Equipment Corporation, Digital Press.

Swade, Doron (1991). *Charles Babbage and his Calculating Engines*, Trustees of the Science Museum.

Turing, Alan M. (1937). "On computable numbers with an application to the Entscheidungsproblem," *Proceedings of the London Mathematical Society* **42**, pp 230–267. Correction, **43**, pp 544–546.

von Neumann, John (1945). "First draft of a report on the EDVAC," privately circulated; reprinted (1973) in *The Origins of Digital Computers, Selected Papers*, Brian Randell, editor, Springer-Verlag, Berlin.

Waldrop, M. M. (1992). *Complexity: The Emerging Science at the Edge of Order and Chaos*, Simon & Schuster.

Weik, Martin H. (1961). "The ENIAC story," *Ordnance* (Journal of the American Ordnance Association) (January–February), pp 3–7. (also posted at http://ftp.arl.mil/~mike/comphist/eniac-story.html)

Weik, Martin H. (1955). *A Survey of Domestic Electronic Digital Computing Systems*, Ballistic Research Laboratory, Aberdeen Proving Ground, MD.

Weiss, Eric A. (1997). "Computer technology commemorative postage stamp" ("Happenings" column), *IEEE Annals of the History of Computing* **19**, No. 2 (April–June), pp 77–78.

Wiener, Norbert (1961). *Cybernetics*, 2nd ed., MIT Press and John Wiley & Sons, Inc. New York. [1st ed., 1948, MIT Press]

Wiener, Norbert (1950). *The Human Use of Human Beings*, Avon Books, New York.

Wilkes, M. V. (1980). "Early programming developments in Cambridge," in *A History of Computing in the Twentieth Century*, N. Metropolis *et al*, editors, Academic Press, pp 497–501.

Williams, Michael R. (1997). *A History of Computing Technology*, second edition, IEEE Press, Los Alamitos, CA. [1st ed., 1985, Prentice Hall]

Winegrad, Dilys (1996). "Celebrating the birth of modern computing: The fiftieth anniversary of a discovery at the Moore School of Engineering of the University of Pennsylvania," *IEEE Annals of the History of Computing* **18**, No. 1 (Spring).

www.ingramcontent.com/pod-product-compliance
Lightning Source LLC
Chambersburg PA
CBHW082122230426
43671CB00015B/2773